MARKET GEOGRAPHY OF KASHMIR

MARKET GEOGRAPHY OF KASHMIR

(A Case Study of Srinagar)

A. Sami
A. Q. Khan

RAJESH PUBLICATIONS
NEW DELHI-110002

ISBN : 81-85891-13-3
First Edition : 2000

Published by :
M. L. Gupta
Rajesh Publications,
1, Ansari Road, Darya Ganj,
New Delhi-110 002
Phone : 3274550

Lasertypesetting by :
Sanjay Gupta
Sanjay Enterprises
New Delhi-2

Printed at :
Graphic Print, New Delhi-2

Preface

The Economy of a nation is closely related to the commercial process of marketing and market places where this activity actually take place. A market centre, in economic parlance, is area within which the prices of demand and supply operate.

The study of intra-urban market centres is relatively a new offshoot of urban geography. The market places within cities have proved to be of paramount importance in urban life. In fact the relative importance of a city can often be related to the shopping facilities it possesses.

The city of Srinagar is one of the most beautiful tourist centres of the world, which has now acquired considerable commercial importance. With the rapid growth of population it has witnessed during the last few decades, the city has experienced an uprecedented expansion in its commercial activities. New market centres have come up in many areas, while the older ones have declined in importance.

It is the purpose of this work to identify various market centres of Srinagar city. It is also proposed to determine the hierarchy of market centres and to analyse their functional character; physical condition and land values. The study is based largely on primary data collected and generated by the authors in the course of field investigation.

The present volume is a part of a Major Research Project, sponsored by the University Grant Commission, New Delhi.

The book is divided into seven chapters. The theoretical approach and the methodology used are discussed in the first chapter. The next Chapter deals with the geographical personality of the study area. The Chapter III attempts to identify different market centres and hierarchy of commercial complexes of the city of Srinagar. The next chapter is devoted to the study of functional character of the market centres of different levels. The examination of the internal structure of markets and an enquiry into the commercial land values from the basis of study in chapter V and VI respectively. The last chapter summarises the study and highlights the major findings.

Profound thanks and grate fulness least that we can offer in return for the untiring help, and constant encouragement extended to us by respectable Prof. L. N. Ram, Pro-Vice Chancellor, Patna University.

We find words inadequate to express our deep sense gratitude to Prof. Majid Husain, former Head, Dept. of Geography Jamia Millia Islamia, New Delhi and former prof. & Head, Dept. of Geography University of kashmir, Srinagar, without whose genero-sity and valuable suggestion the completion of this work would not have been possible.

We must express our deep indebtness to Prof. Rais Akhter, Prof. & Head, & Dr. T. A. Kanth, Reader, Department of Geography, University of Kashmir, Srinagar for their constant encouragement.

We are also indebted to Dr. Zubair Khan for his Co-operation. We have no words to express our profound thanks to all our friends for their help and co-operation which they extended to us at all stages of work.

We admit that this work could not have been completed without the help and assistance of number of officials and citizen to whom we owe a good deal. Our thanks are particularly due to different officers of the Srinagar Municipal Corporation, Srinagar Development Authority, Dal Lake Development Authority, Srinagar, Town & Country Planning Organisations, Srinagar, Census of India Srinagar, and various libraries located at Srinagar and Patna. Valuable co-operation was also extended by shopkeepers, salesman, and other business men at different localities of Srinagar in the course of field work, especially at the time of enquiry about land value, rent and premium of shops.

In the end we must thank Mr. Ejaz Rahman of wonder type Ramna Road, Patna-4 for having carefully and painstaking typed the work and Sri M. L. Gupta, Rajesh Publications, New Delhi for readily accepting the typed manuscripts for publication.

Abdus Sami
Abdul Qayoom Khan

Contents

1

Introduction

Geography of Markets is concerned with markets as fixed points on the earth surface. Marketing functions take place at specific centres distributed in an orderly or random way in an area each having facilities of collection and distribution of goods as well as services. Thus a market in economic parlance is the point where the forces of demand and supply converge. Geographically it is a well defined place or area within human habitations be they petty villages or metropolitan centres[1].

According to Belshaw, "Market places are sites with social, economic, cultural and other referents where there are a number of buyers and sellers and where prices offered and paid are affected by their decision"[2].

The word "market" has been derived from the Latin word, "marcatus" which refers to the place or method of contact between buyers and sellers[3]. In the present context, market is a place where sale and purchase of different commodities take place. The commodity might have been brought from other places or might have been produced locally. There are world markets of cotton, rice, wheat, jute, tea and coffee, etc. These are exchanged in specific places. The Chicago wheat pit and the London metal exchange are examples of market places of International importance. Equally important are the thousands of small market centres found all over the world[4]. The market centres are of different order, grade or rank which varies from the rural markets of hamlets or villages to the market complex of metropolitan centres.

The local or village markets must have been the forerunners of markets[5]. The village economy of the middle ages must not have been entirely closed, certain part of the products had to be given as levies and so these products became commercialised. And in this way the markets were born[6]. These often met only once in a month or perhaps once a week. Markets developed contacts between different regions which different goods to trade e.g., towns of the Vosges were built on the line of contact between sandstone and limestone regions[7]. Gradually, market places developed in port towns of different seas or other water bodies, along roads and railway lines. They sometimes started in the form of fairs. In the olden days considerable trade was carried on principally in fairs. The fairs sometimes transformed small local markets into important trading centres[8].

Whether it be a periodical market, a fair, a new shopping centre or a decaying central business district, it is a place where people come to exchange their products with others' products. It is at these centres where demands and supplies are ultimately balanced through the mechanism of price. Producers and consumers come face to face at these centres. The retail stores, service establishments etc. are the end of the chain of production and distribution and the beginning of the process of consumption[9].

The function of the smaller market centres or Major Metropolitan market complexes is to collect products from their surrounding regions or near and far urban places, to store them and to sell them in retail or wholesale form. Those establishments which acquire them in the wholesale form distribute them among smaller retail outlets which ultimately serve the consumers who visit them occassionally to purchase the articles they need[10].

The essence of the geography of marketing is the clustering of retail and wholesale establishments with diverse goods and services. It is said that the relative importance of towns and cities is to be judged on the basis of variety and range of goods offered by them. It is obvious that the large centres have larger number of establishments and greater variety and range i.e. they offer greater volume of trade and business than the smaller ones. Smaller centres generally offer only such consumable for which people frequently prefer minimum travel[11].

The retail shops are the last link in the chain of business activities which reach the goods to the ultimate consumer. The wholesale and retail business includes not only sale of goods, but also services providing such as meals, amusements and lodgings. In order to be successful the establishments require wide contact with the consumer and therefore they are highly sensitive to locational matters. Ordinarily, small and low retail establishments generally deal in goods of daily requirement. On the other hand big market centres or high order centres offer a wide range of goods and services with sizeable stock of goods. The locational advantage of shops thus becomes important and is determined by the rent they can manage to pay. Similarly, since shops prefer busy streets with considerable road space the chief shopping streets are those which are frequented by prospective consumers[12].

1.1 Market Geography

The importance and need for geographical study of retailing[13] was spelled out first by its outstanding practitioner William Applebaum[14]. He pointed out that the well developed topical field of economic geography with the exception of transport geography was concerned with production of material goods. The goods are not only transported from areas of production to areas of consumption, but they change hands from producers to wholesalers, middleman, retailers and ultimately reach the consumers. This change of hands may be called marketing. In his opinion the study of marketing had been neglected by geographers so long despite the fact that a sizeable proportion of the working population was engaged in marketing activities and a substantial part of the urban land was utilised by wholesale and retail trade which were practised through complex system of distribution whereby goods moved from the producers to the consumers[15].

About ten years later it was claimed in the introduction to a collection of papers that marketing geography had "come of age"[16]. The papers had several common characteristics and were concerned with actual business operation of firms. They dealt with the problem of selecting suitable location of new stories. The crux of the problem was the present suitability of the locations and their potentials. Much emphasis was put on how to conduct such studies, which might help to understand better store locations. Evaluation of the sites of the stores and their locational research was recognised as an art rather than a science[14].

Geographers paid a little attention to this aspect of the study and most of the early literature were published by the economists and people of other disciplines. Schwartz pointing out the genesis of serious study of marketing around approximately 1900 opined although this study initially produced a "plethora of facts that seems to add up to very little[15]. However, after the second world war a body of marketing theories emerged to enable people to begin to talk of marketing science[16].

That the marketing geographers should fail to orient their work in accordance with Applebaum's 1954 plea within the framework of marketing science is understandable because for many years geography as a whole was inward looking and often insensitive to the happenings in other subjects[17]. It is not surprising that the geographers did not pay adequate attention to the pioneering work done by Christaller and Losch who presented theoretical models regarding delineating trade areas, selecting retail locations and evaluating markets. These works had been there within geography for at least twenty years before Applebaum prepared his paper on marketing geography[18].

There is dearth of works on marketing geography in India. This is mainly due to the non-availibility of appropriate data. In India most of the studies of the Geography of markets have been undertaken on regional basis. These studies pertain to market towns, rural markets, agricultural markets, fairs, periodical markets and weekly or bi-weekly markets of particular regions or districts. As far as the study of intra-city commercial zones and belts are concerned, a number of Indian geographers have examined this aspect in the course of their overall studies of urban places.

In the western countries most of the aspects of retailing have been studied by different scholors. But in India, where the subject is still under developed the studies do not cover all aspects of the subject. The hierarchy of the commercial centres inside cities has been determined by Alam[19], Dutta[20], Singh[21] and Venugopal[22] by various methods. Only Alam and Khan have studied the functional characteristics of the shopping centres and the market areas of different centres in details.

The inadequacy of the works on intra-city commercial centres in India may be due to the non-availability of data or lack of interest in this particular branch. In the western countries the data are easily available in the form of Census of Business[23]. Volume II (detail trade area statistics) of the Census of Business, contains information about each kind of business, the number of establishments, sale, pay-roll, personnel and number of proprietors for all important cities[24]. In India such data are not available even for Metropolitan cities of Mumbai, Calcutta, Chennai and Delhi. hence the Indian research workers have to depend upon their own field surveys. Obviously it is not possible for an individual to cover all aspects of the subject such as turnover, catchment area of shopping centres and consumer behaviour etc. The services of teams of investigators must be available for undertaking field investigation and collecting data on all these aspects which is sure to involve substantial investment in terms of time and money.

1.2 Problem Under Study

The city of Srinagar be a tourist spot has acquired considerable commercial importance. With rapid growth of population it has witnessed during the last four decades the city has experienced unprecedented expansion in its commercial activities. New retail centres have come up in many areas while the older ones declined in importance in some areas and expanded and diversified their functional character in others. With the growth and expansion, there has developed marked spatial and functional specialisation. At the same time there has taken place nucleated and ribbon developments of shopping areas all over the city.

It is the purpose of this city to identify and study the various market centres of the Srinagar City belonging to different levels of hierarchy and functional specialization. It is also proposed to determine the hierarchy of the nucleated business centres, and to analyse their internal structure, physical conditions, functional character and land values.

1.3 Methodology

A major difficulty faced by the present study was shortage of time and man-power for collecting information. Published materials are lacking or meagre. The work was made doubly difficult because of the general reluctance of the tax paying shop-keepers to disclose the size of their turnovers, cost and profits. They gave vague replies of question on the consumer area served by them. Unlike, western countries no Census of shops or retail trade has been conducted by the local authorities of Srinagar. These handicaps had to be surmounted by the suitable modification of the research techniques and adoptation of methods which suit local conditions.

(a) Source of Data : An invaluable prelude to all research is intensive review of past literature which provides the background information on the subject as well as the theoretical framework for the problems. This is supplemented by published data. The only published data used in the present study is that from the Census of India. This helped in identifying the commercial areas of the city.

Other official data included the records of the J & K State Archives, District Collectorate Record Rooms, State Town and Country planning Department, the Srinagar Municipal Corporation and different research and educational institutions. Most of the information are unpublished and have been used to a limited extent. Some maps, data and literature on land use have also been obtained from the State Town Planning

Office and the Census of India Office of Srinagar.

The following maps have been used in this study :

(i) 1" = 5 miles topographical sheet No. 43, Survey of India, Dehradun.

(ii) Land Use map of Srinagar 1981 (unpublished) Census of India.

(iii) Jurisdictional (S. D. A.) Map, showing ward boundaries obtained from Town Planning Wing of Srinagar Development Authorities.

(iv) Road map of Srinagar obtained from the Srinagar Development Authorities.

(v) Maps included in the master plan of Srinagar and maps from journals and books.

(b) Field Work : It will be seen that data on retail activities of Srinagar were not available either in published or unpublished form. Therefore an intensive field investigation became imperative for obtaining first hand information. Enquiries in different government offices failed to yield much information. Detailed field survey conducted by the author form the basis of all statistical information used in Chapters III to VI.

The first round of field work was undertaken from July, 1989 to November, 1989 on the basis of a questionnaire prepared by the authors (see Appendix). The authors traversed all the major roads of Srinagar city on foot. The authors then compiled complete data on the location of each and every shop of Srinagar, its functional character, road frontage (approximate), physical build, service facilities and some notable features of the commercial character of the streets. To start with the main shopping streets of Central Srinagar (Lal Chowk Complex) were surveyed. This was followed by the shopping areas of Nauhatta and Zaina Kadal areas. Finally, the smaller markets, planned markets and the minor roads having only scatterd shops were surveyed. Since the work was done personally by the authors without the help of anybody else they are fully confident about the accuracy of the data used by them. The field data were computed as soon as possible and plotted on large scale map. Wherever there was any ambiguity the related locality was visited again and the data were subjected to cross checking. The data can with confidence be claimed to be fully reliable. The density and clustering of the shops on the map and field observation helped in identifying the retail nucleations.

The next round of field work was done from February to April. 1990. This was devoted to sample study of the representative commercial centres of different classes or levels of hierarchy. The questionnaire (see appendix) had been designed to obtain information on land values, shop rent and premium, as well as the internal structure of markets and facilities available. The questions were solicited among a large number of shop-keepers and old residents of the area, and as far as practicable, they were cross examined for checking and re-checking information on land value, shop rent and premium in the locality surveyed.

An attempt was also made to collect information on consumer travel behaviour, catchment area of markets and the gross sale of shops and establishments. This survey was confined to the C. B. D., the chief market of Srinagar, but the results obtained were vague and misleading. Neither the shop-keepers nor the customers were interested in giving convincing and correct replies. They were found to be suspicious and evasive. It was felt that the survey was time taking and needed considerable man-power which was not simply available. It was, therefore, given up. Interviewing consumers at their door steps may have given better result, but this would have involved a terrific amount of labour, time, and expense, even if undertaken on sample basis. Counting peak hour pedestrian traffic was not advisable for a single investigator to undertake.

(c) Analysis : All kinds of shops, totalling some 350 of them, were surveyed separately during the field investigation. Many of them belonged to the same generic family, e.g., cloth, cutpiece of cloth, woollen cloth, fabric, upholstary, tapastry, readymade garments, knitting wool, hosiery, bedding, embroidered cloth, tailors, second hand cloth, carpets, shawls, silk-wears, handicrafts etc. Similarly, there were varieties of shops dealing in food stuffs, handicrafts which differed from each other only in details. It was impossible to handle such a large number of functions statistically and cartographically. The exercise would not also have yielded any hierarchical pattern. The shops were, therefore, regrouped on generic consideration into fifty-three functional types. This scheme conforms to the national Industrial Classification. The number (53) of functional types selected thus is neither too large and inconvenient to handle nor is it so generalised and abroad as to conceal the details and to give a vague and misleading picture obtaining in Srinagar. The statistical analyses in Chapters III to VI are based on the latter list.

The study makes use of the available published and un-published maps for determining the extent of the study area, the chronological development of the commercial zones, the road pattern existing and future land use, etc. But more significant are the maps which have been prepared using original data and suitable cartographic techniques.

Various statistical methods such as co-efficient of co-relation, standard deviation, and Kendall's method of ranking have been employed in the present study. The application of sieve technique for drawing generalised but correct conclusions could not have been possible without the aid of maps which constitute an important tool in the present study.

Maps of two different scales have been used for plotting the collected information. The first is 4 inch to a mile road map which has been used as the base map. Individual shops of various functional types were plotted on this map. This exercised yielded forty-two commercial nuclei. The spatial distribution of the nucleations and their major functions and ranking have also been shown on maps of this scale. The remaining maps were drawn on a scale of 2 inches to 1 mile. These are of two types, one showing ward boundaries and other showing major roads.

A number of bar diagrams, pie-diagrams, line graphs and scatter diagrams have also been drawn, particularly for showing the internal structure of individual markets.

The 42 retail nucleations identified in Srinagar were ranked according to their relative importance in the civic life of the city. This was done on the basis of a formula which takes into account the functional specification of individual nucleation in the whole of the city and the number of functional units contained by that nucleation. A detailed discussion of the method applied has been given in Chapter-III. The 42 centres have been classified into six hierarchical groups with the help of a scatter diagram. These are Central Business District. Large Market Centres, Medium Market Centres, Local Market places and Specialised Market Placess. The method applied for the classification has been discussed in Chapter-III. The details of the ranking of functions and functional structure at different levels of hierarchy of markets have been given in Chapter-IV.

The analysis of data relating to build and architecture of shops, their quality and facilities available at different levels of hierarchy has been attempted in Chapter-V. This analysis is supported by a large number of diagrams. Similarly, Chapter-VI is based on the analysis of data relating to the value of land, rent and premium paid in commercial centres of different levels of hierarchy. An attempt has also been made to test the hypothesis that the higher order centres have most specialised functions, better structural conditions and draw higher prices, rents and premiums than lower order commercial centres.

The functional and structural patterns of all markets find place in Chapter-V which also highlights the basic differences between the markets of each level. The analysis here is supported by large scale maps giving the character of large market complexes.

References :

1. Saxena, H. M. : Geography of Transport and Market Centres, S. Chand & Co. (Pvt.), New Delhi, 1975, pp. 1-4.
2. Belshaw, C.S. : Traditional Exchange and Modern Markets, Englewood Cliffs, Prentice Hall, 1965.
3. Encyclopadedia Britannica, vol. 14, p. 912.
4. Berry, B. J. L. : Geography of Market Centres and Retail Distribution, Prentice Hall, Inc., Englewood Cliff , N. J., 1967, p. 1.
5. Gerner, B.J : Urban Geography, Longmans, Green and Co. Ltd.,48 Grasvenor Street London,W.1, 1967, p. 123.
6. Ibid.
7. Ibid.
8. Berry, B. J. L. : Geography of Market Centres and Retail Distribution, *op. cit.*, pp. 1-2.
9. Ibid., pp. 1-2.
10. Ibid., pp. 1-2.
11. Scott, P.: Geography and Retailing, Hutchinson University Library, London, 1971, p. 12.
12. Dickinson, R.E. : City Region and Regionalism, Routladge and Kegan Paul Ltd., London 1947, p. 141.
13. Berry, B. J. L. : Geography of Market Centres, *op. cit.*, p. 125.
14. Applibaum, W.: "Marketing Geography in American Geography, Inventory and Prospect", edited by James, P. E. and Jones, P. E. and

Jones, Q.F., Syracuse, 1954, p. 245.

15. Berry, B. J. L. : Geography of Market Centres, *op. cit.*,p. 125.

16. Murphy, R. E. : Marketing Geography Come of age, Introduction of Store Location and Development Studies, a volume of reprint from Eco. Geography (Worcester Clark University, 1961).

17. Cohen, S. B. and Applebaum, W. : Evolution Store Sites and Determining Store Rent, p. 95.

18. Schwatrlz, G. : Development of Marketing Theory.

19. Berry, B. J. L. : *op. cit.*, p. 126.

20. National Academy of Science - National Research Council, the Science of geography, Publication 1277, 1965.

21. Berry, B. J. L. : *op. cit.*, p. 126.

22. (a) Alam, S. M. : Hyderabad-Secunderabad : Study in Urban Geography, Allied Publishers, Bombay, 1965, pp. 101-104.

    (b) Alam, S. M. : "Commercial Structure of the Cities of Hyderabad and Secunderabad", Journal of the Osmania University, Arts, Commerce and Education, Vol. I, March, 1963, pp.1-10.

    (C) Alam, S. M. and Khan, W. : Metropolitan Hyderabad and its Region : A Strategy for Development, Asia Publishing House, Osmania University, Hyderabad, 1972.

23. (a) Datta, A. K. : Shopping in Calcutta : Town Planning Review, January, 1967.

    (b) Dutta, A. K. : "Daily Shopping in Calcutta :Town Planning Review, January, 1967.

    (c) Dutta, A. K. : "Intra-City Hierarchy of Central Place : Calcutta : A Case Study", Professional Geographers, Vol. XXI, No. 1., January, 1969, pp. 18-22.

24. (a) Singh, U. : "Industrial and Commercial Landscape of Allahabad", National Geographical Journal of India, 1960, 6, pp. 227-41.

    (b) Singh, U. : Allahabad : A study in Urban Geography, B.H.U., Varanasi, 1966.

25. Venugopal, B. : Commercial Structure of Warangal City in Andra Pradesh, India, Proceedings of Symposium of Urban Land Use, 21st International Geographical Congress, India, 1968, National Committee for Geography, Calcutta, 1972, p. 17.

26. Murphy, R. E. : *op cit.*, p. 225.

27. Ibid.

2

Geographical Personality of Srinagar

2.1 The Historical Evolution of the Srinagar City

Srinagar, one of the important tourist centres of the world, is the capital of Jammu and Kashmir State of India. It has nurtured Kashmiri culture, art and learning from time immemorial. Administratively, Srinagar has been the capital of Kashmir for the last more than thirteen centuries[1].

The Srinagar city has a very old history of its origin. As per historical records, the city was founded with the name Srinagari by the Mauryas Emperor in 250 B. C. at Pandrethan, now a village on the right bank of river Jhelum (Vitasta) about five kms. upstream from the present Srinagar city. (Fig. 1).

The name of the city was "Puranadisthan" (the old city) in the 6th century B. C. when Pravarasens II shifted his capital in A.D. 88 to Pradymnapitha (near present Hariparvat) he named it Pravarasenspura. He had divided the city into eight wards which were under ward officers. The wards were as follows.

(I) Rainawari and Dal lake. (II) Sathu, Amira Kadal and Ganpatyar, (III) Haba Kadal (left bank of the Jhelum) and Doodganga (IV) Zaina Kadal (left bank of Jhelum), (V) Beyond Zaina Kadal, (VI) Safa Kadal and Chestibal (VII) Hariparvat, Aali Kadal (right bank), Safa Kadal (right bank), (VIII) Bohri Kadal, Fetha Kadal (right bank) and Zaina Kadal (right bank) (Fig. 1).

The spatial distribution, arrangement and demarcation of the boundaries of these wards indicate that during those days the concentration of settlement was mainly on the right bank of river Jhelum.

Pravaraseknapura was the capital of Kashmir from the 6th century onwards. It is difficult to say how did it lose its name and assume the name Srinagar. Both the cities existed side by side for more than five centuries. Perhaps it was the old name that found favour with the people in preference to the new name. Ultimately, the old familiar name Srinagar seems to have become familiar as the name of the new city of Pravarasenapura[2].

It is not known as to when Srinagar extended to the left bank of river Jhelum (Vitasta). In ancient days the left bank was of secondary importance. It was only during the reign of Anante (A. D. 1028-1063) that the royal palace was constructed on the left bank of river Jhelum[3].

During the Muslim period A. D. 1320-1819 the city used to be called, "Kashmir" after the name of the country[4]. Mirza Haider, Abul Fazal and Jahangir, called it Srinagar, but almost all the other Mughal emperors called it, "Kashmir" or Shahr" (the Persian version of city). Bernier and Desidri, who visited Kashmir during the Mughal period,

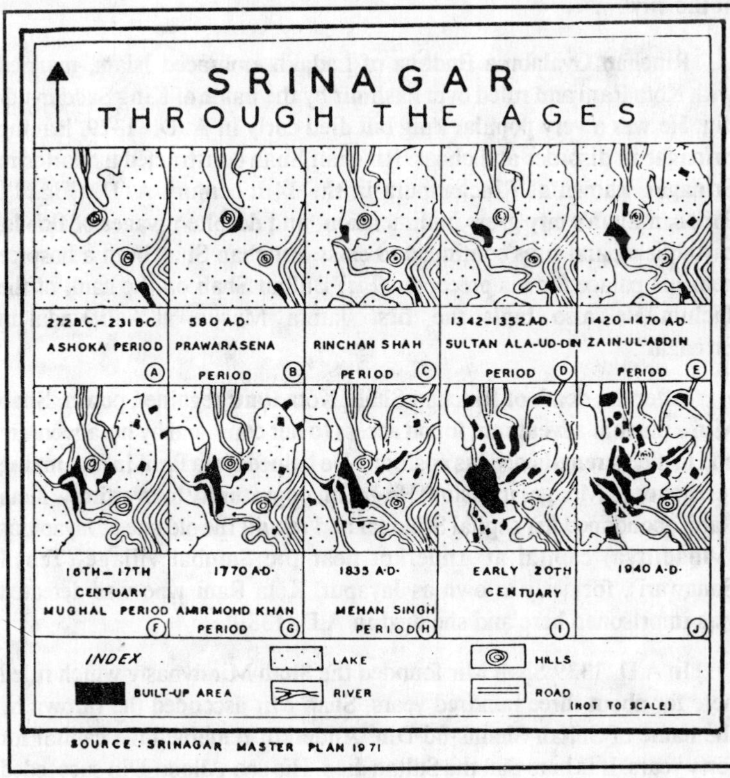

Fig. 1

used the name Kashmir, not Srinagar, for the capital. For centuries together the name Srinagar was unknown. With the advent of the Sikh rule in A. D. 1819 the old name by which it is known at present was restored[5].

With the advent of the Muslim rule, a new era dawned in the history of Kashmir. During this period the Srinagar city underwent a radical change. Though the seat of government changed occasionally, the location of Pravarasenapura on the whole remained unaltered.[6]

In A.D. 1318 Dulchu, a Mongol invader reduced the Pravarasena's city to ashes. Only eleven families survived, who rebuilt the new city of Srinagar. Srinagar and its neighbourhood before the founding of the city were a vast field full of grass with men without food. In A. D. 1318 Kota Rani rebuilt the capital and gave relief to the afflicted population of the city[7].

Rinchan Gyalabu a Budhist of Ladakh embraced Islam, married with Kota Rani and ruled over kashmir by the name of King Saddar-ud-din. He was a very popular king but died early in A. D. 1329, leaving Srinagar in disorder and choas. Rinchan Shah constructed a quarter in Srinagar, known as Rinchanpura in the 14th century A. D. (Fig. 1). Rinchan Shah's city grew in dimension, and despite ravages of floods, earthquake, and fires continued to exist. Rinchan Shah built a hospice near his palace for his preceptor (Pir) Bulbul Shah on the bank of the Jhelum. He also built the first Jamia Masjid at Aali Kadal in Srinagar[8].

After the death of Rinchan Shah, Kota Rani regained power. Shah Mir, a muslim adventurer, found access to her court and by his adventure and tact he strengthened his position. He helped Kota Rani in organizing resistence to Mongol invasion. He got an oppurtunity to overthrow Kota Rani, abondoned her capital Srinagar and rebuilt the old site of Jayapidas (Vinadittya) capital at Anderkot near the Sambal village (Tehsil Sonawari), formerly known as Jayapur. Kota Rani who was defeated was imprisoned here and she died in A.D. 1339[9].

In A.D. 1339 Shah Mir founded the Shah Mir dynasty which ruled here for about three hundred years. Shah Mir ascended the thrown by the name of Sultan Shams-ud-Din. Anderkot remained the capital for forty years. It is here that the Sultan died. His son Allaud-Din succeeded him. He erected many buildings and laid out gardens here. The centre for propagation of Islam had by then been established near Jamia Masjid in Srinagar. Allaud-Din shifted his capital from Ander Kot to the vicinity of the old site of Rinchanpur (Aali Kadal) and called it Allauddinpura, presently Khanqahi Maulla and its suburbs[10]. (Fig. 1).

Srinagar experienced a devastating flood in A. D. 1361. It swept away men and material. The Jhelum and its tributaries were in spate and the lowlands of Srinagar were submerged. The flood made people to suffer and damaged crops. To obviate danger from flood, the Sultan's son Shahab-ud-Din (in 1356-74) changed the capital. He selected the elevated and healthy area around Kohimaran (Hariparvat hill) for his capital and named it Lakshmipur or Shahabuddinpur, now Shahampur, a mohalla near Nowhatta. This new city extended from Nowhatta to Lal Bazar and included the present Malkhha graveyard and Zadibal. Military barraks were constructed here. Srinagar came to be called "Shahri Kashmir"[11].

Sultan Qutub-ud-Din, the son of Shahabu-ud-Din, settled the localities, between Zaina Kadal and Aali Kadal, on the left bank of river Jhelum and called it Qutub-ud-Din Pora. He built the wooden mosque of Khankahi Mualla in A. D. 1395[12].

Sultan Sikander founded a town Sikandarpur between A. D. 1389 and 1413 and built a magnificient palace and the grand Jamia Masjid. He also laid the foundation of the Idgah of Srinagar which was completed by his son Ali Shah. He built Khanquahs (hospices) besides mosques[13].

Sikandar's son Zain-ul-Abi-Din (A. D. 1420-1470) founded the new town of Nowshahr, now a part of Srinagar and made it his capital (Fig. 1). he called it Zainanagar. He adorned it with splendid houses for his officers, courtiers and learned men. He constructed a wooden palace which had twelve stories, each containing fifty rooms, halls and corridors. It was surmounted by a golden dome and its spacious halls were lined with glass[14]. The construction of Zaina Kadal, started by Sikander, was completed by him. In A.D. 1430 he constructed the Zaina Khul (Zaina canal), commonly known as Lachma Khul. It was the main source of drinking water for the people of Srinagar. Its head regulator was Sindh river (Ganderbal). During this period the Dal lake was connected with river Jhelum at Haba Kadal. The Sultan closed it and allowed the city to expand southward. He dug Nallamar in the city and connected the Dal Lake with the Anchar Lake. This navigable channel had cottage industries on its banks. Zaina Kadal, the first bridge across river Jhelum, was built by him which initiated the expansion of the city to the other side of the river Jhelum. The Soona Lank and Rupa Lank, the two artificial isles in the Dal Lake, are known at present as Teen Chinar and Chhar Chinar. These had been constructed by him. He introduced new industries manufacturing shawls, carpets, papier machies, and paper and wood carving. Namdah and Gabha of the Srinagar city and the fame of city rests on these industries[15].

Sultan Haider Shah shifted the seat of his government from Nowshahr to Nowhatta in 1470 - 72 but during Sultan Hussan Shah's reign A. D. 1472 - 84 the capital was shifted to Nowshahr again[16].

During A. D. 1540-50 Mirza Daughlat founded the city of Srinagar. It was densely populated. Many buildings were constructed with fresh cut pine during this period. Most of these buildings were five storied and contained apartments, halls galleries and towers. There were (retail) grocer's, drapper's, shops etc. There were no bazar's for wholesale business[17]. Mirza Haider died in A. D. 1550. His death was followed by civil war in Srinagar which ended in A. D. 1555 when Nasir-ud-Din Mohd. Ghazi Shah ascended the throne. He laid the foundation of the Chak dynasty. The Chak rule of Kashmir was marked by internal feuds. This led to the Mughal occupation of Kashmir[18].

During the medieval period a number of madarsas maas (schools) were opened in different parts of the city of Srinagar. In Mohalla Qutub-ud-Din Pura a residential schools and University were opened. These had hostels attached to them both for teachers and taught. One more college was opened in Saraf Kadal. A meteorological observatory was located in Pari Mahal. Madarsa Darushafa (Medical College) was opened on the eastern spur of Kohi Maran (Hariparvat) near the present Central Jail[19].

Akbar erected a wall around Hariparvat hill. The town within this wall was called, "Nagar Nagar": (Fig. 1). This wall can still be seen around Hariparvat fort. During the reign of Jahangir (A. D. 1605-28), there were eight hundred gardens in the vicnity of the Dal Lake[20].

During Aurangzeb's period the Aali Masjid was constructed in Idgah in A. D. 1664-65. Saif-Khan a Mughal Governer, laid out the garden of Saifabad on the bank of the Dal Lake. During his second governorship (1669-72) he spanned the Safa Kadal bridge over the Jhelum in Srinagar in A. D. 1670[21]. Fazil Khan (A. D. 1698-1701) built the bund of Hafat Chinar, near Hazuri Bagh in order to save it from the ravages of the Doodganga river. The bund was lined with Chinar trees in order to strengthen it [22].

The Mughals also laid out the Shalimar, Nishat, Chashmashahi, Naseem Bagh, Harwan, etc. gardens, which are still important tourist points. They also erected Parimahal, Pather ke Masjid and constructed Mosques and forts and repaired the bridges, which had been damaged by the floods[23].

After the Mughal rule ended Kashmir came under the occupation of Afghans in A. D. 1753. They ruled Kashmir from A. D. 1753 to 1819. Some Afghan governors did much for the development of the Srinagar city. Amir Khan Jawansher (A.D. 1770-1776) reconstructed the Sona Lank in the Dal Lake and raised a seven storied mansion on it. He rebuilt the Amira Kadal bridge which was washed away in A. D. 1772. He also laid out the Amira-abad and built the fort of Shergari (Fig. 1). Another Afghan governor Sardar Atta Mohd. khan Barakzai (1806-13) constructed the fort of Hariparvat[24].

The Pathans had divided the city of Srinagar into sixteen zillas of parishes, each being under the management of a Kotwal and other officials. These have now been reduced twelve Zilla is again sub-divided into mohallas or districts. The Pathans had divided the city into the following zillas[25].

(1) Drogjun includes 23 mohallas and lies west of the Takht-i-Suliman and south of the Tsent-i-Kol Canal

(2) Ahkbanur includes three mohallas on the right bank of the Jhelum and lies north of the Tasont-i-Kol canal.

(3) Kunyan includes fifteen mohallas north-east of Brarinambal and the Mar canal.

(4) Rainwari includes fifteen mohallas west of the Dal and south-East of Hariparvat.

(5) Nawetter includes twentyone mohallas lying between the Mar canal and Hariparvat.

(6) Sangin Darwaza includes thirteen mohallas north and north-west

of Hariparvat.

(7) Zaina Kadal includes fourteen mohallas lying in the middle of the town on both sides of river Jhelum.

(8) Buldimur includes twenty seven mohallas of the right bank of the Jhelum at the north-western of the town.

(9) Chutsabul includes ten mohallas of the left bank of the Jhelum at the south-western end of the town.

(10) Taswun includes nine mohallas of the left bank of the Jhelum.

(11) Nursingud includes five mohallas by the Kuti-Kol canal north of Sherghari.

(12) Sher Gud includes four mohallas found in the vicinity of the palace.

With the advent of the Sikh Emperior, the old name of the capital (Srinagar) was restored in A. D. 1819. During this period the general and physical condition of the city was not good. Poor buildings, narrow and filthy streets, poor drainage system and insanitary conditions prevailed in the whole of the city of Srinagar[26].

The Dogras came in power in Jammu and Kashmir during A. D. 1846-1890. During the early part of the Dogra rule Srinagar presented a sad picture. There was deterioration in the physical appearance of the city. The city was full of filth and had poor drainage which caused epidemic cholera during A. D. 1888-92. It is during this period that the high embankment was erected and a very big flood control canal (Sonti Kaul) was constructed for draining out the flood water from the city to the Wular Lake. Mehan Singh constructed a Gurudwara in the southern vicinity of the fort wall and dug a spill channel known as Chunti Khul (Nallah) connecting river Jhelum with the Dal Lake to Basantbagh (Fig. 1)[27].

In the 19th century, when residency was established, new schools and the first Intermediate College (S. P. College) was opened, a library and piped water were provided to the people of the city[28].

Silk and wool factories were established in the early 20th century. A Convent School was also opened. Barber Shah bridge at Chunti Kohl was constructed. The Ganderbal Road, Anantnag Road and other roads of Srinagar were metalled. The Gopkar road was widened and the Boulevard was constructed. The Zunimar area which has thirty six mohallas and Batamalina, Baghi Nand Singh, Sonawar, Bonamsar, Shivpora and Rathpora villages were added to the Municipality during the same period[29]. (Fig 1).

The history of the development of Srinagar city dates back to 1886 when the first municipal act was passed. In 1913 another act on the governance of local bodies of Srinagar was enacted and the Municipality was authorised to elect its Vice-President in 1921[30].

Works started for the development of the Srinagar city include improvement of sanitary condition, construction and repair of roads and bund, improvement of the drainage system of the city and construction of many metalled roads. Certain amenities and facilities such as footpath along roads of the civil lines area, widening of roads, construction of Pratap Park and many other gardens for the convenience of the people were also provide in the city. The government laid a sewerage line from Sara-i-bala to Chattabal[31].

The kerosene oil lamp postes along the roads and streets of Srinagar were replaced in 1920 by electric lamp posts[32]. Another problem faced by the Srinagar Municipality was the congestion of the city, This was due to neglect and the political instability of the 19th century. The Afghan, Sikh and early Dogra did not pay attention to town planning. A large number of villagers immigrated to the Srinagar city during the Dogra rule. This led to the haphazard development of the Srinagar city[33].

According to the Census of 1891, Srinagar extended over about two miles along the bank of river Jhelum[34]. In 1911 the city extended over more than three miles and had an area of 5,139 acres[35].

The suburbs of Buchwara and Zadibal were included in the municipality in 1915[36]. The municipality expanded further during 1920-21 with the addition of the Zunimar tract containing thirty six mohallas and the village of Batmaloo, Bagh Nand Singh, Sonawar, Bonamsar, Shivepura and Rathpura[37].

As a result of these additions Srinagar expanded rapidly. By 1941 the city was four miles in length and about 2 miles in width[38]. In addition were the housing colony of Bemina, the Kashmir University, the Nehru park, the Tourist Reception Centre, hospital, stadium and the Medical College areas, (Fig. 1).

Since 1940 the city moved downwards occupying the area between Parvarapura in the north and Jawahar Nagar and Kurso Rajbagh in the south and then got stuck up from moving further south and west. These areas of the south are really lowlaying have high water table and serious flood problem. In course of time the pressure on urban land increased steadily and a process of spill over is visible across the flood spill channel. Barzulla, Nattipora, Hyderpora and Baghat lying in the flood absorption basin are growing faster than ever. This leapfrog development is likely to continue in the flood affected areas and serious problems of road construction, drainage development and providing other infrastructure will arise, unless a planned development of this area is initiated.

Business establishments have also moved from north to south in sympathy with the physical expansion of the city. The old business area was in Maharaj Ganj. It extended further south on both sides of the main roads. The development of the north has resumed, partly, due to betterment of urban infrastructure and transportation facilities.

At present Srinagar is well connected with other parts of the country by networks and roadways and airways. The National Highway number IA passing across the Banihal pass through the Jawahar tunnel connects it with Jammu, and other parts of the country. National Highway IA actually handles all inward an outward movements of goods to and from for Srinagar. About 1000 light and heavy vehicles ply from each side. Winter season creates trouble for the transporters, especially when there are heavy snowfalls.

Regular bus services handle the traffic between the city and the peripheral and other commercial towns of the valley. The city has four bus stands and two metador stands. Out of the four bus stands two are used by the state run buses and two by the private owners buses.

Srinagar is also connected by airways with Jammu, Leh and Kargil and other parts of the country, such as Amritsar, Chandigarh, New Delhi, etc.

2.2 Site

The exceptional position of Srinagar can safely be attributed the natural advantages of its site. Srinagar has benefited by its being a riverside town. It occupies a site close to the centre of the valley. It also has abundant transport and communication facilities which no other site could offer. Before the advent of vehicular traffic, the river along which the city is settled, provided all season and most convenient trade route. Goods traffic moved both up and down the valley, that is, from Khanabal town of Anantnag district to Khadanyar of Baramulla district. The lakes such as Dal and Anchar, which flank Srinagar, assured an abundant supply of fresh vegetables for the large city population.

On account of its central location the Srinagar city has close relations with the two other main commercial towns of the valley, Baramula and Anantnag which are almost equidistant, thirty kilometres each from it. As a result of this Srinagar developed as the main centre of trade and

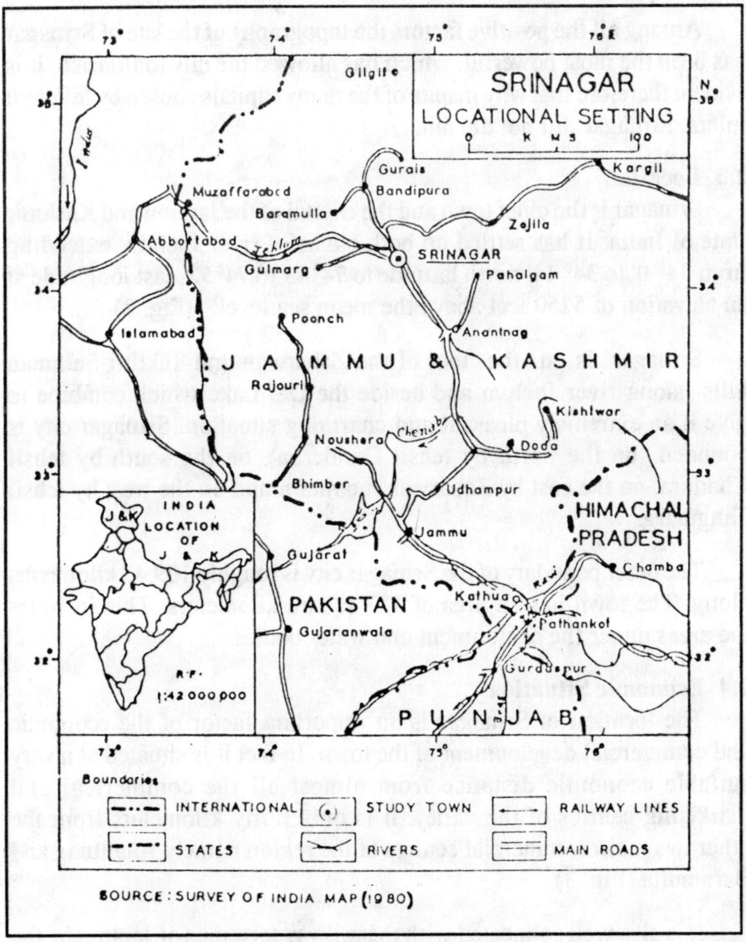

SOURCE : SURVEY OF INDIA MAP (1980)

Fig. 2

commerce. As Srinagar occupies a riverside location riverway must have played a vital role in the origin and growth of the city. Srinagar being the master centre and the chief town of the Kashmir valley, its markets attract people from all parts of its surrounding region.

Srinagar also attracts a large number of tourists from other parts of the country and other countries of the world and as such it has developed into a tourists' paradise. This has helped the growth and development of trade and commerce, specially cottage industries and hotels, houseboats, guest houses, and transoport facilities.

Among all the positive factors the topography of the site of Srinagar has been the most powerful, which has allowed the city to flourish. It is evident therefore that why inspite of the many capitals chosen by different rulers, Srinagar did not die out.

2.3 Location

Srinagar is the chief town and the capital of the Jammu and Kashmir state of India. It has settled on both banks of river Jhelum, extending from 34^0 0' to 34^0 14' north latitude to $74^0$43 to $74^0$52' east longitude at an elevation of 5250 feet above the mean sea level[39] (Fig. 2).

Srinagar is at the foot of the Zabarwan and Takth-i-Sulaman hills along river Jhelum and beside the Dal Lake which combine to give it an extremely pleasant and charming situation. Srinagar city is bounded on the north by tehsil Ganderbal, on the south by tehsil Chadura, on the east by Zabarwan mountain and on the west by tehsil Tangmarg.

The outer boundary of the Srinagar city is roughly 109.43 kilometres along. The town has an area of 157 square kilometers. This includes the areas under the cantonment and water bodies.

2.4 Economic Situation

The location of Srinagar is an important factor of the economic and commercial development of the town. In fact it is situated at a very suitable economic distance from almost all the commerical and marketing centres of the valley. It is only thirty kilometers from the other two main commercial centres of the region namely Anantnag and Baramulla (Fig. 3).

It is also well connected with the railway terminus of Jammu by the National Highway and airway. Direct buses ply between Srinagar, and

Jammu, Udhampur, Doda, Rajouri, Pathankote and Delhi. In addition to these more than three hundred loaded trucks with different commodities come to and go out of Srinagar every day. It is also connected with the Kargil and Leh towns of the Ladakh region. The Mughal road will be a new booster for commerce and trade. It is under construction and will connect Srinagar with Punch and Rajouri districts of the Jammu region. It will help the growth and development of commercial activities of the city.

River Jhelum has acted as an important route of trade and commerce and passanger movement in the past. This is the reason why the main bazars of Srinagar are on the right bank of the river from where goods could easily be carried by boats to different places of the valley.

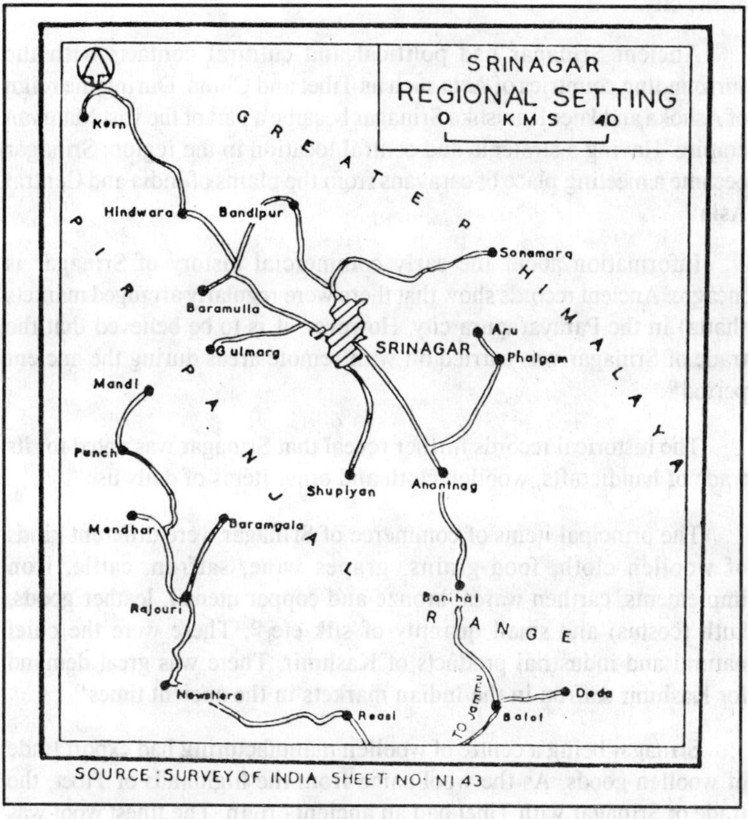

Fig. 3

Srinagar was from early times, and still is, the focal point of trade routes and beacuse of the convergence here of some many routes. It grew as a nodel town of the Kashmir valley.

2.5 Early History of Commercial Activities

Every nucleated settlement whether hamlet, village, town or city is in varying degree a service centre for a surrounding area[40]. In fact cities do not grow of thier own, the countryside set them up to do tasks that must be performed in central places[41]. The essence of a town is grouping together of centralised services in an accessible place.

The emergence of Srinagar as an important commercial and trading centre is not a recent phenomenon. The origin and evolution of commercial areas within the city are related to the history of the growth of the city.

Ancient Srinagar had political and cultural contacts with the surrounding countries of Asia such as Tibet and China. During the reign of Ashoka and later Kanishka Srinagar became a part of the vast Mauryan empire. Having a strategic and central location in the region, Srinagar became a meeting place of caravans from the plains of India and Central Asia[42].

Information about the early commercial history of Srinagar is meagre. Ancient records show that there were regularly arranged markets (hatta) in the Paravarapura city. However, it is to be believed that the trade of Srinagar was carried on with remote areas during the ancient period[43].

The historical records further reveal that Srinagar was noted for its trade of handicrafts, woollen cloth and other items of daily use[44].

The principal items of commerce of Srinagar were different kinds of woollen cloth, food-grains, grapes wine, saffron, cattle, iron implements, earthen wares, bronze and copper utensil, leather goods, kuth (costus) and small quantity of silk etc.[45]. These were the chief natural and industrial products of Kashmir. There was great demand for Kashmir saffron in the Indian markets in the ancient times[45].

Srinagar being a centre of woollen manufacturing had export trade of woollen goods. As the wool came from the highlands of Tibet, the trade of Srinagar with Tibet had an ancient origin. The finest wool was imported from the markets of Turfan, Tien Shen mountains[47]. The wool traders exchanged their raw wool for manufactured shawls and other goods and sold them in various markets of Central Asia. From there these goods were exported to the famous cities of Asia and Europe[48].

Silk, Muslin and Kabala were the products of ancient Srinagar. Woollen, silken and cotton cloth were also produced in Srinagar[49].

Due to the internal disorder and instability, Srinagar had remained cut off and uninfluenced by exogenous influences as far as its trade and industry were concerned, for a long time. The invasion, loot and plunder by Zulchu towards the end of the 13th centrury brought about the complete ruin of the whole economy of Kashmir[50].

Sultan Zain-ul-Abidin, who ruled Kashmir from A.D. 1420 to 1470 was popularly known as Bud Shah or great king. He had introduced most of the industrial art and crafts which made Kashmir of world fame. He reorganised the silk industry and Srinagar began to export silk to as far as Damascus[51].

Manufacturing of shawls reached its zenith during the Mughal period (A. D. 1586-1750). They were produced in large numbers and exported[52]. During this period the trade of shawls was started in the open markets. Before this period the trade of shawls was carried on from the houses.

During the Afghan and Sikh rule the shawl industry was subjected to heavy taxation. The noteable development of this period was the prosperous trade in shawls with Europe, Persia, Turkey etc. France alone accounted for importing 80% of the shawls exported from Kashmir, the U.S.A imported 10%, Italy 5% Russia 2% U.K and Germany 1% each. From the 17th century up to 1870 Kashmiri shawls dominated the world of textiles in the whole of the world[53]. This trade brought huge profits to Kashmir. In the words of "Shah Toash" the shawls of Kashmir were so fine that they could pass through a ring[54].

The silk industry of Srinagar was considerably developed during the different historical periods, but this industry faced stiff competitions with China and Japan which had captured the international markets due to their large-scale production and comparatively lower prices than Kashmir. Due to this the Kashmiri silk was deprived of its overseas markets[55].

Sultan Zain-ul-Abidin introduced carpet industry in Srinagar. He invited the craftsmen from Persia and Samarkand to Kashmir and gave them all facilities so that the Kashmiris learn the art from them. The carpets were generally exported to the U.S.A., U.K. and Australia[56].

Fresh fruits such as apples, grapes, walnut, almonds etc. were not exported in sufficient quantities and more frequently though fresh fruits were in great demand in northern India. This was because transport was difficult[57].

Srinagar had regular trade relations with the countries of central Asia from the period of Kusana conquest of the valley to that of Ashoka[58]. It had commercial relationship with Leh also[59].

The main items of imports in to Srinagar were salt, spices, cotton and silk cloth and metals, specially copper and brass[60]. Coral which was brought from the western parts of the world had good market in Kashmir[61].

The internal trade of Srinagar was confined to food grains, cattle, agricultural implements, earthenwares, metallic vessels, and minor agricultural and industrial products[62].

Most of the goods of trade were moved on river Vitasta (Jhelum) and its tributaries. The boats were the principal means of transport and communication[63].

The import and export of goods to and from Srinagar were carried along various routes leading to various parts of Asia, mainly Tibet and China. The various passes through which trade moved served as customs posts (Sulkasthane) and were officially known as Saulkikas and duty was realised on the goods coming in and going out of Srinagar[64].

In A.D. 399 the Chinese traveller Fa-hien started from the northern shore of the Volur lake and travelled through the present villages of Atawat and Vijjemarg to the Astor and Balti territories on the Indus. In ancient days this route served as the second important route of commerce with Central Asia and China. The trade links with the Darad territory were maintained by this route[65].

Towards the east from Kashmir there was a third route leading to Ladakh, Tibet and China. It passed through the present Zoila pass[66]. This pass had played a vital role in the political, cultural and commercial interactions between Tibet and Srinagar[67].

There were several routes to the valley of Kashmir from the south across the Pirpanjal range. The Banasala or Banihal pass on the eastern range provided links with Punjab[68]. The Siddhapatha pass is on the west of Banasala. This pass linked Srinagar with Sailkot ancient Sakala[69].

In ancient days it was the chief route between Srinagar and Central Punjab. This route was used mainly for salt trade between Srinagar and Punjab.

The routes through which trade was carried on, were well protected from the danger of plunderers and each one had a vigilence post at its terminus. Soliders and custom officers were posted on these routes in order to collect duty from the traders[70].

The commodities coming and going across the vigilence posts were stamped and registered by the custom officers and duty on export and import of articles realised[71].

2.6 Medieval History of Commercial Activities

Trade relations of Srinagar of the ancient times with Tibet, China, Central Asia and Persia continued in the medieval period also[72].

Srinagar was accessible by twentysix different routes[73]. These routes were the highways of commerce with several countries. During the Mughal period two main routes leading to western Punjab and the western plains of India passed through Bhimber and Pakhli. The Bhimber route had three branches, viz. the Hastivanj, Pir Panjal, and Tangtallah routes. The Tangtallah route does not exist today[74].

The trade relations between Central Asia. Tibet etc and Srinagar was so strong that they did not break altogether. The merchants took a longer and strainuous route. From Srinagar, they went to Patna (Bihar), thence to Nepal and by way of the Kuti (Nilam) Pass to Shigatge and thence to Lhasa. There was a trade route from Lhasa to Sinning Fue on the Chines frontier northeast of Khasai and Charingnor[75].

The principal commodities imported were salt and wool for shawl manufacturing. Most of the salt came to Srinagar from Punjab across the Pir Panjal pass but some salt came also from Ladakh and Changtheng[76]. Caravans loaded with musk, crystal, jade and two kinds of fine wool came to the markets of Srinagar[77]. In addition to wool for shawl manufacturing the Tibetans brought gold to Srinagar. Woollen cloth was brought from Ladakh by the Ladakhi traders[78]. Jade, silk, carpets, pottery, brass and copper vessels were imported from Khotan to the markets of Srinagar. Agate. Opal, Turquoise and other varieties of precious stones were imported to Srinagar from Badakshan, Bukara and Yarkand[79].

The most important item of export from the city was Kashmiri shawl, which found ready market in most of the large cities of India. Other items of export were woollen goods, blankets, fresh and dried fruits, saffron, timber and horses[80].

The bazars of Srinagar were visited by the Turkish, Tibetan, Indian and Nepali traders who had built their rest houses and godowns here[81].

The following table gives an idea of the imports and exports during the Muslim rule.

Table 2.1

Showing articles of export and import from and to Srinagar

Place	Export	Import
Rest of India	Fruits, (fresh and dried), saffron, shawls, woollen stuffs, silk fabrics, horses, woodwork, metal & stone-work.	Precious metals for coinage and ornaments, salt, cotton piece goods and spices.
Central Asia	Saffron, wood-work and metal-work	Shawl wool, woollen cloth, Musk, crystal jade, salt, tea kuhruba & Mumiranchini etc.

Source : A History of Kashmir by P. N. K. Bamzai.

During the medieval period, particularly during Jahangir's reign, the bazars of Srinagar were of different type. The number of exclusive commercial establishments were very few on the roads and streets of the city. Most of the producers, druggists, beer seller and bakers transacted their business in their residential houses. This was true of the silk and shawl merchants also. However, drappers and retail dealers of food materials were found transacting their business in shops. During the Mughal period this tradition seems to have ended. Bernier, who visited Srinagar during Aurangzeb's time mentioned that trade was very brisk in the city and the streets were lined with long rows of shops offering various commodities for sale[82].

Trade in grains, however, was controlled by the goverment all through the medieval period. The State share of the produce was stored in the granaries and was sold to the people at controlled rates[83]. This naturally had a stabilizing effect on the prices in times of scarcity. The government came forward to sell its surplus grains.

Though the chief means of transport were the river boats, ponies were also used for carrying paddy and other food grains from the distant villages to the Srinagar markets[84].

2.7 The Commercial History of the Sikh Period

At the begining of the sikh period in India, Srinagar was not only a centre of intra-provincial trade but also of international trade, with Tibet, China, Afghanistan, Iran, Punjab and other parts of British India[85]. The trade with Sinkiang and even with Russia was carried on through Ladakh[86]

The trade of Srinagar within the valley was carried on the Baramulla-Muzaffarabad-Mansera route. The trade with British India was carried on the Banihal-Jammu-Najibabad route and with Ladakh on the Ganderbal-Gangangir-Leh route[87].

Due to the Sikh-Afghan hostility in Punjab in the early 19th century the traditional routes connecting Punjab with Kashmir became unsafe and remained usually closed[88]. However, soon after the Afghans were exturned from Kashmir and Punjab, the Banihal-Jammu-Akhnoor and the Pirpanjal-Bhimber-Rajouri-Gujarat routes became important for the trade of Srinagar again. The Muzaffarabad-Mansera route remained closed until 1831, when Prince Sher Singh crushed the revolt of Ahmed Brelavi. Custom check-posts were established along these routes and in the year 1936-37 there were fortytwo such check-posts to control the internal as well as external trade[89].

During the Sikh period the commodities sent from Srinagar to other parts of the country were properly packed and sealed before being dispatched to their respective destinations[90].

The internal trade of Srinagar was carried on by boats playing on the Jhelum and the lakes around the city[91]. Vehicular modes were unknown in the Kashmir valley and waterways were the chief routes of transport of internal and external trade of Srinagar up to the exit points from where they were transported across the Banihal Pass[92]. The goods sent to Afghanistan, Iran and Turkey were first brought to Baramulla by boats[93].

The shawl industry of Srinagar was one of the biggest of its kind in the world. Its finished products had key position in the foreign trade of Srinagar until the early Dogra period. The main sources of shawl wool were Tibet and Ladakh. About 2000 traders with 800 loaded horses carrying shawl and raw wool used to come to Srinagar and its adjoining regions annually[94].

The main items of export from Srinagar to Russia, Great Britain, Turkey, Turkistan, Bokhara, Baghada, Armenia, France and Germany during this period were shawl and woollen goods[95]. The Sikhs encouraged the Kashmiri and Punjabi traders. They were given trade contracts and also credit through the bankers in the form of hundis. These hundis were negotiable and safe and very helpful in promoting trade. Special arrangements were also made for the traders for sending their expensive parcels and business letters to various countries through the Government Parcel Department.

From the very beginning Srinagar had been a centre of art and crafts and handicrafts occupied an important place in the commerce of the city. In 1921 there were fifty factories of wood work in the Srinagar city. Carpets produced in the city were sent to different countries of Europe. Namda was another article of trade produced in the city of Srinagar. The handicrafts articles of Srinagar such as Gubba, Pattu, copper work, silver work, papier machie and jewellery were in great demand in both inside and outside the country. Both raw and manufactured silk were exported to different states of India and Europe. The total export value of "silk raw and cocoon" in 1925-26 was rupees 15,83,184[96]. In 1922 the Government established a department of commerce and industry for the expansion of these activities[97].

The Dogras realised that without a good network of transport and communication the progress of trade and commerce was impossible. As such they developed the Jhelum valley road and constructed the Banihal Cart Road. Previously almost all trade between Srinagar and British

India was carried by way of the Jhelum valley Road. The necessity of Banihal Cart Road was felt after the great famine of 1877-79. The Banihal Cart Road connects the two capitals Jammu and Srinagar and stimulated inter-provincial trade[98].

The Treaty high road connected Srinagar with Yarkand through Ladakh and formed an important trade route between British India and Central Asia[99]. The Jhelum river remained the chief line of transport. Through this river goods came from Baramulla and Khanabal to Srinagar. A postal system was started by the Dogras which was later taken over by the British government in 1894. It was used by the traders for importing and exporting light weight articles. On the roads the main means of transport were Ekkas, Tongas, Hill Carts and Bullocks[100].

Motor vehicles were introduced in 1931 and the number of slow moving vehicles such as bullock-carts and ekkas declined. The main items of import were liquor, metals, salt, tea, sugar and raw cotton. Snuff, tobacco etc. were also imported from outside the valley. The Karan Singh Woollen Mill was started at Srinagar in 1934. The mill was taken over by the State Government in 1954. The work in the mill started with grinding, spinning and worsted sections. These sections comprised of 2,000 wool and 1,600 worsted spindles and allied machinery. Some 12,000 worsted spindles with allied machinery were imported from Japan in 1961[101].

2.8 Recent Commercial Development

With the growth of its population and the gradual expansion of city, commercial areas emerged within the city. Zaina Kadal grew as an important commercial area. Moreover, shops came up on both banks of river Jhelum. Commercial activities began to develop along the main streets and roads in nucleations and new commercial areas came into existence. Upto the first quarter of the present century, Zaina Kadal, Maharaj Ganj, Haba-Kadal, Fetha-Kadal and Rainawari were the main thorough fares of old Srinagar. As a result many businessmen specially confectioners, cloth, shawl, and carpet delaers, coppersmiths, silver smiths, goldsmiths and general merchants settled along the roads and started their business.

A new commercial area developed in the beginning of the present century in the south central part of the old city after the coming up of the Chunti Khul bridge which provides connection with the southern part of the city. The Amira-Kadal area also developed into a commercial-cum-residential area. A large number of retail establishments were opened along the roads in this area. Recently the main commercial activities have shifted from the old section of Srinagar, that is, Nowhatta, Haba-Kadal, Fetha-Kadal to the Lal Chowk area. This is a newly developed and purely commercial area of the city. Lal Chowk is noted for its fashionable articles of daily use such as costly cloth, readymade garments, shoes and ladies sandles and shoes, tailoring, electrical appliances, hotels and resturants. This is actually the CBD of Srinagar. At present more than 32% of shops of Srinagar are located here.

Presently, Srinagar is the chief commercial centre of the Kashmir valley. The commercial activities of the city have witessed rapid development. While the old commercial areas have added to the volume of their trade, intensity of shops and modernizing their premises, a number of new business nucleii are emerging rapidly in other parts of the city.

The existing roads of Srinagar city which carry on commercial activities can be divided into two groups, one group running north to south and other east to west.

The Maulana Azad road and the Residency road which run east to west are the most important roads of the Srinagar city. Almost all other roads such as Boulevard, Nishat & Harwan, Nowhatta-Ganderbal, Haba-Kadal, Fetha-Kadal, Nalamar, Baramulla, Chhanapura and Jawahar Nagar Roads and the national Highway IA etc. meet these two roads. Thus the two roads form the backbone of the city. These roads are broad and well maintained.

One of the important roads of the second group having commercial activities is Haba-Kadal-Zaina-Kadal road. It takes off from the commercial hub of old city and runs south to north. This road is comparatively narrow and as such only light vehicles are allowede to run on this road. Other roads such as the Batmaloo, Karan Nagar, Karalkhud-Khyam roads and many lanes meet this road.

The other road of second group running north to south connects the city with its northern parts. It is called Ghulam Ahmad Ashai road (Dargah road).

The other important road is Nowhatta-Ganderbal road. It runs from Lal Chowk in the south to Khanyar, Nowhatta, Zadibal, Nowshera and Soura in the north.

The next important from the commercial point of view is the Channapura road. It connects the southern part of the city with Lal Chowk. This road has commercial establishments on both of its sides.

Outside the main areas there are a few commercial pockets, in the north, east and west, on the Batmaloo-Baramulla, Harwan, Ganderbal roads and on the Boulevard. The Boulevard-Harwan road is very important from tourist industry point of view and Nishat, Shalimar, Harwan and Chashmashahi gardens are located on this road.

2.9 Major Commercial Areas

The fact that Srinagar was an important trading centre in the past has already been seen in the preceding pages. At present the main concentrations of commercial activities are found in Lal Chowk, Haba Kadal-Fetha Kadal, Zaina kadal, Nowhatta, and along Ganderbal road, Boulevard, Nalamar road, Batmaloo, Jawahar Nagar road and Hazratbal (Ghulam Ahmad Ashahi) road.

Lal Chowk Commercial Complex

It is located in the south-central part of the city on both the banks of river Jhelum. It includes Maualna Azad road, Residency road, Bund, Hari Singh High street, Hazuri Bagh and Government Central Market, area. Lal Chowk complex is the central business district of the Srinagar city. People from all parts of the city flock in this area for retail and wholesale purchases, specially, for purchasing specialised goods and services, fashionable items, readymade garments, cloth, shoes, food materials, sweets, electronic goods etc.

Zaina-Kadal-Nowhatta Commercial Complex

This is the old commercial area of Srinagar. It is located in the central part of the city. It includes the middle part of the Nalamar road up to Rajouri Kadal, Zaina Kadal, Maharaj Gang, Bori Kadal and Nowhatta. Copper and brass utensils, cloth, general merchandise, gold and silver ornaments are the main attraction of this area.

Haba Kadal-Fetha Kadal Complex

Haba kadal-Fetha Kadal area is also one of the important commercial areas of Srinagar. It is located on the Haba Kadal-Zaina Kadal road. It extends up to the Hospital Road in the west across river Jhelum, in the south up to Tankeypora, in the north up to Khankhahi Moulla and in the south-east up to Basant Bagh. This complex is noted for general merchandise, cloth, leather goods, embriodery and cosmetics etc.

Rainawari

Rainawari market is also one of the important commercial areas of the city, located on the Hazratbal road. It extends from the the Hazratbal road in the west to Jogi Lanker in the east. This commercial area is important for consumable items of daily use such as fruits, vegetables, fish, meat, chicken, general merchandise, ordinary cloth and hosiery goods.

Jawahar Nagar

It is a linear market extending from Jawahar Nagar Metador Stand, in the south to river Jhelum (Lal Mandi) in the north. Meat, Hardware, Tea Stall, General Stores, Chicken etc. are the main articles sold here.

Karan Nagar

This market is located on the Safa Kadal road. It is also linear and extends from Karan Nagar Chowk in the south to Safa Kadal bridge in the north. Cosmetics, fashionable goods, medicines, cloth, readymade garments etc. are the main items sold in this market.

Besides in these market centres, scattered shops occur on both sides of some other roads of the city. They are scattered to the extent that they do not form any compact commercial centre. These scattered shops have been excluded from the present study.

Besides these commercial complexes and market centres, there are a number of retail centres in the city of Srinagar located on the main roads of different areas. The important among them are Hazratbal, Nowshera, Nagin-Saida Kadal markets found on the northern parts of the city. Batwara-Sonawar, Panthachowk and Chhanapura roads. Boulevard and Batamaloo markets are situated in the eastern and western parts of the city. Moreover, there are few specialised markets located in different parts of the city. Important among them are the Nishat and Shalimar markets, located near the gardens. They specialise in the items of tourist interest. Parimpora fruit mandi is located in the western part of the city. This is purely wholesale vegetable and fruit market.

2.10 Population

The visible landscape of a city perhaps is the most obvious object of geographical study. At least it provides a starting point for study by urban geographers. Associated with the morphology of city are its past and present populations, which establish certain social and economic institutions, required to be housed and follow distinctive occupations.

Even such a crude measure as total population has certain relevance to the importance of a city. The size of the total population provides a rough indication of the size of the working force and the nature of the specialised services which a city is likely to offer. The distribution of population as well as its size have important geographical consequences. In many cities there is a regular decrease in the density of population from the city centre towards the periphery. It is related probably to the intensity of residential landuse[102].

The growth and development of the Srinagar city is related to the growth of its population, development of economic activities, traditions and professions of the people and the heavy pressure of tourist traffic[103].

The first population census in the Srinagar city was taken in 1891[104]. No information is available on the pre 1891period. The population of the Srinagar city shows a tremendous increase between 1891 and 1981 (422.5%). Table 2.2 gives and idea of the growth of population of Srinagar between 1891 and 1981.

Table 2.2
Population Growth in the Srinagar city 1891-1981

Census Year	Total Population	Decadal increase
1891	1,18,960	-
1901	1,22,618	+3.07
1911	1,26,334	+3.03
1921	1,41,735	+12.19
1931	1,74,459	+23.09
1941	2,09,596	+20.14
1951	2,50,724	+19.23
1961	2,91,853	+16.40
1971	4,23,253	+45.02
1981	6,21,621	+46.87

Source : District Census Handbook, Srinagar District, (1981).

The population of the Srinagar city grew at a slow pace during the pre 1911 years. The population increased from 1,18,960 in 1891 to 1,22, 618 in 1901 and to 1,26, 344 in 1911. The decadal variation remained constant. The 1891-1901 and 1901-1911 growth rates of the population were 3.07 and 3.03 percent respectively.

It is noteworthy that between 1911 and 1931 the city witnessed a phenomenal increase in its population, rather a meteroric rise, which can only be attributed to immigration. From 1931 onwards until 1961 the population of the city was 1,74,459 which rose to 2,09, 596 by 1941, to 2,50,724 in 1951 and to 2,91,853 in 1961. The population grew by 23.09%, 20.14% 19.63% and 16.4% respectively between 1921-31, 1931-41, 1941-51 and 1951-61.

The decline in the growth rates during the successive deades since 1931 was due to the drought conditions of 1931-32, limited amenities and facilities and especially the partition of India (1947) and the aggression over Jammu and Kashmir by Pakistan. The people were forced to migrate to Pakistan by the last two events.

The decade 1961-71 witnessed a population explosion. In 1971 the city had 4,23,253 persons as against 2,91,853 in 1961. The growth rate rose from 16.40% in 1951-1961 to 45.02% in 1961-1971. This increase was due to improvement in the social amenities and facilities, control over (reduced) death rate, the development of household industries, trade, commerce, transport and communication and the all round development of the city. These factors acted as some kind of a centripetal force and attracted people from the surrounding areas of the city (Fig. 4).

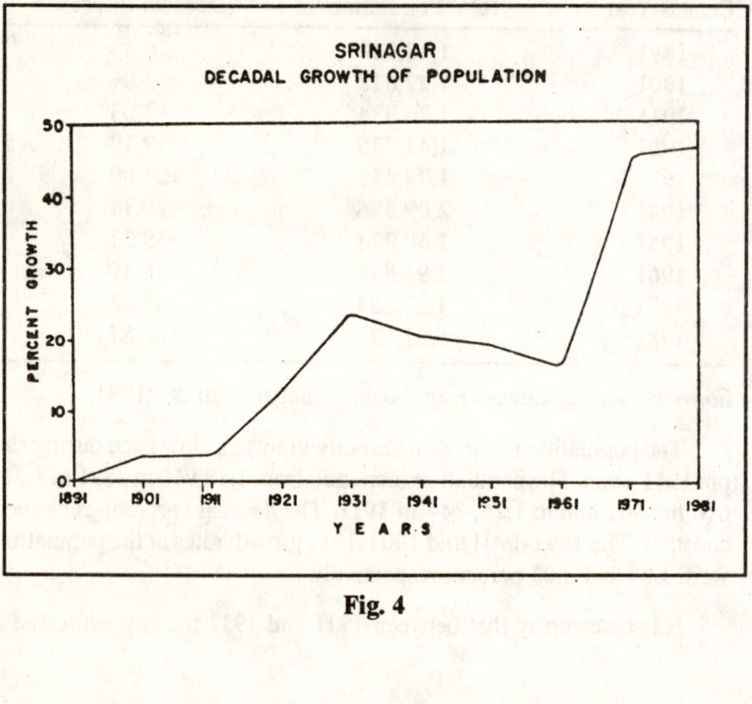

Fig. 4

The census of 1981 showed an increase in the population form 4,23,253 (1971) to 6,21,621 and the growth rate showed a slight increase from 45.02% to 6\46.87%. This almost constant growth rate during the decade 1971-81 was despite the popularity of family planning measures, specially among the literate and conscious people of the city.

Density

The distribution of density of population in the Srinagar city is directly related to the functional character of the land, being high in the commercial areas and decreasing steadily towards the peripheral agricultural belts of the city. The Lal Chowk area provides an exception because though having commercial function it does not have as many people as the other commercial areas of the city.

In 1891 the total area of Srinagar which confined to the right bank of river Jhelum was 22 square kilometers containing 1,18,960 persons. At present (1981) the Srinagar Municipal Corporation covers an area of 157.30 square kilometers including the cantonment and the areas under water bodies.

The overall density of population of the Srinagar city in 1891 was 5,407 persons per square kilometer. At present it has 3,952 persons per square kilometers.

Considering the increase in the population between 1891 and 1981 the decrease in overall density from 5407 (1891) to 3952 (1981) is apparantely due to the addition of new lands to the Municipal area which has more land under agriculture than under settlements. The inclusion of water bodies in the Municipal area is also a major factor.

The density of population varies greatly ranging from 4 persons per acre in ward number one to 195 persons per acre in ward number eight.

On the basis of the density of population Srinagar can be divided into five sections. (Fig. 5).

1. Very low density areas.
2. Low density areas.
3. Medium density areas.
4. High density areas.
5. Very high density areas.

1. Very Low Density Area

The areas having population density below 10 persons per acre may be called very low density areas. Four wards come under this group. They are ward numbers 1,4, 16 and 17. The density of population among the areas of this category ranges from 3.73 in ward number one, which is the lowest density in the whole of the city, to 8.46 persons per acre in ward number four. The other two wards, i.e. 16 and 17, have almost

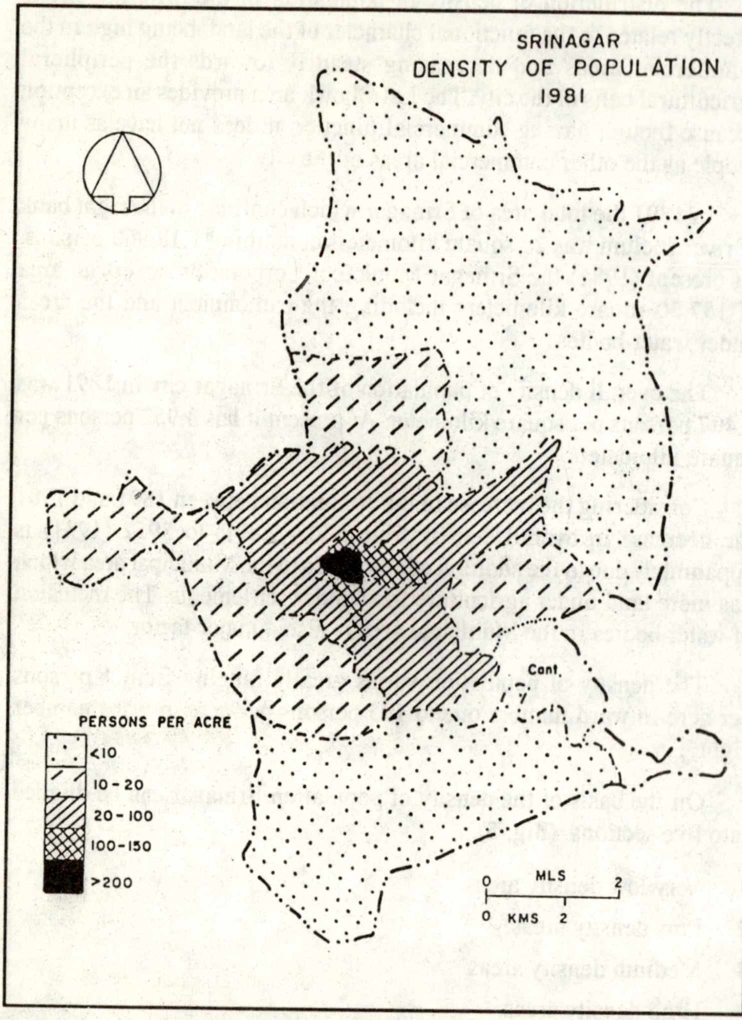

Fig. 5

equal density of population. They have 5.17 and 5.32 persons per acre respectively. These very low density areas are found on the periphery of the city mainly in the northern, eastern, western and southern parts of Srinagar. In these areas most of the land is under agricultural use. The famous Dal Lake, the mountains and forests are also included in these very low density areas of Srinagar.

2. Low Density Areas

The parts of the city with population density ranging from 10 to 20 persons per acre are grouped under the low density areas. Ward numbers 2, 5 and 15 are included in the areas of this category. The density in the wards is 17.80, 14.37 and 11.22 persons per acre respectively. All of these three low density wards are found between the very low and medium density areas of the city. While ward number 15 is located in the northern part, ward numbers 5 and 2 are located in the south-western and south-eastern parts of the city respectively.

3. Medium Density Areas

The wards having population density ranging between 20 and 100 persons per acre are categorised as medium density areas. Seven wards come under this group. They include ward numbers 3, 6, 9, 11, 12, 13 and 14. All of these wards are close to the high density areas of the city and are found in its central part. The density of population within these areas ranges from 21.12 persons per acre in ward number 12 to 78.64 persons per acre in ward number 13. Ward numbers 9, 6 and 11 of this group show relatively higher density of population i.e. 70, 79 and 51.61 persons per acre respectively. The two remaining, wards namely ward numbers 3 and 14, have density of only 24.69 and 21.24 persons per acre respectively.

All these wards are mainly residential. There are some commercial establishments in ward numbers 6, 9 and 13. Ward number 3 (Lal Chowk area) of this group is purely commercial, yet the density of population in this ward is only about 25 persons per acre. This shows that the main commercial centre of Srinagar is to a considerable extent non-residential and has the character of a true central business district.

4. High Density Areas

The areas with density ranging from 100 to 150 persons per acre are classified as high density areas. Only two wards, namely ward numbers 7 and 10 come under this group. The density figures of ward numbers 7 and 10 are 141.13 and 115.92 persons per acre respectively.

These wards comprise the old residential-cum-commercial areas of the city. They are found close to the very high density zone and are located in the middle part of Srinagar.

5. Very High Density Areas

Very high density area is found in the heart of the city of Srinagar. This area having more than 200 persons per acre may be called very high density area. Ward number 8 is the only one which comes under this group. It has a density of 194.86 persons per acre which is the highest density in the whole of the city of Srinagar. This (Zaina Kadal) area is the oldest part of the city and is characterised mainly by residential function (Fig. 5).

The density of population in a section of a city is determined to a considerable extent by the function the section discharges. In general people are inclined to settle nearest to the heart of a city However, lack of space and high land value compel them to settle away from the city centre. The main business area of Srinagar city, Lal Chowk, is moderately populated which clearly indicates that the CBD of Srinagar is purely commercial. The other business areas of Srinagar such as Zaina Kadal, Maharajganj, Bori Kadal, Nowhatta, Haba Kadal, Fetha Kadal and their surrounding areas have highest density of population. The density of population is comparatively higher in the residential-cum-commercial core of Srinagar.

The study of the spatial distribution and density of population of Srinagar reveals that the highest density of population is found in mainly residential areas. The main commerical area of the city (Lal Chowk) is located away form the residential core (Zaina Kadal). It has relatively lower density of population. While the CBDs of most Indian cities are characterised by maximum concentration of population as they have mixed landuse commercial as well as residential, the commercial core of Srinagar has lower density because it has less residential (night) population.

2.11 General Land Use

Preparation of a land-use inventory and its analysis are essential prerequisites of the preparation and administration of a comprehensive city plan[105]. Urban land use planning is one of the important ingredients of urban planning which aims at orderly and balanced spatial arrangement of all the uses of urban land.

The land-use pattern of a city or town is essentially a reflection of its economic and social form and structure. In view of the diversity of the economic and social structure of cities and towns, there are nearly as many patterns of land-use and city layout as there are cities and towns. Cities and towns tend to have certain characteristics which smaller rural settlements do not have. For a proper understanding of the basic characteristics of cities and towns and for gaining an insight into the maladjustment in the land-use pattern, it is useful to undertake a scientific study of the existing land-use pattern of the cities and towns of the

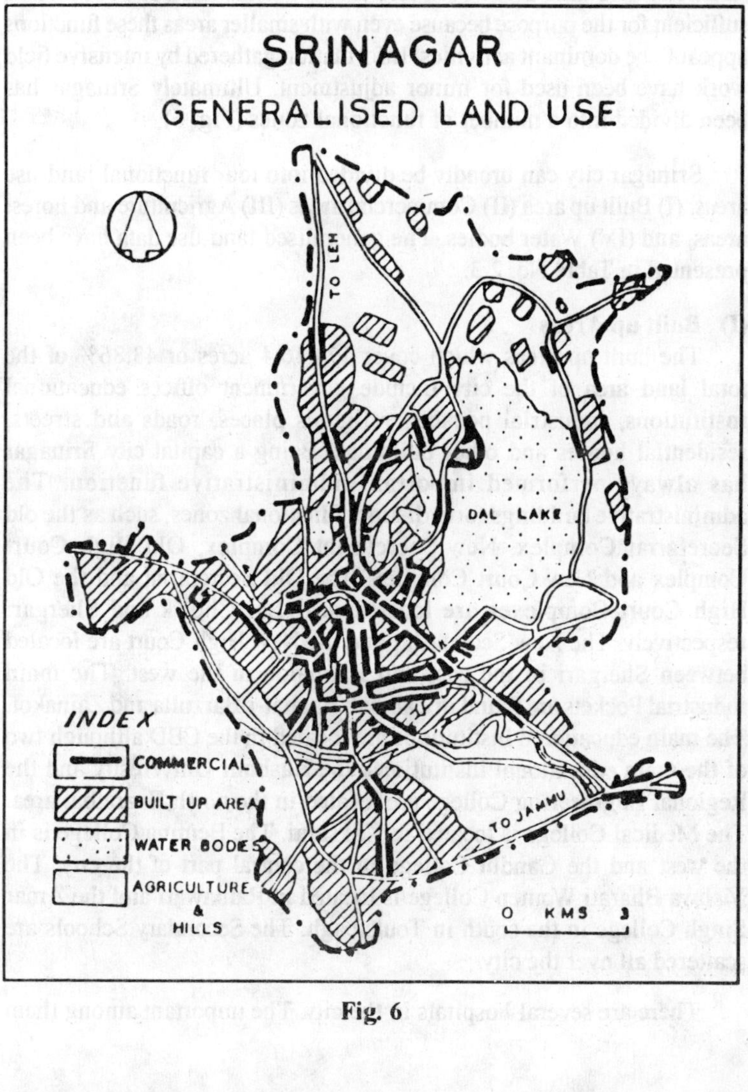

Fig. 6

country.

A general land use map has been use in the present study as the base map for the generalised classification of Srinagar's land use. The land areas under individual uses have been computed graphically. If the land area under a particular use is found to exceed 20 acres in a particular area that area has been designated as one of that particular function. A departure has been made in the case of commercial, medical and transport functions, and land areas even less than 20 acres has been considered sufficient for the purpose because even with smaller areas these functions appear to be dominant activities. Information gathered by intensive field work have been used for minor adjustment. Ultimately Srinagar has been divided into a number of functional zones (Fig. 6).

Srinagar city can broadly be divided into four functional land-use areas. (I) Built up area (II) Commercial areas (III) Agriculture and Forest areas, and (IV) Water bodies. The generalised land-use data have been presented in Table No. 2.3.

(I) Built up Areas

The built up areas which cover 17,046.4 acres or 43.86% of the total land area of the city include government offices, educational institutions, industrial pockets, religious places, roads and streets, residential houses and other buildings. Being a capital city Srinagar has always performed important administrative function. The administrative buildings form distinct functional zones, such as the old Secretariat Complex, New Secretariat Complex, Old High Court Complex and New Court Complex. The Old Secretariat and the Old High Court Complexes are located near Lal Chowk and Shergari respectively. The New Secretariat and the New High Court are located between Shergari in the east and Batmaloo in the west. The main industrial Pockets are found in Zadibal, Baghat-i-Barzulla and Zainakot. The main educational institutions are located in the CBD although two of the main educational institutions, the Kashmir Univeresity and the Regional Engineering College are located in the north Hazratbal area. The Medical College is located in Kaksarai. The Bemina College is in the west and the Gandhi College in the central part of the city. The Vishwa Bharati Women College is located in Rainawari and the Amar Singh College in the south in Toulsibagh. The Secondary Schools are scattered all over the city.

There are several hospitals in the city. The important among them are the Soura Medical Institue of Soura, the S.M.H.S. Hospital of Karan Nagar, the L.D. Hospital of Hazuri Bagh and the Nehru Memorial Hospital of Rainawari.

Srinagar is less developed industrially. Some important industries are Saw mills, carpet weaving factory, silk factory, Govt. Woollen Mills, H.M.T. Watch Factory, Steel Industry etc. which are located in different parts of the city.

There are stone quarry and stone carving industries in the Srinagar city. Other cottage industries are distributed all over the city found especially in the residential areas.

As far as the residential areas are concerned, the central and south-central parts of the city have maximum concentration of residential houses. The eastern part has low density of residential houses due to the presence of the mountain and forest. The northern part of the city has comparatively less residential buildings.

Table 2.3
Generalised Land-Use in Srinagar

Generalised land-use	Area in acres	% of total area
1. Built up areas	17046.40	43.86
2. Commercial belts	729. 60	1.87
3. Agriculture & forest	14549.76	37.43
4. Water bodies	6542.44	16.84
Total	38867.20	100.00

Source : Field work.

(II) Commercial Belts

About 730 acres of Srinagar's total land area is under commercial use which comes to about 2 percent of the total area of the city. Cities like Bombay and Calcutta have respectively 9 and 6 percent of their land under commercial use. On the other hand Kanpur and Lucknow have less than 2 percent of their lnad area under commercial use. The average proportion of land under commercial use of cities with population of 2 to 5 lakhs is only 3.5 percent[106]. The land under commercial use in Srinagar is comparatively less than an average town of India.

Almost all the important roads have commerical establishments on their flanks with intermittent breaks. The most important and the busiest retail shopping areas of the city are found on the residency road, right from the office of the Public Service Commission in the east to Government Central Market (Hazuribagh) in the west. The Maulana Azad Road also has commercial units between Golf club in the east and Amira Kadal (second Bridge) in the west. The two other important shopping centres are the Haba Kadal-Fetha Kadal and the Zaina Kadal-Nowhatta complexes. These two commercial complexes are located in the central and north-central parts of the Srinagar city.

Besides these the Chanapura road in the south has also commerical belts with intermittent breaks. Retail shops are also found on the National Highway in the south-east. Other important roads such as the Boulevard-Harwan road, Lal Chowk-Dargah road and Lal Chowk-Soura road, Nalmar road and Batmaloo, Baramulla road have continuous lines of shops.

Besides these linear occurrences of shops along the important roads, there are a number of other commercial pockets scattered all over the city arranged on both sides of the roads.

(III) Land Under Agriculture & Forest

Large chunks of land now within the Municipal Corporation boundary are under such uses as agriculture, parks and play grounds, forests and hills. The total area under agtriculture and forest comes to 14,549.76 acres which constitutes about 37 percent of the total area of the Srinagar Municipal Corporation. This proportion is high. This is due to the incorporation of new land by the Corporation in 1981. All the newly incorporated areas are agricultural on account of which the proportion of land under this category has increased. The agricultural land is found on almost all side of the city except the west, which is mostly forested and hilly. Besides, there are a number of public open spaces. The chief among them are the Pologround, Iqbal Park, Bakshi Stadium, Sheri-Kashmir, Golf Clubs, Nishat garden, Shalimar garden, Chashmashahi and Harwan. These are located in different parts of the city.

(IV) Water Bodies

The Srinagar city is gifted with the world famous Dal Lake which adjoins it. River Jhelum divides the city into two parts and flows through the middle of the town. Other water bodies include the Khushalsar, Brarinambal and Nagin Lakes. The total area under water bodies is 6,541 acres (16. 84%). The Dal Lake is situated in the north of the city.

It extends from the Dal Gate in the south to Telbal in the north. This lake is very important from the tourist interest point of view. In ancient times this lake and river Jhelum were the chief lines of transport and communication. About 3.93% of the total population of the Srinagar city resides on house boats over the Dal and Nagin Lakes and river Jhelum. Some of the tourists reside on the commercial house boats.

The Nagin Lake is situtated between Lal Bazar and Saida Kadal while the Khushalsar is located in the West of Hawal.

2.12 Land-Use Pattern associated with Commercial Belts

Almost all the commercial establishments are located on the flanks of important roads. These include commercial offices, different kinds of shops, marketing centres, small manufacturers and order suppliers. Most of the streets have houses used both for residential and commercial purposes. The shops occupy the street frontage and the ground floor, while the family resides at the back or on the first or second floors.

The Residency road and Maulana Azad road have the major shopping complexes of the city. Buildings on both flanks of these roads are purely commercial. The front and back portions and even upper floors of the buildings are used for commercial purposes. This is the most important commercial area of the city.

The land within the commercial belts of the Haba Kadal-Fetha Kadal and Nowhatta, Zaina Kadal commercial complexes are almsot purely residential with dense settlement amd closely built houses, which are now dilapidating into slums. The front portions of the ground floors of buildings which have road frontage have been converted into shops, while their back portions are used for residential purposes.

Besides these commercial commercial complexes, Jawahar Nagar, Chhanapura, Karan Nagar, Safa Kadal, Qamarwari, Soura, Dargah, Rainawari etc. are scattered commercial areas in different parts of the city. Among small and dispersed commercial ribbons, Saderbal Lal bazar, Soura and Nowshera are in northern Srinagar. These dispersed centres have small number of and a few types of establishments. They are in predominatly residential areas. They deal in mostly consumer goods of daily use.

There are a few specialised markets in Srinagar. They include Boulevard, Nishat and Shalimar markets and the Parimpura Fruit Mandi. The Parimpura Fruit Mandi is located in the eastern part of the city.

The Boulevard market is situated in the east and the Nishat and Shalimar markets are located in the north-eastern part of the city. The Boulevard, Nishat and Shalimar markets specialise in goods of tourist interest while the Parimpura fruit Mandi of the west is deals in fruits and vegetables only. The buildings housing them are purely commercial.

2.13 Future character of Commercial Belts

The futrue development, growth and extension of the commercial belts are likely to follow the distribution of population in the city. The population is moving rapidly from the congested central areas of the northern, southern and western parts of Srinagar. The eastern part is restricted by the presence of the mountains. These mountains are actually natural barriers for eastward expansion of the city. Therefore the future expansion is sure to take place in the northern, western and southern parts of the city. As such the existing small markets of the Rajbagh and Rawalpura areas of the south, the Bemina, Parimpura and Zainakut areas of the west and the Lal Bazar, Soura, Butchpura, and Hawal areas of the north are likely to form large commercial zones.

It will be clear from the subsequent pages that the Lal Chowk complex is expanding towards the south and the Chanapura-Nattipura market is expanding towards the north. New commercial units are coming up in between these markets. It appears that these two commercial centres will soon be merged and a greatly enlarged commercial complex will come into existence which will function as a more effective central business district of Srinagar.

References :

1. Stein, Sir M. Aural, Rajatarangini of Kalhana Volume II, Motilal Banarsidas Publisher, New Delhi (1900), p. 104.

2. Stein, Sir, Adfural, Kalhana's Rajatarangini, Volume III, Motilal Banarsidas Publisher, New Delhi, (1900), p. 95.

3. Stein, Sir M. Aural, Rajatarangini of Kalhana, Volume I, Banarasidas Publishers, New Delhi (1900) p. 274

4. Gazetter of Kashmir and Ladakh, Vivek Publishing House, Delhi-7 (1974), p. 770.

5. Stein, Sir M. Aural, Rajatarangini of Kalhana, Volume II, op.cit. (1900), p. 294.

6. Bamzai, P. N. K. A History of Kashmir, Metropoliyan Publishers,

Pvt. Ltd. New Delhi (1962) pp. 463-464.

7. Rabbani, G. M. Kashmir Social and Culture History. Amol Publishers, New Delhi-51 (1986) pp. 20-21.

8. *Ibid.*

9. Robbani, G. M. Kashmir Social and Culture History *op. cit.* pp. 12-19.

10. *op. cit.*

11. Rabbani, G. M. Kashmir Social and Culture history, *op. cit.*

12. *op. cit.*

13. *op. cit.*

14. Kashmir Under Sultans, pp. 63-64.

15. Khan, Mohd. Ishaqe, A History of Srinagar 1846-1947, A Study in Socio-Cultural Change, Amir Publisher, Srinagar (J&K) 1978, p. 11.

16. *Ibid.*

17. Robbani, G. M. Kashmir Social and Culture History, *op. cit.* p. 20.

18. *op. cit.*

19. Sofi, G.M.D. Kashmir, being a history of Kashmir from the earliest time to our own. Light and Life Publishers, New Delhi (1974) pp. 38-49.

20. Allami, Abul Fazal, The Ain-1-Akbari, Munshilal Manoharlal Publishers Pvt. Ltd. New Delhi-55, pp. 232-237.

21. Ibid.

22. Ibid.

23. Ibid.

24. Robbani, G.M. Kashmir Social and Cultural History op. p. 21.

25. Gazetteer of Kashmir and Ladakh ; Vivek Publishing House, New Delhi-7 (1974), pp. 770-795.

26. Sufi, G.M., Kashmir, Being a History of Kashmir from the earliest

time to our own, Volume I ; Light and Life Publishers, New Delhi, (1974). pp. 38-49.

27. Bamz ıi, P. N. K., A History of Kashmir ; op. Cit. pp. 601-631.

28. Master Plan of Srinagar City, Town and Country Planning Department, Govt. of J & K, Srinagar (1970), pp. 1-3.

29. Ibid.

30. Annual Administrative Report of Municipal Committe, Town Area adnd visitors Bureau Deparment (J&K) (1940) p.37.

31. Report on Srinagar Municipal Administration (J&K), 1920-1921.

32. Ibid.

33. Ibid.

34. Census of India, Series Jammu And Kashmir, 1931, p. 20.

35. Ibid.

36. Koul, P.A ; Report on Srinagar Administration (J&K) op. Cit. p.1

37. Census of India, Series Jammu and Kashmir, 1931, p. 20.

38. Administrative report of J&K (16 oct. 1941-43).

39. Lawrance, W.R. : Provincial Gazetteer of Kashmir ; Rima Publishning House, ER-10, Inderpuri, New Delhi (1985), p. 116.

40. Dickinson R. E. City Region and Regionalism, London, (1960), p. 52.

41. Jaferson, M : The Distribution of World City Folk, G.R. volume XXI, (1931), P.453.

42. Bamzai, P. N. K., A History of Metropoliton Publication Pvt. Ltd., New Delhi (1962), pp. 227-228.

43. Ray ; Sunil Chandra ; Early History and Culture of and Kashmir, Munshilal Manoharlal, New Delhi, p. 128.

44. Stein, Sir M. Aruel ; Kalhanas Rajatarangini Volume IV Motilal Banarsidas Publication, New Delhi (1990), p. 208.

45. Ibid.

46. Bamzai, P. N. K., A History of Kashmir ; op. cit. p. 227.

47. Bamzai, P. N. K., A History of Kashmir ; op. cit. pp. 227-28.

48. Ibid.

49. Hussnain, F. M. Heritage of Kashmir ; Gulshan Publishers, Srinagar (J&K) (1980) pp. 156-169.

50. Ibid.

51. Hussion, F. M. ; Heritage of Kashmir ; op. cit. p. 128.

52. Allami, Abul Fazal, Ain-i-Akbari; op. cit. pp. 448-49.

53. Koul, G. L. ; Kashmir now and than ; (1972) ; p. 73.

54. Matto, A. N. Kashmir Geographia "Our Loagg", Kapoor & Brothers, Srinagar (J&K) (1954), pp. 72-80.

55. Husnain, F. M. Heritage of Kashmir ; op. cit. pp. 100-199.

56. Husnain, F. M., Cultural Heritage of Kashmir, op. cit. p. 199.

57. Allami Abul Fazal, Ain-i-Akbari, op. cit. p. 449.

58. Ray, S. C. The Early History of Kashmir ; op. cit. p. 129.

59. Stein, M. A. Kalahana's Rajatarangani, Volume, III, op. cit. p. 10.

60. Bamzai, P. N. K. : A History of Kashmir, op. cit. p. 329.

61. Ibid, p. 329.

62. Ibid.

63. Bamzai, P. N. K., A History of Kashmir, op. cit. p. 329.

64. Ibid.

65. Ibid.

66. Stein, M. A. Kalahana's Rajatarangani, Volume VIII, op. cit. p. 495.

67. Ibid.

68. Stein, M. A. Rajatarangani of Kalhana Volume VII, op cit. p. 495.

69. Op. cit.

70. Op. cit., p. 1221.

71. Op. cit., p.2010.

72. Bamzai, P. N. K. A History of Kashmir ; op. cit., p. 494.

73. Op. cit.

74 Op.cit.

75. Bamzai, P. N. K. A History of Kashmir; op. cit. pp. 494-496.

76. Ray, S. C. Early History and Culture of Kashmir, op. cit. pp. 125-225.

77. Op. cit.

78. Op. cit.

79. Bamzai, P. N. K. A History of Kashmir; op. cit. p. 495.

80. Op. cit.

81. Husnain, F. M. Heritage of Kashmir, p. 157.

82. Bamzai, P. N. K. A History of Kashmir; op. cit. p. 497.

83. Elias, N. : Tarikh-i-Rishidi; op. cit. p. 425.

84. Sharma. D. C.; Kashmir under the Sikhs, Seema Publications, Delhi-7 (1983). p. 215.

85. Ibid.

86. Ibid.

87. Ibid.

88. Sharma, D. C. : Kashmir under the Sikhs, op. cit. p. 214.

89. Op. cit. p. 215.

90. Op. cit. p. 217.

91. Op. cit. p. 218.

92. Sharma, D.C.; Kashmir under the Sikhs, op. cit. p. 218.

93. Moorcroft, William, Travels part II Published by Directer Languages, Deptt. Punjab, Patiala (1970), pp. 398-471.

94. Sharma, D.C. op. cit. pp. 398-471.

95. Op. cit. pp. 219-223.

96. Bamzai, P. N. K . A History of Kashmir, op. cit. pp. 594-654.

97. Op. cit.

98. Master plan of Srinager city, Town and country- planning Department, Govt. of J&K, srinager (1970). pp. 10-20.

99. Ibid.

100. Ibid.

101. Ibid.

102. Kornhauser, David; Japan : Geographical background to urban industrial development. Longman Group Ltd., Longman House, Burnt Mill, Harlow, Essex, U.K. (1982), pp. 22-32.

103. Kornhauser, David; Japan : Geographical background to urban industrial development. op. cit. p. 30.

104. District Census Handbook of Srinagar District.

105. Bartholomew, H : The Land-Use Survey, Published in Readings in urban Geography by H. M. Mayor and C.F. Kohn, Central Book Dept Allahabad, (1967), p. 168.

106. Report on Land use Pattern of India's Cities and Towns, Town and Country Planning Organization, Govt. of India New Delhi (1966), pp. 29-40 (unpublished).

3

Activities : Identification and Hierarchy of Market Centres

In the city of Srinagar the commercial activities multiplied several times in the last few decades, partly because the city is the capital of the state and its central location enables it to serve the vast valley region. It has an efficient network of transoprt and communication connecting it with the different parts of the valley.

The commercial activites of Srinagar have developed in phases. The unplanned growth of the city has led to haphazard development of the city settlement area and the whole town has lost its physical coherence. The growth and development of shopping areas of Srinagar are therefore, mostly strip-development along one or both sides of the roads with intermittent breaks. Not a single market of Srinagar had been planned properly, before the development of the Lal Chowk area.

Till recently Nowhatta, Zaina Kadal and Haba Kadal were the main shopping centres. The Lal Chowk and Government Central Market are the products of recent commercial development.

At present the concentrations of commercial activities are found on almost all major roads up to Soura and Hazratbal on the Gandarbal and Ghulam Ashai roads respectively on the north, upto Chana Pura and pantha Chowk on the Chana Pura and Srinagar-Jammu roads (N.H.A) on the South and South-West respectively, on the Baramulla road upto Parimpura Fruti Mandi on the west and on the Boulevard in the east.

3.1 Identification and Delmitation of Market Centres

The preliminary task before the market geographers is to demarcate and delimit the different market centres existing within the city. Previous researchers have relied generally, upon self perception and extensive field work[1]. However, delimitation of market centre should be done scientifically and uniformity must be maintained in this task.

In the present study the boundaries of the retail centres have been drawn mainly on the basis of the distribution of shops, their compactness, and breaks in the continuity such as presence of river bridges, the presence of open spaces, and dominance of other than commercial landuse as observed in course of the field work. At few places the market centre have been demarcated simply on the basis of the nomenclature of the markets. Though there is an apparant continuity of shops along one road, it is actually two markets outgoing in ribbon development, form two separate, nucleii, in which there is a marked difference in their functional character as well as a drastic fall in the density of shops at their mutual junction. These two different markets take the name of the respective roads, streets or mohallas.

Unlike other cities and towns of India, Srinagar does not have street hawkers. However, a few shops are found on the foot-paths under the open sky in Lal Chowk, Batmaloo and Nowhatta. These are mainly fruit, fur and leather garment shops. Neither their number nor their type is fixed. Obviously, they are temporary in character and have been ignored by the present study.

Every permanent shop whether it is in a pucca, semi-pucca, kutcha building or stall or is located on the ground, first, second, or third floor has been taken as one unit. In cases of shops selling a variety of articles the dominant item (article) has been taken to determine their type. After collecting the relevant information from the field, the retail establishments were plotted on a large-scale road map of the Srinagar city using separate symbols for their types.

While making use of the break in the continuity of shops as a basis for delimiting the boundary of market centres a linear scale has been fixed. Approximately fifty shops or more per thousand feet of street frontage has been taken as the limiting factor for identifying individual market centres. It is found that the number of shops rises towards the market centre but falls to around 25 shops or less per thousand feet towards the margin or the boundary between two markets. In most cases this transition is extremely sharp and clearly discernible. At the same time there is a marked change in the functional character of shops, (lower order function) and landuse (non-commercial landuse is predominating). Even in areas of ribbon development, sharp change in number and functions is obvious and cannot be missed. The question, of course, does not arise in the case of smaller and newer markets which constitute a different commercial nucleus. In this way 42 market centres have been identified within the boundary of the Srinagar Municipal

Corporation (Fig. 7).

The greatest concentrations of shops are in Zaina Kadal, Haba Kadal and Lal Chowk areas. The arrangement of shop on the different projecting roads presents a picture of radiating ribbons which combine to form a clear nucleus. Basically, such nucleii are formed in Batmaloo, Chota Bazar, Karan Nagar, Qamarwari, Safa Kadal, Rajouri Kadal, Nawa Kadal, Zaina Kadal, Bohri Kadal, Nowhatta, Zaidibal, Khanyar Chowk, Khyam Chowk, Barbar Shah, Lal Chowk and Jawahar Nagar.

Most of the shopping centres are formed in the form of strips and ribbons along the main roads of the city. In a few areas the ribbons are very long and continue up to other intersections and parallel roads of the same area. Such continuity is observed along the Haba Kadal-Fetha

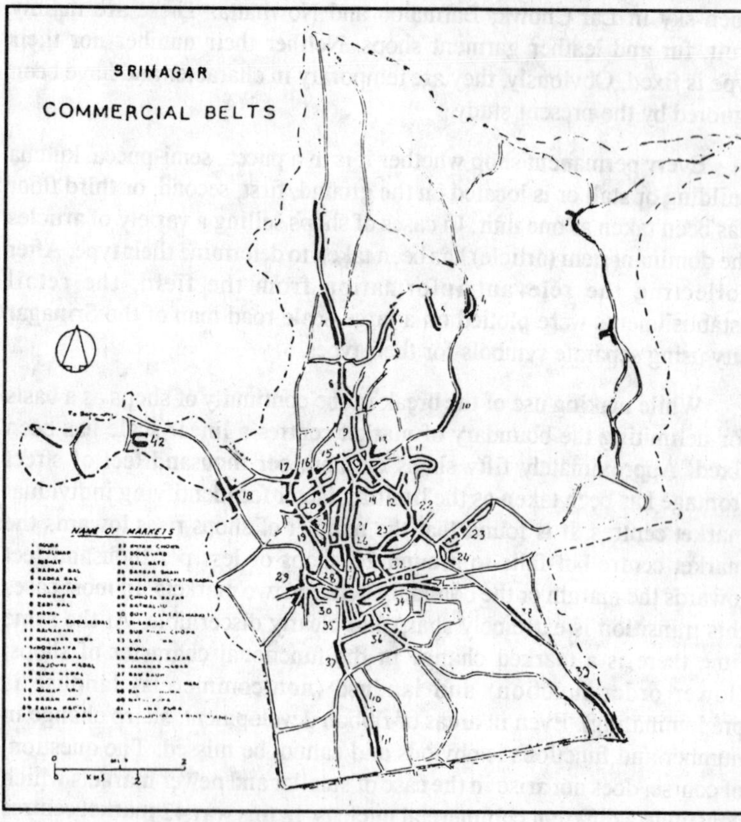

Fig. 7

Kadal,.Nalamar and certain other arterial roads. The identified centres of these areas form, large clusters. They appear to be parts of each other and present a picture of one shopping centre but locally they have different nomenclature and hence the designation of shopping centres in these areas is based on local names (Fig. 7).

The central, north-central, south-central and eastern parts of Srinagar are the important commercial areas of the city. The northern part includes, Soura, Nowshera, Zaidibal, Nagin-Saida Kadal, Lal Bazar, Sadrabal, Hazratbal, Nishat and Shalimar markets which contain 6. 30% of the total number of the shops of the city. The north-central part includes, Hawal, Nowhatta, Rainawari, Khanyar Chowk, Bohri Kadal, Maharaj Ganaj, Zaina Kadal, Safa Kadal and contains 26. 66% of the total number of the shops of the city. The central part shares 17.76% of the shopping units. This includes Haba Kadal, Fetha Kadal, Azad Market, Chhota Bazar, Barbar Shah, Khyam Chowk and Karan Nagar.

The south-central part has 36.56% of the total number of the shop of Srinagar. It includes Lal Chowk, Bund, Bud Shah Chowk, Sher Ghari, Maharaj Bazar, Govt. Central Market, Batmaloo and Jawahar Nagar.

The southern, eastern and western parts of the city contain 6.32%, 3.76% and 2.43% of the total number of the shops of the city respectively.

Table 3.1

42 Market Centres Identified in Srinagar

Sl. No.	Name of the markets	No. of establishments	Type of establishment	Percentage
01	Lal Chowk	1414	51	11.77
02	Bund	82	16	0.69
03	Bud Shah Chowk	805	47	6.70
04	Sher Ghari	248	20	2.07
05	Maharaj Bazar	1066	50	8.87
06	Govt. Central Market	130	5	1.09
07	Nowhatta	649	44	5.40
08	Bori Kadal	344	35	2.87
09	Maharaj Ganj	474	33	3.94
10	Zaina Kadal	433	41	3.60
11	Rajouri Kadal	120	27	1.00
12	Haba Kadal-Fathe Kadal	794	43	6.60

13	Azad Market	250	31	2.08
14	Chhota Bazar	353	39	2.93
15	Jawahar Nagar	386	37	3.21
16	Rainawari	329	36	2.73
17	Karan Nagar	326	41	2.71
18	Nawa Kadal	278	32	2.31
19	Batmaloo	259	32	2.16
20	Khanyar Chowk	244	33	2.02
21	Dal Gate	222	31	1.84
22	Khyam Chowk	221	31	1.83
23	Chhana Pura	211	31	1.76
24	Safa Kadal	202	34	1.69
25	Hazrat Bal	198	25	1.64
26	Qamarwari	197	32	1.63
27	Barbar Shah	194	30	1.61
28	Pantha Chowk	179	21	1.49
29	Ram Bagh	150	28	1.24
30	Hawal	132	28	1.10
31	Natti Pura	127	25	1.05
32	Nagin-Saida Kadal	122	21	1.01
33	Batwara-Sonawar	117	23	0.98
34	Lal Bazar	83	17	0.70
35	Zadi Bal	81	20	0.68
36	Nawshera	70	21	0.64
37	Soura	77	21	0.64
38	Sadrabal	36	08	0.30
39	Boulevard	231	20	1.92
40	Parim Pura Fruit Mandi	95	01	0.80
41	Shalimar	49	06	0.40
42	Nishat	36	04	0.30
	Total	12022	53	100

Source : Field work

3.2 Identified Markets of Srinagar

Shops on both sides of the Chhanapura road, from Lal Nagar to Nattipura High School, constitute the Chhanapura shopping centre. This centre includes the retail units of Chhanapura and Lal Nagar. 127 shops and 27 types of functions are found here. With 211 shops and 31 types of functions Nattipura market is located on the same road. It extend from Nattipura high school on the south to Majhoor bridge on the north.

This is linear in pattern and shops are found on both sides of the Chhanapura road. These newly developed commercial centres are located close to the newly developed colonies of the southern part of the city.

Continuing towards the north on the airport road are two commercial centres namely Rambagh and Maharaj Bazar markets, having 150 and 1050 shops and 28 and 50 types of functions respectively. The Rambagh retail centre extends from near Majhoor bridge on the south to the Bakshi stadium on the north.

It includes the shops of Solina, Hab Chinar and Rambagh markets. It generally has, grocery and cloth stores. Further north, on the eastern side of the same road, is the Maharaj Bazar. This retail centre extends from the Iqbal Park on the south to the Janghir Hotel Chowk on the north. This market centre includes retail establishments of Hanuman Mendhar, Hari Sringh High Street, Charas ghali, Huzuribagh, Shah Market, Cheap market, Gonikhun, Maharaj Bazar, Saribala, and Magar Mahalbagh market. This commercial area is very compact and occupies the second position in number of establishments. This market centre contains 8.87% of the total number of the shops of Srinagar.

Four market centres are identified on the Srinagar-Baramulla road. These market centres are Government Central Market, Batmaloo, Qamarwari, and Parimpura Fruit Mandi.

With 130 shops and 5 types of functions the Government Central Market is located on the south of the Srinagar-Baramulla road close to the Lal Chowk. This market centre specialises in articles of tourist interest. It is the only commercial centre in the whole of Srinagar city which is fully planned. It is circular in plan and is owned by the government. There are shawls, carpets, wood carvings, dry fruits and jewellery shops here. It shares 1.09% of the total number of the shops of the Srinagar city. Further west, on the same road is a radiating market centre named Batmaloo. It extends from the opposite side of the office of the Srinagar Development Authorities on the south-east to the Batmaloo bus stand on the north-west. It includes Batmaloo, Wani and parts of Magar Mahal Bagh markets. There are 259 shops and 32 types of functions in this retail centre. Spare parts, grocery, auto-repair shops are common in the market. This market centre constitutes 2.16% of the total number of the shops of the city. Further north-west, on the same road, is a nucleated retail centre with 197 shops and 32 types of functions. It is known as Qamarwari retail centre. It extends from the Shah Cinema

Hall on the south to the Petrol Pump on the north. The Qamarwari market, with 197 shops and 32 types of fuctions, shares 1.63% of the total number of shops of the Srinagar city. Further west, on the southern side of the Baramulla-Srinagar road, is a specialised market centre. It is known as Parimpura-fruit mandi. It has 95 shops and only one type of functional units. This market centre is important for fruits and vegetables and constitutes 0.80% of the total number of the shops of Srinagar.

The shops on both sides of the Safa Kadal-Lal Chowk road are identified as the Chhotta Bazar shopping centre. With 353 shops and 39 types of functions this retail centre forms a nucleated centre. Its outer boundary touches the New Secretariate on the south and S.M.H.S. Hospital on the north. It includes the Chhota Bazar, Neelam Cinema Chowk and Shaieed Ganj. This retail nucleation contributes 2. 93% of the total number of the shops of Srinagar. Further north, on the same road, from Karan Nagar Chowk on the south to Safa Kadal bridge on the north is Karan Nagar market. It contains 326 shops and 41 types of functions. This market centre shares 2.71% of the total number of the shops of the city of Srinagar. Further north, on the same road, at the crossing of Safa Kadal-Lal Chowk and Nalamar roads is another retail nucleation. It is named Safa Kadal market. Here there are 202 shops and 34 types of functions. This commercial centre extends from the Safa Kadal bridge on the south to Nalamar Road on the north. It includes Safa Kadal, Nawampura and Daresh Kadal markets. This market centre shares 1.69% of the total number of the shops of the Srinagar city.

The Jawahar Nagar Market is located on the Chinar-Jawahar Nagar road of southern Srinagar. It extends from the Jawahar Nagar Metador stand on the north to Lal Ded hospital on the south. It includes the commercial strips of Jawahar Nagar, Chinar Jawahar, Wazirbagh, Lal Ded Hospital road and Municipal markets Lalmandi. The commercial strips have 386 shops and 37 types of them. They have 3.21% of the total number of the shops of Srinagar. The Bund market is located north of the Jawahar Nagar Market mainly on the road parallel to River Jhelum extending from the General Post Office on the east to the Amira Kadal bridge on the west. This market centre has 82 shops and 16 types (functional) of them.

On the Residency and Maullana Azad roads are two main business centre of Srinagar namely the Lal Chowk and Bud Shah Chowk markets. These two commercial centres are the city's very important ones. The Lal Chowk market is on the residency road. It is a large market centre and has 1414 shops and 51 types of them. This market is located in the south-central part of the Srinagar city. It extends from the office of the J & K Public Service Commission on the east to the Amira Kadal first bridge on the west. It includes Shere-Kashmir Central Market, Ghantaghar, Khowaja Mohalla, Kokar Bazar, Arts Market, Parts of Maisuma, Pladium Chowk, Aftab market, Lal Chowk, Regal Chowk, Municipal Market and Lumbert market. This is an important commercial centre of Srinagar. Most of the buildings here are purely under commercial use. This commercial centre shares 11.77% of the total number of the shops of Srinagar. On the opposite side of this market centre is another market on the Maulana Azad Road. It is known as Bud Shah Chowk market. It has a total of 895 shops and 47 types of functions. It extends from the Golf Club on the east to the Amira Kadal second bridge on the west. It includes Bud Shah Chowk, Gom Kadal, Exchange road parts of Maisuma, Awqaf Market and Red Cross road markets. This business centre contributes 6.70% of the total number of the shops of the Srinagar city.

On the north of Lal Chowk on the Lal Chowk-Nawa Kadal road there are four market centres. These markets, from south to north are the Sher Ghari, Azad market, Zaina Kadal and Nawa Kadal markets. The Sher Ghari market extends from Janghir Hotel Chowk on the south to Zaldagar bridge on the north. There are 2.48 shops and 28 types of functions. It includes Sher Ghari and parts of Shaieed Ganj. It shares 2.07% of the total number of the shops of Srinagar. Further north, on the same road is the Azad market. It has 250 shops and 31 types of functions. It extends from Tenkeypura on the south to the Haba Kadal bridge on the north. It includes the Azad market, Zaindar and Tenkeypura markets, which shares 2.08% of the total number of the shops of the Srinagar city. On the north Zaina Kadal market on the same road has 433 shops with 41types of functions. It extends from the Nawa Bazar bridge on the west to the Zaina Kadal bridge on the east and from Zaldagar on the South to the Zaina Kadal bridge on the North. It includes parts of Zaina Kadal, Pathar Ki Masjid, Dalal Mohalla, Sayied Hamidura, Siraj Bazar, Kalamdanpura, Nawa Bazar, Shah Mohalla, Chattabal, Zaldagar and Aishan Sahib-markets. From Pathar Ki Masjid to Zaldagar the shops occur in a scattered way but the rest of the market has high concentration of them. Zaina Kadal accounts for 3.60% of the total number of the shops of Srinagar. The Nawa Kadal market is situated further north, partly on the same road and partly on the Nalamar road. It extends from Bulbul Lanker on the south to the Nalamar road on the north and forms a nucleation with 278 shops with 32 types of functions. It includes Wanganpura, Bulbul Lanker, Nalbapura, Nawanpura and Nawa Kadal. This business centre shares 2.31% of the total number of the shops of Srinagar.

Linking Lal Chowk with Haba Kadal-Fetha Kadal and Nalamar road is the Haba Kadal-Fatha Kadal road. There is a concentration of a large number of shops on this road, specially form Basantbagah, just opposite of the Bud Shah Chowk market on the south, to Khankhai Mulla on the north. This retail centre is known as the Haba Kadal-Fetha Kadal market. It forms a long and continuous belt of commercial activities and is occurs in the central part of Srinagar. There are 794 commercial units with 43 types of functions here, on both sides of the Haba Kadal-Fetha Kadal road. It includes Khankhia Mulla, Dukan-Sangin, Qaziya, Buna Mohalla Mallapora, Chandkar Mohalla, Shalyar, Baha Kadal, Safiyar, Keral Khud, Ganpatyar, Malyar, Badiyar and Basantbagh. These are parts of the old city. The roads are narrow and congested. Only light vehicles are allowded to ply on these roads. This market center is of linear pattern and shares 6.60% of the total number of the shops of the city. Further north, on the same road, is Maharajganj, another important commercial centre. The Maharajganj and Zaina Kadal market centres are located practically in the Zaina Kadal area, but River Jhelum, the cultural barrier, divides them into two parts. The Maharajganj market extends from Zaina Kadal Metador Bus stand on the south to Zaratkhana on the north. It includes Maharajganj and parts of Khankohia Muhalla market. There are 474 shops with 33 types of functions here. This market had 3.94% of the total number of the shops of the city. On the north of Maharajganj market, on the Nalamar road, is the Bori Kadal market. It extends from Naid Kadal on the east to Kadi Kadal on the west and has 344 business establishments with 35 types of functions. It includes Naid Kadal, Bori Kadal, Sarat Kadal, Baba damb, Kadi Kadal, Kamangarpura and Zaratkhana markets. This nucleation shares 2.87% of the total number of the shops of the city. Further north, on the Nalamar road, is another nucleated retail centre named Rajauri Kadal market. Here there are 120 shops with 27 types of functions. This market centre extends from Kadi Kadal on the east to Kowdhara on the west. It includes Kowdhara and Rajouri Kadal markets. This retail centre contains 1% of the total number of the shops of Srinagar.

On the Barbar Shah road, which is a link between Khyam Chowk and Lalchowk markets is named Barbar Shah market. It is a nucleated commercial centre having 194 shops and 30 types of fuctions. It extends from the north of S.P. College on the south to the Khayam Cinema Hall on the north-east. It includes only two small retail centres, namely Barbar Shah and Nageshpora markets and has althogether 1.61% of the total number of the shops of Srinagar.

The Pantha Chowk and Batwara-Sonawar markets are on the Srinagar-Jammu National Highway in the south-eastern part of the city. The Pantha Chowk market extends from Pantha Chowk on the south to Panderthan on the north. This includes the Pantha Chowk, Athwajan and Panderthan markets and has 179 shopping units with 21 types of functions. Stone carving is the chief function of the establishments of this market. It shares 1.79% of the total number of the shops of Srinagar. Further north, on the same road, is the Batwara-Sonawar market. It has 117 commercial establishments with 23 types of functions. it is a linear commercial centre located near the Broadway cinema hall and includes the markets both of Batwara and Sonawar. It shares 0.98% of the total number of the shops of the city. There are eight commercial centers on the Srinagar-Ganderbal road. These, from south to north, are the Dal Gate, Khyam Chowk, Khanyar Chowk, Nowhatta, Hawal, Zadibal, Nowshera and Soura markets. The Dal Gate market is located at the southern end of the Dal Lake. Here there are 222 shops with 31 types of functions. This market centre extends from just opposite of Burnhall school on the south to the Boulevard road on the north. It includes the Suleman shopping complex, Druguan and Dal Gate markets and shares 1.84% of the total number of the shops of the city. Further north is the Khyam Chowk market. it extends from the Dal Gate bridge on the south to Hotel Kahakashan on the north. It has 221 retail establishments and 31 types of functions. It includes the Noupora, Khyam Chowk and Khuna Khan markets. This market shares 1.83% of the total number of the shops of the city.

Next to Khyam Chowk, on the north on the same road lies the Khanyar Chowk market. It is a nucleated commercial centre and has 244 shops and 33 types of functions. It extends from Noupora on the south to Khwaja Mohalla on the north. The small retail markets included in this market centre are Budoobagh, Shiraz Chowk, Akilmir and Khanyar markets. They together share 2.02% of the total number of the establishments of the city. Another large nucleated commercial centre is situated on the same road, north of Khyam Chowk. It is named Nowhatta market. The Kowajabazar lies on the south and Gojwara lies on the north of this market centre while Mallaratta is on its west and

Nowhattta police station is on its east. It has 649 commercial establishments with 44 types of functions. The Nowhatta market includes Gojwara, Nowhatta, Awqaf market, Hak Bazar, Panthan, Mallaratta, Tujgri and Khoja Bazar. They together share 5.40% of the total number of the shops of Srinagar. Continued towards the north of Nowhatta on the same road, is another commercial ribbon named the Hawal market. It has 132 shops and 28 types of functions. It extends from Gojwara on the south to Chowk Muntazariabad on the north. It includes the Muntazariabad and Hawal markets. This commercial ribbon has 1.10% of the total number of the shops of the city. Further north, on the same road, is the Zadibal market. Zadibal extends from Muntazariabad on the south to the steel industrial complex on the north. Here there are 81 shops with 21 types of functions. This is a small market centre of Srinagar and shares only 0.64% of the total number of the shops of the city. It includes Alamgari Bazar, Auqeat market and Zadibal market.

The Nawshera market is on the same raod, north of the Hawal market. It extends from the Animal Husbandary Institute on the south to Soura Polic Station on the north. It is also a small market in the form of a ribbon and has only 78 shops wiyh 21 types of function and shares 0.64% of the total number of the shops of the city. After a gap is the Soura market on the northern end of the Ganderbal road. It is near the Institute of Medical Science. It is also in the form of a ribbon and is a small commercial centre. It extends from the Soura Medical Institute on the south to Butchpura Chowk on the north. Here there are only 77 shops with 21 types of functions. It has only 0.64% of the total number of the shops of Srinagar.

The Rainawari, Nagin-Saida Kadal and Hazratbal markets are on the Ghulam Mohammad Ashi road in north Srinagar. Rainawari extends from just opposite of the Shiraz cinema hall on the south to Chattipadshi on the north encompassing the commercial activities of Jogilankar on the east. This market centre has 329 business establishments and 36 types of functions. The areas included in this market centre are Mughal Mahal, Kralyar, Rang peeristan, Surting, Jogilankar, Chattipadshi and Rainawari. It shares 2.73% of the total number of the shops of Srinagar. Nagin-Saida Kadal is also on the same road, north of the Rainawari market. It extends from Chattipadshi on the South to Nagin Police Station on the north. It includes the Nagin, Ashibagh and Saida Kadal markets and has 122 shopping units and 21 types of functions. The shops are situated on both sides of the road in Saida Kadal and Ashibagh, but at

Nagin they are only on the eastern side of the road. It shares 1.01% of the total number of the shops of Srinagar. Further north, on the same road, is another retail business centre. It is known as the Hazratbal market. It is also known as the Dargah market. It extends from just opposite of the Regional Engineering College on the south to the Dargah Bus stand on the north. Here there are 329 shops and 25 type of fuctions. The shops are situated on both sides of the road. There are 1.164% of the total number of the shops of Srinagar in this market.

There are two retail centres on the Lal Bazar-Hazratbal road. They are the Sadarbal and Lal Bazar markets. Lal Bazar is of linear parttern. It is very small and has only 83 shops with 17 type of functions. It extends from the northern end of the Industrial Estate of Srinagar on the south to the Umar Colony on the north. The shops are arranged on both sides of the road. This retail centre contains only 0.70% of the total number of the shops of Srinagar. Further east, on the same road, with 36 shops and 8 types of functions is the smallest business centre. It is named Sadarbal market. It is very close to the Hazratbal market and extends from the northern end of Sadarbal on the north to University town on the south. It shares only 0.30% of the total number of the shops of Srinagar.

There are three commercial strips on the Boulevard-Harwan road on the east of the Dal Lake. These are the Boulevard, Nishat and Shalimar markets. These markets are important in so far as they specialise in the items in which tourists are interested. The Boulevard market extends from the southern end of the Dal Lake to the Nehru park along the eastern bank of Dal Lake. The shops are situated only on the eastern side of the road. Here there are 231 shops with 20 types of functions. Carpets, shawls, handicraft goods, dry fruits, hotels and restaurants are the major functional units of this market. The Boulevard market has 1.92% of the total number of the shops of Srinagar. Further north, on the same road, is the Nishat market. It has 36 shops and four type of functions. It is near the Nishat Garden. Leather and fur goods, wood carvings, photographic studios and tea-stalls are the important functional units of this market. It shares only 0.30% of the total number of the shops of Srinagar. The Shalimar market is located on the same road, north of the Nishat market in front of the Shalimar garden (Fig. 7). It is also a small market with only 49 shops and 6 types of functions. This market centre accounts for 0.40% of the total number of the retail establishments of the city. It also specialises in the items of tourist interest such as leather goods, fur goods, wood carvings and photographic studios etc.

There are in all 12022 establishments in the above mentioned 42 commercial centres of Srinagar. The scattered shops and establishments situated on the different roads and mohalla do not form any belt or nucleii. These have been ignored by the present study. It may be noted that commerce has not been fully activised in the extreme southern, western and northen parts of the city because of lower density of population and lower purchasing power. With the expansion of the city on the west and south-west, new colonies are developing. These colonies may attract the shopkeepers and the present situation may change. New commercial development is already taking place at Rajbagh, Shivpora, Baghati-Barzalla, Rawalpura and Bemina areas of the city.

3.3 Functional specialisation of the Markets

It has already been seen that the different retail centres vary greatly as regards the number of retail shops and the number of functions they have. This will be clear from table No. 3.1. It is, however, impotant to bear in mind that while almost all large markets discharge a number of functions the intensity of occurrence of the functions varies greatly. To illustrate this point, a number of maps have been drawn showing the percentage share of shops discharging various functions. These maps have superimposed proportionate pie diagrams depicting various combinations of functions. They bring out the functional specialisation of the markets.

Figure 8 shows the distribution of shops dealing in leather goods, suit cases, spectacles, wine shops and bars and cinema halls. Such shops are not found in all the markets. They confined to some markets only. The cinema halls have a high concentration in Lal Chowk (25%), and are found also in the Maharaj Bazar, Qamarwar, Chhota Bazar etc. (12.5% each). Suit cases and leather goods shops are concentrated in Bud Shah Chowk (34. 49%), Maharaj Bazar (13.80%). Khyam Chowk (13. 80%), Haba Kadal-Father-Kadal (10.34%). Qamarwari and Jawahar Nagar have 3.44% of the leather goods shops each.

Similarly the spectacles shops are concentrated in Haba Kadal-Fathe Kadal (29.03%) and Lal Chowk (22.59%). Although wine shops are found in ten of the markets of Srinagar, they are concentrated in Lal Chowk (32.60%) and Maharaj Ganj (26.09%). Maharaj Bazar and Bud Shah Chowk have 10.86 and 6.52 percent of the wine shops respectively, while Jawahar Nagar, Batmaloo, and Batwara-Sonawar have 4.35% of the wine shops at each centre.

The car and auto sale shops are concentrated only in two commercial centres. More than 96% of the car shops are found in Lal Chowk and the remaining 33.33% of them are in the Batwara-Sonawar market of southern part of Srinagar. Machine and refrigerator shops are observed to be concentrated mostly in the three markets of the central part of the city (Fig. 9). Bud Shah-Chowk has the largest share (50.00%). Sher

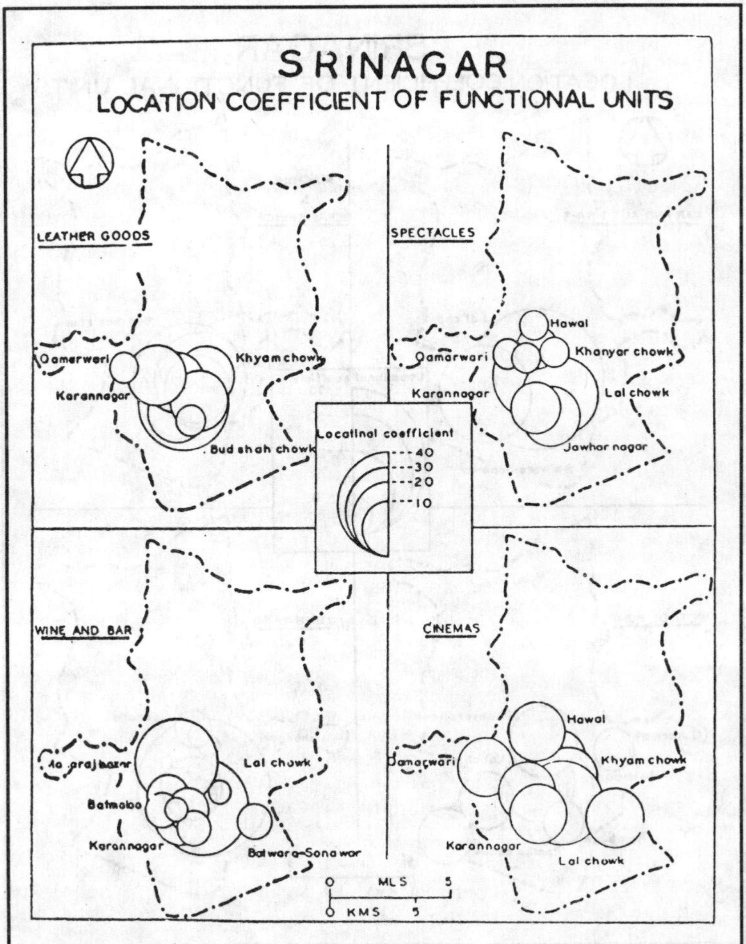

Fig. 8

Ghari has a third (33.33%) and Maharaj Bazar a sixth (16.67%) of the total number of them. Junk yard shops occur in some markets of the city, but are concentrated mostly in Sher Ghari (68.83%), followed by Bud Shah Chowk (13.95%). Nawhatta, Lal Chowk and Maharaj Bazar each have 4.19% of the Junk shops. Petrol pump stations are also found in quite a few markets almost in equal proportions. Lal Chowk and Bud Shah Chowk each have 23.52% of the petrol pump stations, followed by Khanyar Chowk (17,67%). Again Batwara-Sonawar and Pantha Chowk each have 11.77% of the Petrol pump stations, followed by

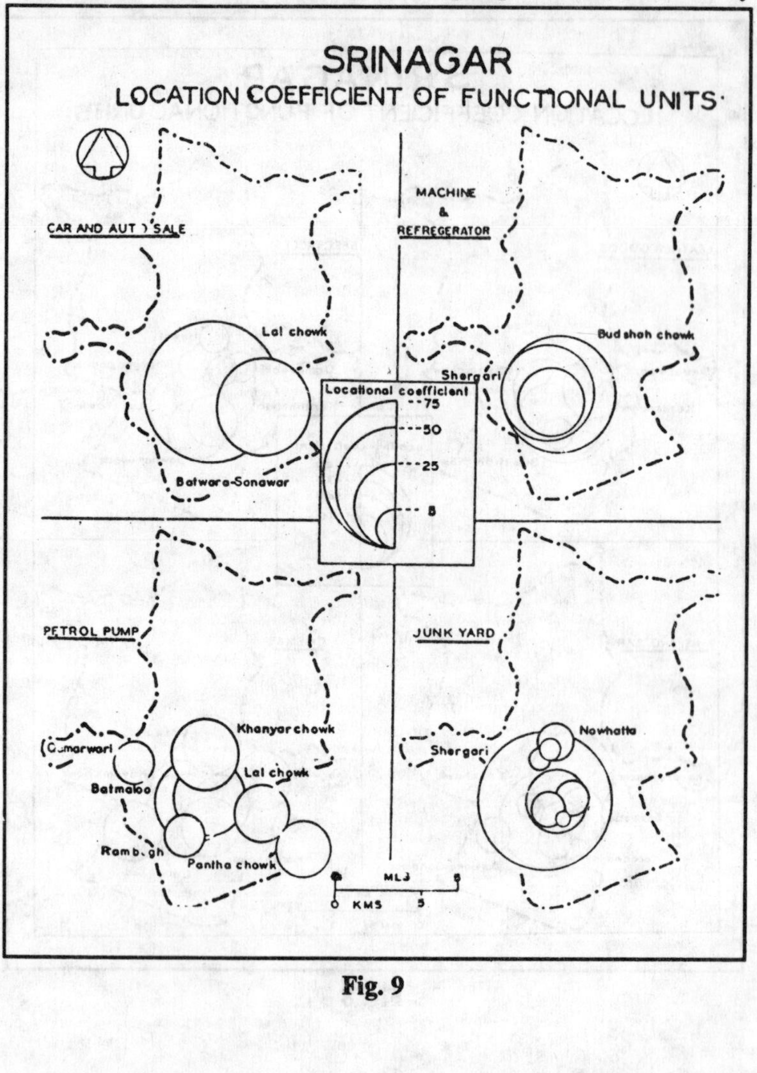

Fig. 9

Rambagh and Qamarwari each with 5.89% of the Petrol pump stations (Fig. 9).

The agricultural implement, non-electrical machine, bokhari & black smithy and kangri and earthen pottery shops are found in a number of markets but their number is higher in a few market centres. Nawhatta is specialised in non-electrical machine (20.46%) and bokhari & black smithy shops (15.52%). On the other hand in Haba Kadal-Fathe Kadal and Rainawari, the majority of the shops deal in agricultural implements

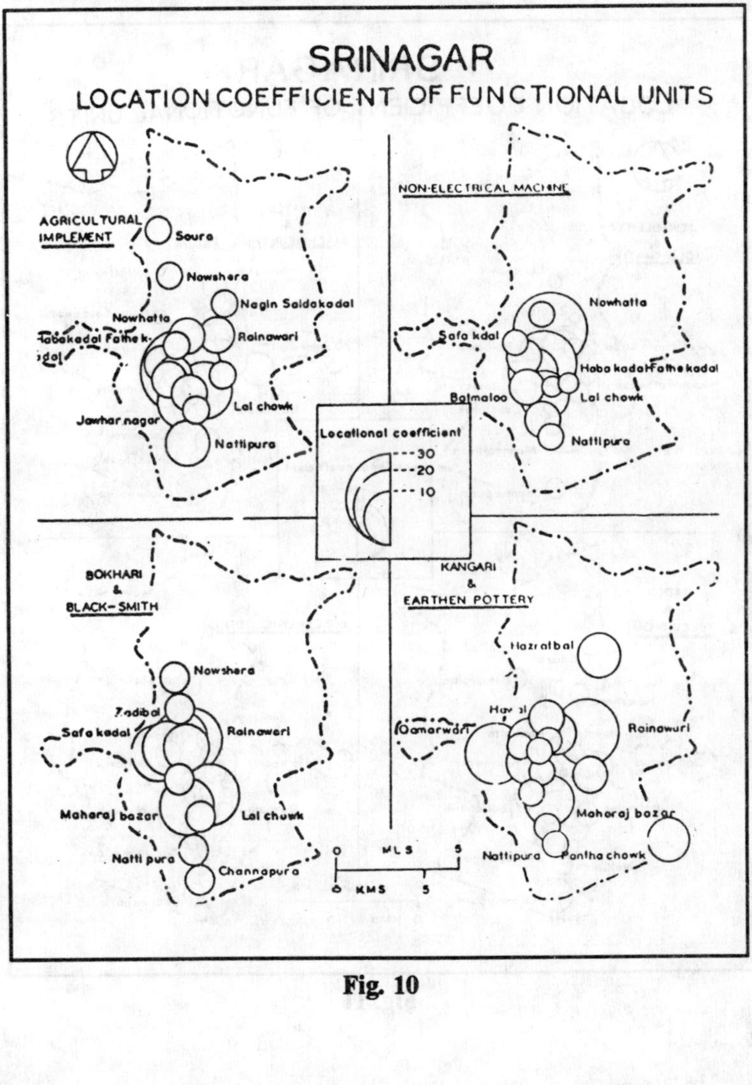

Fig. 10

(26.82%) and Kangri (15.91%) respectively. The distribution of these shops is shown in figure 10. Establishments discharging all these functions are found in other markets also, but the percentages they share are very low. While the non-electrical machine shops occur in the central part of the city, the agricultural implement, bokhari and kangri shops are found scattered here and there in almost all parts of the city.

Figure numbers 11 and 12 show the spatial distribution of shops dealing in costly items such as jewellery, watches and machines, radios

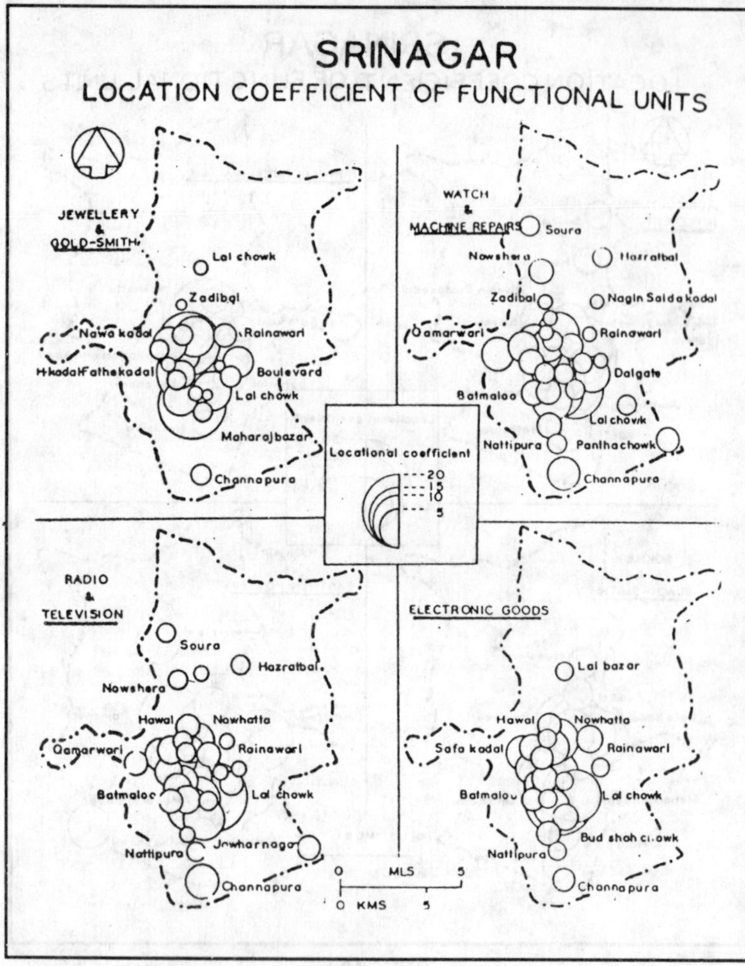

Fig. 11

and televisions, electrical goods, steel & wooden furniture and metal engineering products. These shops are found in considerable numbers in many commercial centres but they concentrate in some particular market centres. The Bud Shah Chowk market specialises and it alone has the largest percentage of shops dealing in steel furniture (22.22%), metal engineering goods (21.38%), building materials (19.17%) and electrical goods (17. 59%). The next in importance in these functions is the Maharaj Bazar. It has shops dealing in steel furniture (15.55%) and building materials (18.02%). Nawhatta specialises in metal engineering

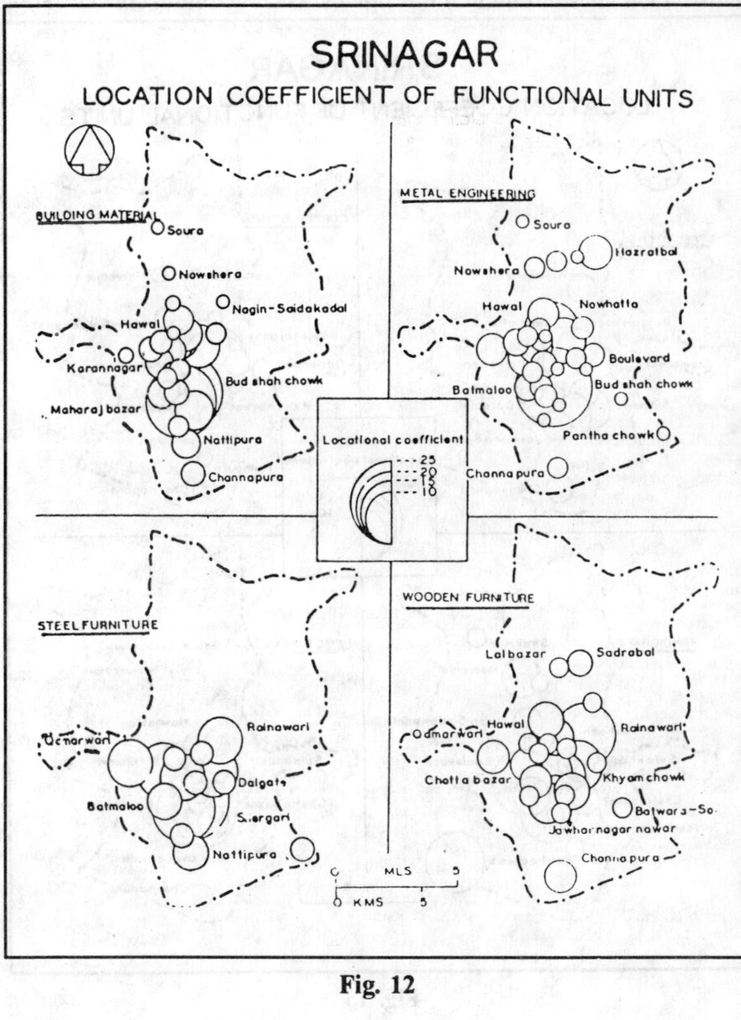

Fig. 12

goods (10.34%) and Haba Kadal-Fathe Kadal in electrical goods (12.07%). Lal Chowk has the largest number of shops dealing in watches and machines (18.85%) and radios and televisions (18.58%), followed by Bud Shah Chowk (8.89%) and Haba Kadal-Fateh Kadal (8.92%) respectively. All these are large markets and occur in the central part of the city. The per cent share in these functions of other markets is insignificant. Steel and copper utensils are other costly items of daily use. The establishments dealing in these goods are scattered in some markets but concentrate in a few others. The maximum concentration

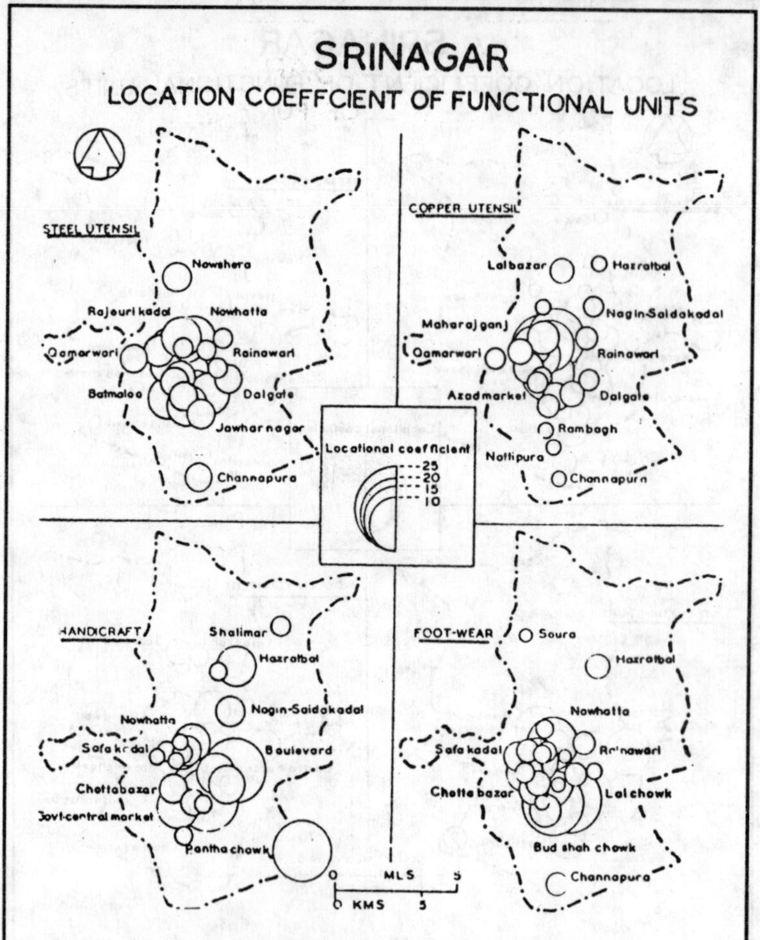

Fig. 13

of the steel utensil shops is found in Zaina Kadal (11.19%) and Bud Shah Chowk (9.32%). Nawhatta and Haba Kadal markets each have 7.46% of the steel utensil shops. Similarly the maximum number of the copper utensil shops are found in Maharajganj (18.96%) and Nawhatta (14.21%). Fathe Kadal-Haba Kadal and Bori Kadal have about 14% of the copper utensil shops each. The distribution of these markets is shown in figure 13.

Handicrafts and foot-wear shops are also found in most of the

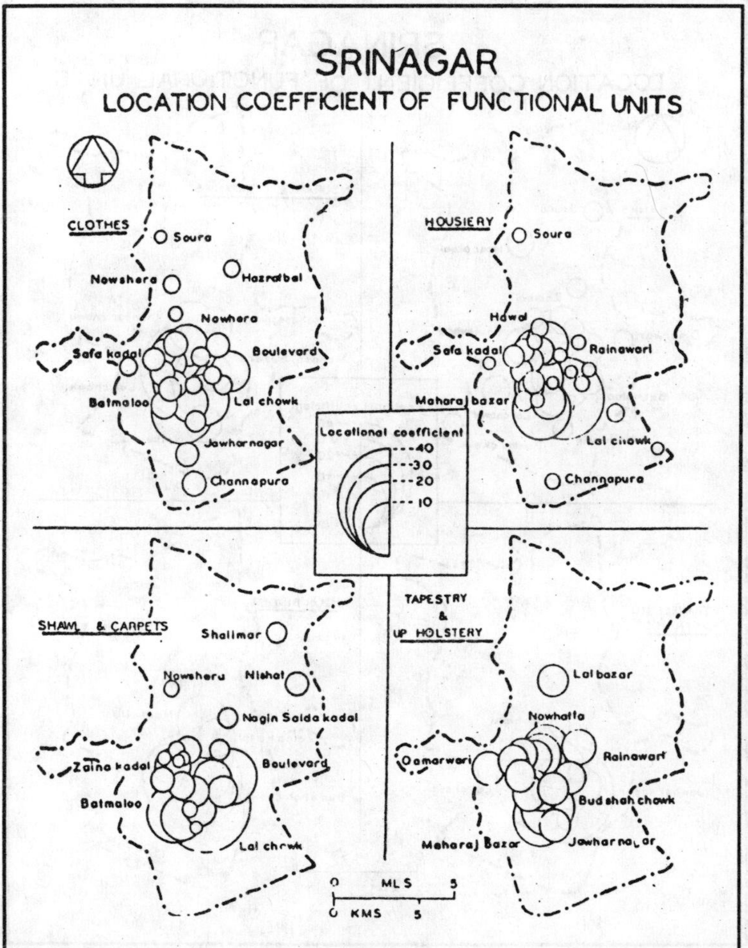

Fig. 14

markets (Fig. 13), but their number is comparatively larger in some commercial centres. The Boulevard and Lal Chowk markets specialise in handicrafts and have 14.45% of handicrafts shops each. Lal Chowk has the largest number of foot-wear shops (15.74%) followed by Bud Shah Chowk (14.57%). All of these markets occur in the central part of the city and have tourist attraction also. Markets specialised in these functions are Pantha Chowk (13.00%), Government Central Market (6.50%) and Hazratbal (6.13%) markets in handicrafts and Haba Kadal-Fathe Kadal (12.20%), Nawhatta (9.44%) and Zaina Kadal (7.09%) in

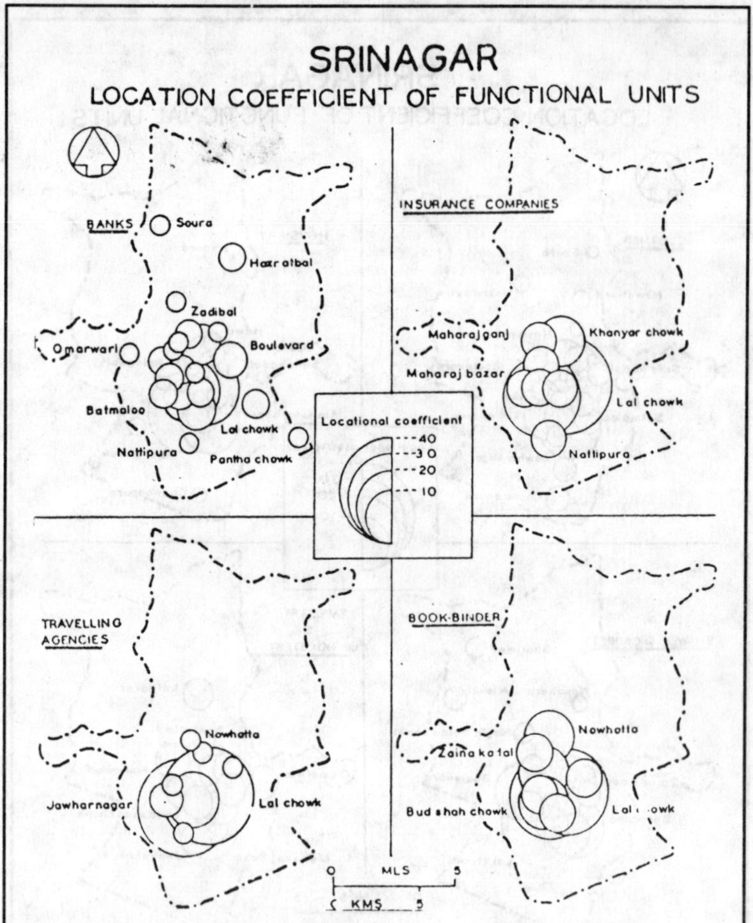

Fig. 15

foot wear. The share of other markets in all these functions is very low and without significance.

Figure number 14 shows the distribution of the markets dealing in cloth, including tapestry and upholstry. Though such shops are found in about fifty percent of the market centres of the city, there are specialised markets dealing almost exclusively in these goods. While the Lal Chowk market specialises in hosiery (24.70%) and shawls and carpets (32.20%), Maharaj Bazar occupies the first position in cloth (14.89%), tapestry

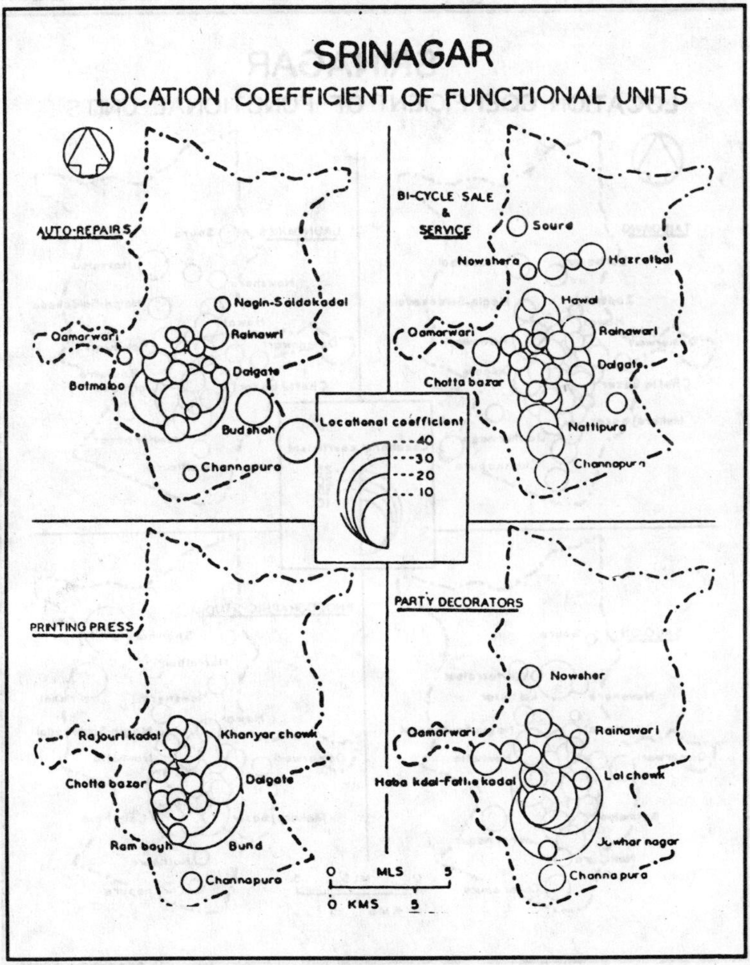

Fig. 16

and upholstry (11.88%). Maharaj Bazar, Haba Kadal-Fathe Kadal, Govt. Central Market and Bud Shah Chowk occupy the second position in hosiery (13.43%), cloth (13.37%), shawls & carpets (12.36%) and in tapestry & upholstry (10.89%) respectively. Hosiery and cloth shops are well distributed and are found in most of the market centres of Srinagar. On the other hand shawl and tapestry shops are found only in about thirty per cent of the market centers of the city, all confined to its central part. Service establishments such as insurance companies, travel agencies and book binding are highly concentrated and are found only in 20%

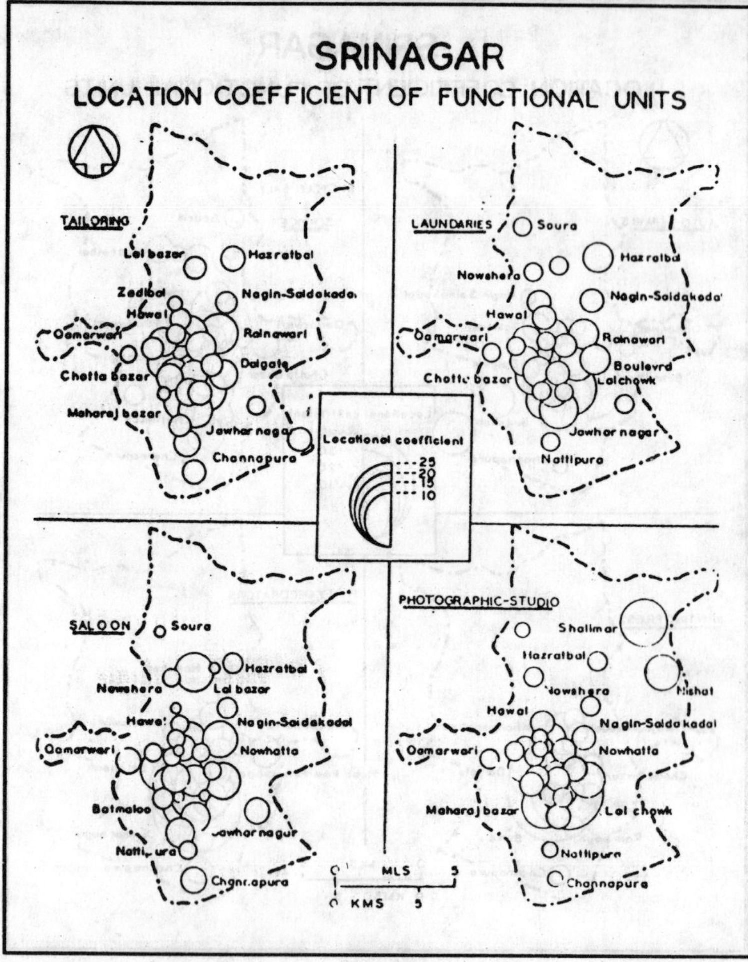

Fig. 17

particular commercial centres of city (Fig.15). Lal Chowk and Maharaj bazar specialise in these functions. They have more than 70% of the service establishments. Insurance companies are concentrated in Lal Chowk (38.09%). Maharaj Bazar (23.70%) and Khanyar Chowk (9.52%). Six other markets namely Batmaloo, Sher Ghari, Bund, Nattipura and Maharajganj have 4.77% of the insurance companies each. Similarly travel agencies are concentrated in Maharaj Bazar (37.14%), Lal Chowk (35.71%) and Bud Shah Chowk (11.42%). Batmaloo, Khanyar Chowk, Nawhatta, Rambagh and Boulevard market

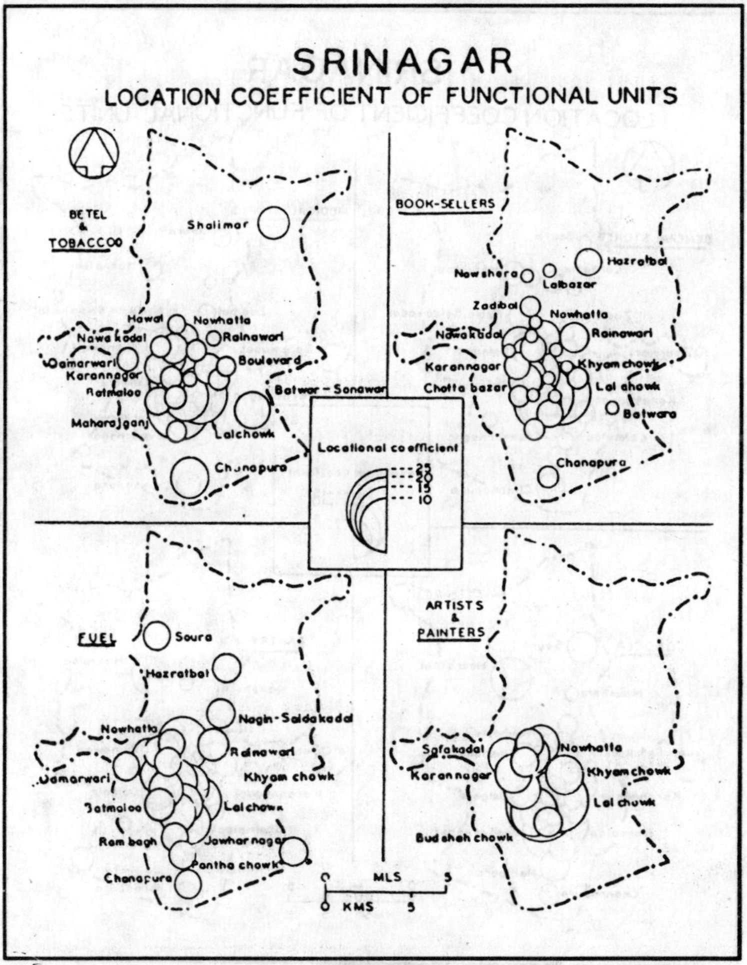

Fig. 18

centres have less than 5% of the office of the travel agencies each.

Fifty per cent of the book binding shops are in Bud Shah Chowk (25.00%) and Lal Chowk (25.00%) only. Nawhatta, Haba Kadal-Fathe Kadal, Maharaj Bazar and Nawhatta markets have 10.00% of the book binding each. Four other markets namely Zaina Kadal, Dal Gate, Sher Ghari and Jawahar Nagar have only 5.00% of the book binding shops each.

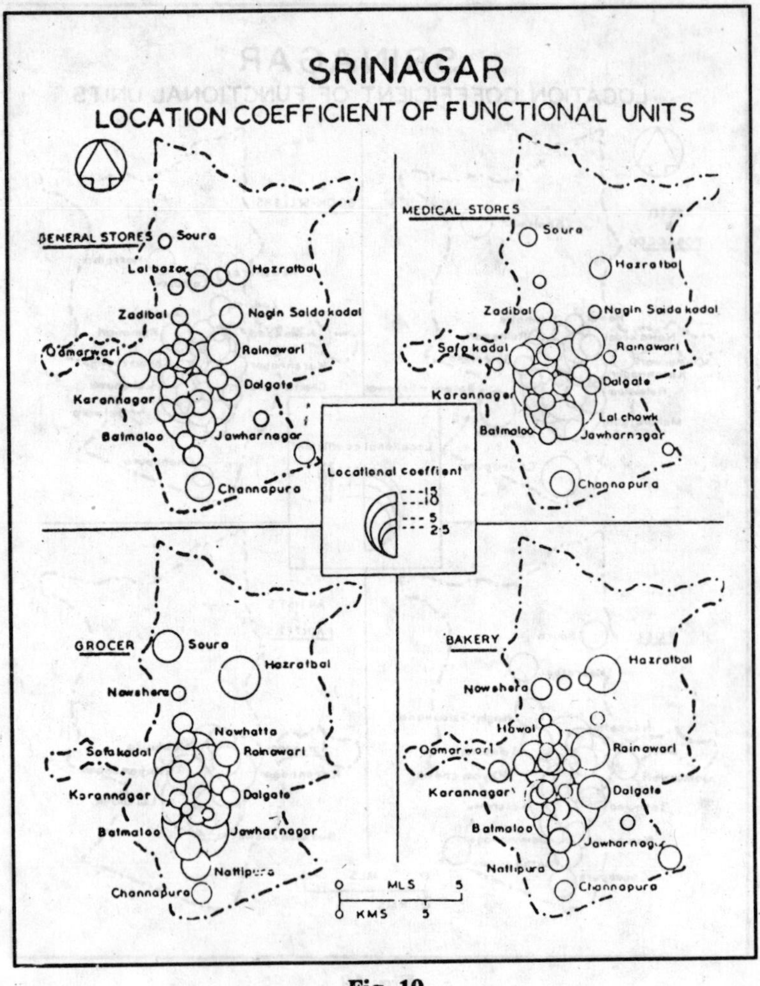

Fig. 19

Financial service institutions such as banks are found more than a half of the commercial centre of Srinagar, but there are markets which specialise in this function. Lal Chowk specialises in banking service (119.71%), followed by Bud Shah Chowk (15.16%). Khanyar Chowk, Maharaj Bazar, and Jawahar Nagar markets have only 6.07% of the banks each. Other nineteen commercial centres have only less than 5% of the banks each. It is important to note here that while the financial service institutions such as banks are uniformally distributed over the city, offices of the insurance companies, and travel agencies and book

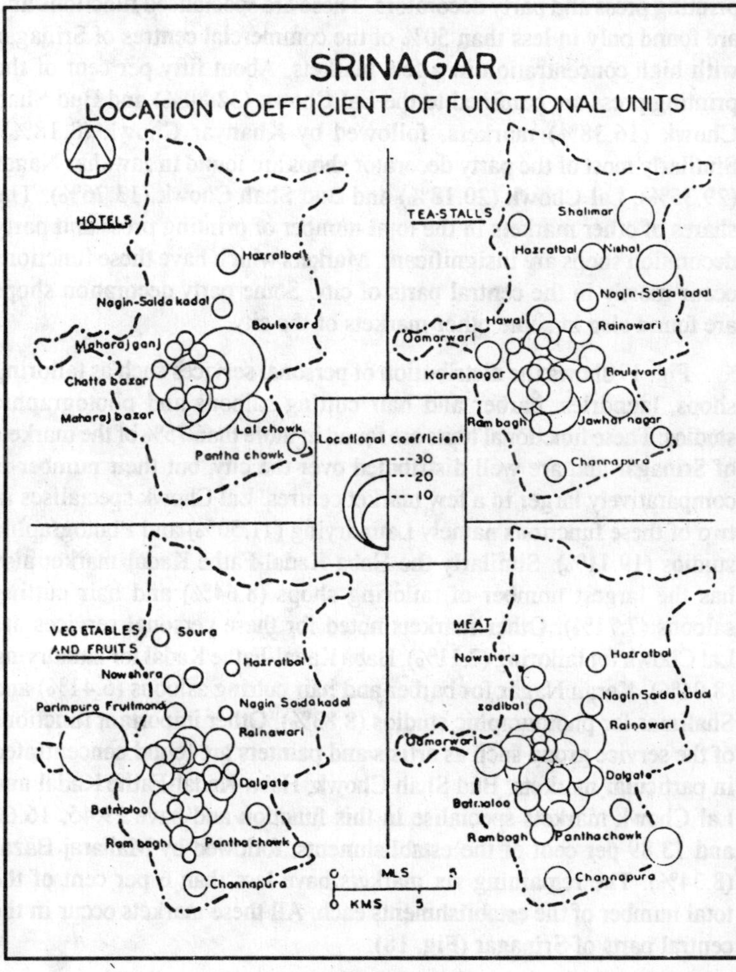

Fig. 20

binding shops occur in the central part of Srinagar (Fig. 15).

Auto-repair and cycle repair & sale establishments are found in most of the markets, but their number is larger in a few of them. The majority of the auto repair shops are found in Bud Shah Chowk (27.60%), Batmaloo (14.48%) and Lal Chowk (9.05%). Lal Chowk, Hawal and Maharaj Bazar markets have 7.10% of the cycle repair & sale shops each. These functions are scattered in almost all over Srinagar (Fig. 16). Map number 16 also shows the distribution of services such as printing press and party decorators. These are specialised functions and are found only in less than 50% of the commercial centres of Srinagar with high concentration in a few markets. About fifty per cent of the printing press are confined to the Lal Chowk (32.80%) and Bud Shah Chowk (16.38%) markets, followed by Khanyar Chowk (8.18%). Similarly most of the party decorator shops are found in Jawahar Nagar (29.35%), Lal Chowk (20.18%) and Bud Shah Chowk (13.76%). The shares of other markets in the total number of printing press and party decoration shops are insignificant. Markets which have these functions occur mostly in the central parts of city. Some party decoration shops are found also in some other markets of the city.

Fig. 17 shows the distribution of personal services such as tailoring shops, laundries, barber and hair cutting saloons and photographic studios. These functional units are found in more than 75% of the markets of Srinagar and are well distributed over the city, but their number is comparatively larger in a few market centres. Lal Chowk specialises in two of these functions namely Laundrying (11.50%) and Photographic studios (19.11%). Similarly the Haba Kadal-Fathe Kadal market also has the largest number of tailoring shops (8.64%) and hair cutting saloons (7.71%). Other markets noted for these personal services are Lal Chowk for tailoring (7.11%), Haba Kadal-Fathe Kadal for laundrying (8.04%), Karan Nagar for barber and hair cutting saloons (6.41%) and Shalimar for photographic studios (8.83%). Other important functions of the service group such as artists and painters are found concentrated in particular markets. Bud Shah Chowk, Haba-Kadal-Fathe Kadal and Lal Chowk markets specialise in this function and have 19.45, 16.66 and 13.89 per cent of the establishments, followed by Maharaj Bazar (8.34%). The remaining six markets have less than 6 per cent of the total number of the establishments each. All these markets occur in the central parts of Srinagar (Fig. 18).

Shops dealing in betel & tabacco, books, and fuel are shown in figure 18. Lal Chowk occupies the first place and has the largest number of shops dealing in books (13.91%) and the second position in betel (11.89%) and fuel (8.43%). Maharaj Bazar and Nawhatta markets specialise in betel (16.86%) and fuel (12.02%). The other important book selling (13.04%), Haba Kadal-Fathe Kadal in betel (8.20%) and Barbar Shah in fuel (7.23%).

Figure number 19 shows the distribution of non-specialised functions, such as general stores, grocery shops, bakeries and medical stores. These functions are found in all markets found almost all over the city. However, their number varies considerably from one market to another. Maharaj Bazar has the largest number of grocery shops (13.00%) and general merchandise stores (10.00%) followed by Jawahar Nagar (10.03%) and Lal Chowk (7.43%) respectively. Nawhatta and Khanyar Chowk have 6.02% and 5.28% of the total number of the general stores of Srinagar respectively. Nawhatta and Maharajganj have 7.48% of the grocery shops each.

Similarly bakeries are concentrated in Haba Kadal-Fathe Kadal (8.07%) and in Lal Chowk (7.80%) followed by Karan Nagar (6.89%) and Maharaj Bazar (6.30%). The medical stores are found mostly in Lal Chowk (10.40%), Maharaj Bazar (9.47%), Chhota Bazar (8.31%), Haba Kadal-Fathe Kadal (7.86%) and Nawhatta (6.23%). The shares of all other markets dealing in these goods are very small.

The last map of this series (Fig. 20) shows the spatial distribution on food materials. These includes tea-stalls, vegetable & fruit shops, meat shops and hotels. All of them except hotels are common to all commercial centres of Srinagar. They can therefore be called non-specialised functions. Hotels and restaurants are not found in all the markets. They are highly concentrated in Lal Chowk (28.22%), and Bud Shah Chowk (10.49%). Maharaj Bazar and Khyam Chowk have 8.07% and 5.25% of all the hotels and restaurants respectively. Vegetable and fruit shops are found mostly in Parim Pura Fruit Mandi (17.09%) and Maharaj bazar (7.20%). The tea-stalls and meat shops and fish and egg shops are of common occurrence in most of the commercial centres. The tea-stalls concentrate in Lal Chowk (10.56%). Maharaj Bazar (8.66%), Jawahar Nagar (7.21%), Bund (6.25%) and Nishat markets (5.77%). Meat, fish & egg shops are found mostly in Nawhatta (8.16%), Rainawari (6.30%), Nawa Kadal (5.82%), Zaina Kadal (5.60%) and Maharaj Bazar (5.12%). These shops are found also in other commercial centres of the city, but their shares in the total is negligible.

The preceding analysis of the thirteen maps reveales that some functions of the city of Srinagar are specialised. These are found highly concentrated in only a few markets. The specialised functional units deal in auto sale, television and refrigerator, leather goods, wine and bar, spectacles, financial service institutions such as insurance companies and other services such as traval agencies and artists and painters.

Shops and establishments dealing in steel furniture, tapestry and upholstry, hotels and restaurants and bank, printing press and party decorators are moderately concentrated, in about 50 per cent of the commercial centre of the city. On the other hand are the non-specialised functions which have common occurrence in almost all the markets of the city. Important among them are general stores, fruit and vegetable shops, grocery shops, medical stores and personal services such as tailoring, laundring etc.

The specialised functions are found generally in the larger market centres, which have bigger catchment areas extending sometimes beyond the city limits. An attempt has been made in the following pages to determine the ranks of the various market centres on the basis of their functional specialisation.

3.4 Ranking of the Market Centres

After identifying the market centre and studying their functional specialisation the next logical step is ranking them. This involves determination of the relative importance of the 42 market centres on the basis of the cumulative functions they discharge. This is necessary before and attempt is made to put them into groups of various hierarchical orders suh as Central Business District, Large Market Complexes, Large Market Centres, Medium Market Centres, Local Market Centres and Specialised Markets.

Kendall's method has been used for ranking the 42 market centres identified in the city of Srinagar. To begin with the absolute numbers of shops and establishments discharging various functions in a market centre were converted into the percentages of the total number of shops and establishments occurring in that market. This exercise was repeated for all the 42 market centres. This gave the share (in percentage) of each function in the cumulative functions discharged by each of the 42 market centres. The percent share accuring to an individual function (say grocery shop) in the 42 market centres were summed up and divided by 42. This gave the mean percentage of the shops and establishments discharging that function. This computation was repeated for all the 53 functions. The per cent shares accuring to any particular function (say grocery shops) in the 42 market centres were then divided by their mean. All product values of a function (say grocery shops) were awarded weightage. Higher product values were alloted lowest weightage. The quotients have been taken as the index value of the function in question in each of the 42 market centres. Higher index value is taken as indicative of greater concentration of the funciton in question in the market centre in question. The index values of various functions accuring to each of the 42 market centres were summed up. This gave the composite index values of each of 42 market centres. These values were ranked in descending order. Larger the composite value of a market centre higher its rank, i.e., its position in the hierarchical order of markets.

The composite index of any markets is calculated with the help of following formula :

$$IJ = \sum_{i=1}^{n} RIJ$$

Where IJ is the composite index of the different markets. n is the number of selected fuctions and RIJ is the rank of the ith function in the Jth areas. The composite indices of the different market centres are shown in Appendix no.1

This method of ranking the markets has been used because it is capable of dealing simultaneously with any number of functions and functional specialisations occurring in any particular market centre. The number of functional units (shops) is indicative of the size of the market centre while functional specialistaion indicates the relative importance of the market centre in a particular function in the overall commercial activities of the city.

The forty two markets can be put into five groups on the basis of their composite indices. The spatial distribution of these markets with their number of functional units are shown in figure No.21.

Markets with index values ranging between 900 and 1,000 have been put into the group of very high order, markets those with index values ranging between 800 and 900 have been classified as high order markets, and those with index values between 200 and 800 as average order business centres. It the index values range between 100 to 200 the group is called low order market and if they range berween the 0 and 100 group is called very low order market.

Of the total of markets of Srinagar 5 are in very low order, group, 7 belong to the low order and 25 are grouped into average order category. Only 3 retail nucleations are classified as high order and 2 as very high order commercial centres.

Lal Chowk and Maharaj Bazar are the only markets which belong to the very high order group. Their index values are 973.5 and 948.5 respectively. These two markets occur in the south and cental parts of the city very close to each other. Lal Chowk is actually the C B D of

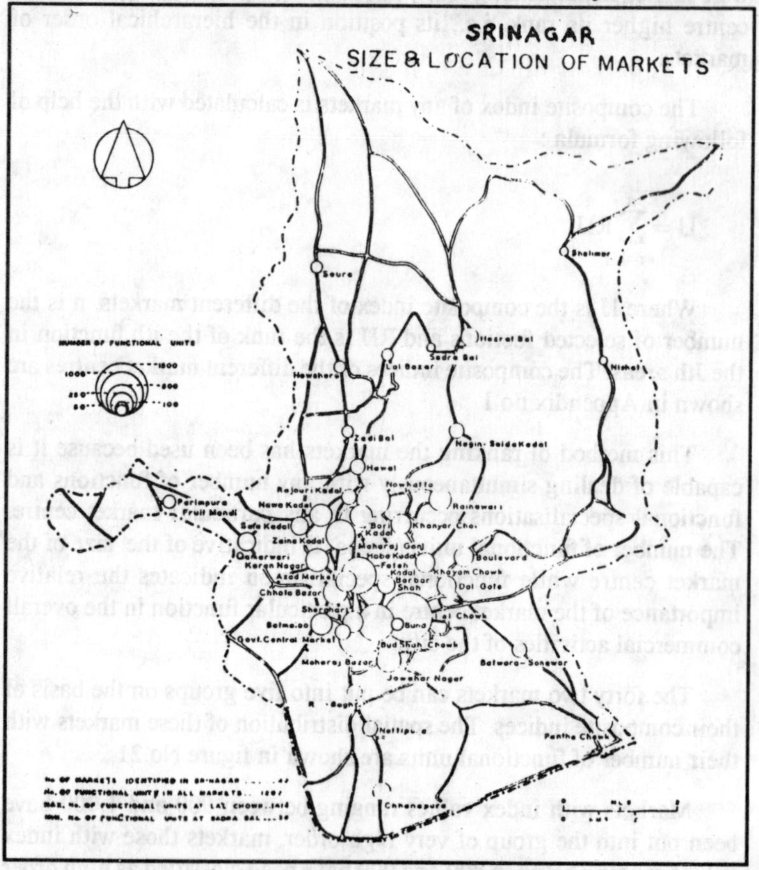

Fig. 21

Srinagar.

Nowhatta, Bud Shah Chowk and Haba Kadal-Fathe Kadal markets come under the high order group. Their index values are 844.5, 840.5 and 884.5 respectively. Nowhatta occurs in the north central part of city, Bud Shah Chowk is in the south-central part very close to the Lal Chowk market and Haba Kadal-Fathe Kadal is in the central part of the city.

The majority of the markets come under the average rank order group. Important among them are Karan Nagar, Chhota Bazar, Zaina Kadal, Jawahar Nagar, Rianawari, Nawa Kadal, Khanyar Chowk, Azad Market, Maharaj Ganj, Batmaloo, Bori Kadal, Qamarwari, Hazrat Bal, Dal Gate, Safa Kadal, Chhana Pura and Khyam Chowk with composite index values of 6.23, 589.5, 582.84, 537.33, 526.00,494.8, 473.5, 474.5, 439.00, 420.65 400.33, 399.00, 390.00, 385,83, 397.00,368.00, 345.00 respectively. Other markets of this group are Hawal, Barbar Shah, Sher Ghari, Rambagh, Natti Pura, Batwara-Sonawar, Rajouri Kadal and Pantha Chowk, with composite index values of 326.50, 301.33, 290.15, 281.83, 246.20, 235.53, 235.00, 294.63, respectively. These markets are located in the different parts of the city. Karan Nagar is in the western part of the city. Zaina Kadal, Nawa Kadal, Maharaj Ganj and Bori Kadal markets are in the north-centre part of Srinagar.

Seven markets namely Boulevard, Nagin-Saida Kadal, Lal Bazar, Nowshera, Soura, Bund and Zaidi Bal are of lower rank order and are highly dispersed. All of these markets have index values between 100 and 200.

The value of the Boulevard (197.5) is the highest in this group, while Zaidi Bal's index value (145.5) is the lowest in this group.

The remaining five markets, namely Shalimar, Govt. Central Market, Nishat, Sadra Bal and Parim Pura-fruit mandi are of very low rank order. They have index values between 0 and 100. The index value of Shalimar (95.5) is the maximum and that of Parim Pura fruit mandi is the minimum (36.00).

It will be seen in the map (Fig. 21) that the higher order markets are concentrated in the central part of the city. They are surrounded by relatively lower order markets. The lowest order markets are found away from the city centre mostly in the residential areas in the outer zone of the city.

3.5 Identification of Commercial Complexes in Srinagar

A close examination of the location and distribution of fortytwo market centres, identified in Srinagar, reveals that there are three major commercial complexes in the city, namely, the Lal Chowk, Nowhatta-Zaina Kadal and Haba kadal-Fathe Kadal. These complexes are located in the south-central, north-central and central parts of the city.

In south-central Srinagar, Lal the Chowk, Bud Shah Chowk, Bund, Maharaj Bazar, Sherghari and Government Central market have been grouped together under the name the Lal Chowk Commercial Complex. These market units are spatially close together under the name the Lal Chowk Commercial Complex. These market units are spatially close

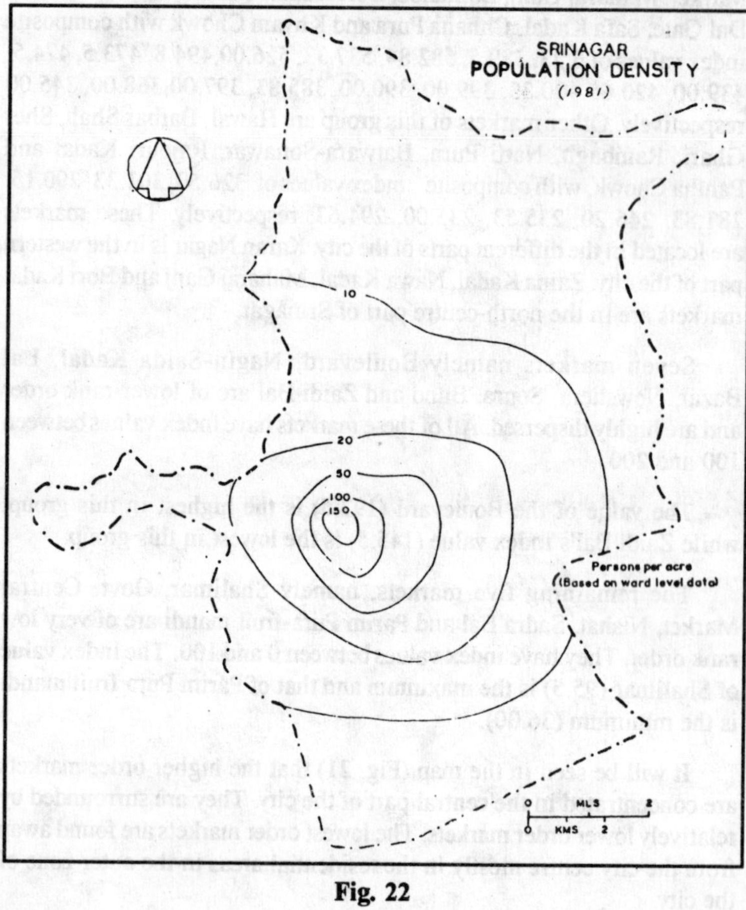

Fig. 22

together and make a single major market complex.

The next grouping occurs in the north-central part of the Srinagar city under the name Nowhatta-Zaina Kadal Complex. The different units included in this complex are, Nowhatta, Bori Kadal, Zaina Kadal, Maharaj Ganj and Rajouri markets.

The third grouping Haba Kadal-Fathe Kadal complex occurs in the central part of Sirnagar. It includes Haba Kadal-Fathe Kadal, Azad Market and Chotta Bazar. The distribution of these three market complexes shows a close relationship with the distribution of the density of total population (Fig. 22) density of shops per acre (Fig. 23) and number of shops per thousand of the total population. This can be seen

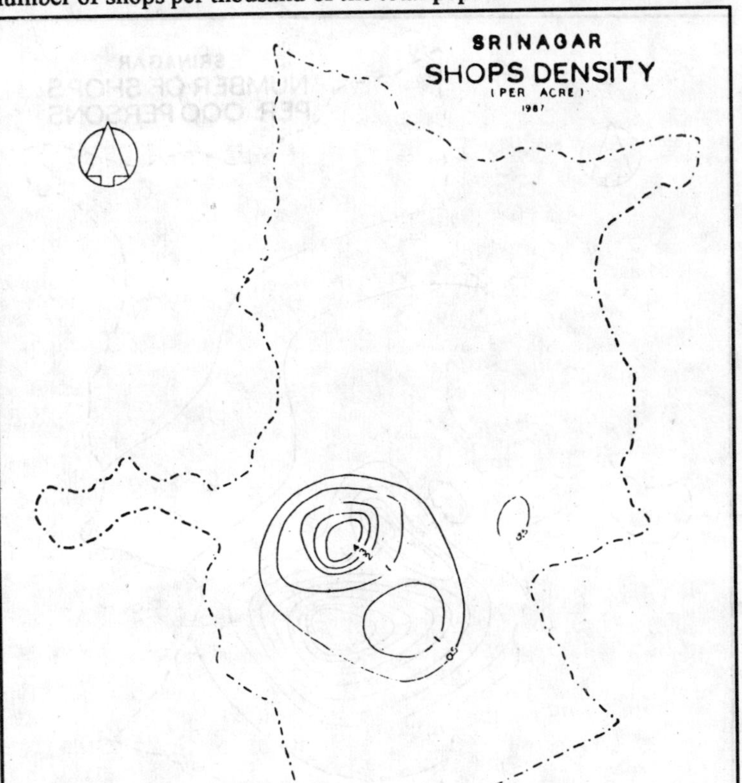

Fig. 23

by superimposing these latter maps on the map of the distribution of market complexes.

The boundaries of the above mentioned commercial complexes have been drawn on the basis of the density of shops per acres (Fig.23), number of shops per thousand of the total population (Fig. 24) and the density of population (1981) (Fig. 22). Many samller markets, recognised as such, are intergral parts of these three large compexes on account of their areal association and functional unity with them. Nonetheless for the sake of convenience of analysis and description they have been regrouped into thirtyone major market centres. These are listed in the Table 3.2.

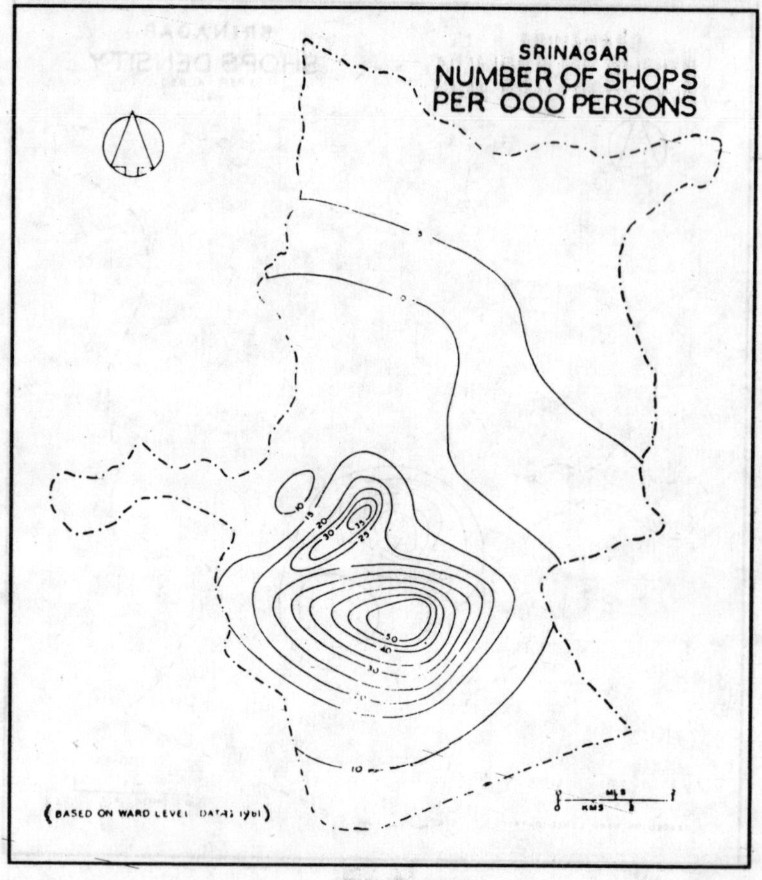

Fig. 24

Table 3.2
Major Market Centres

Sl. No.	Market Centres	No. of Functional units	Types of Functions
1.	Lal Chowk	3745	53
2.	Nowhatta-Zaina Kadal	2020	47
3.	Habakadal-Fathe Kadal	1397	49
4.	Jawahar Nagar	386	37
5.	Rainawari	329	36
6.	Karan Nagar	326	41
7.	Nawa Kadal	278	32
8.	Batmaloo	259	32
9.	Khanyar Chowk	244	33
10.	Dal Gate	222	31
11.	Khyam Chowk	221	31
12.	Chhana Pura	211	31
13.	Safa Kadal	202	34
14.	Hazratbal	198	25
15.	Qamarwari	197	33
16.	Barbar Shah	194	30
17.	Pantha Chowk	179	21
18.	Ram Bagh	150	28
19.	Hawal	132	28
20.	Natti Pura	127	24
21.	Nagin-Saida Kadal	122	21
22.	Batwara-Sonawar	117	23
23.	Lal Bazar	83	17
24.	Zadibal	81	20
25.	Nowshera	78	21
26.	Soura	77	19
27.	Sadrabal	36	08
28.	Boulevard	231	20
29.	Parimpura Fruit Mandi	95	01
30.	Shalimar	49	06
31.	Nishat	36	04

Source : Field work

3.6 Hierarchy of the Commercial Centre of Srinagar

The word 'hierarchy' means grouping or classifying any parameters into different order, grade or rank.

Although, each market has its individual status it forms an integral part of an urban system and has funtional and spatial relationship with other markets. Thus the study of the hierarchical pattern of the market centre assumes importance in geographical study. The study of the hierarchical pattern is necessary for understanding the (1) spatial interdependence of the centres, (ii) functional wholeness of the system and (iii) discrete stratification of centres and also because (iv) it provides a base for regional development planning.

The hierarchy of the commercial centres of the Srinagar city has been determined with the help of the relationship between the number of establishment and the number of types of business. This technique has been preferred because the market centres of Srinagar are characterised by a high degree of variability in their overall size as a result of the initial differences in the size of their constituents. The distinction between the markets is not so clear in the case of their functional types. Secondly, the number of occupied establishments and types of business seem to offer more information pertinent to the underlying objectives of this study. Moreover, the total number of units and the introduction of higher order functions depend directly upon the size of the catchment area and the nodality of the market. The application of this technique therefore gives a better picture of the hierarchy of the markets other empirical methods.

The hierarchical ranks of the market centres have determined with the help of the two variables mentioned above by graphical method. The 31 market centres were plotted on a semilog graph paper. The scatter diagram shows the number of commercial units along y axis their functional types along the x axis[1]. The diagram brings out clearly the arrangement, or for that matter, the hierarchical order of the market centres. The nucleations (markets) have been grouped into six categories, namely, I, II, III, IV, V and VI, which are named. The CBD, Large Market Complexes, Large Market Centres, Medium Market Centres, Local Market Places and Specialised Markets Centres respectively (Fig. 25).

The break between any two hierarchical order is manifestly clear. The distribution among Medium Market Centres, Local Market places and Specialised Markets is slightly disturbed, the aberrations having been made smooth by the dots representing the Boulevard and Sadrabal. These two markets are closer to Medium Market Centres and Specialised Markets respectively. In the course of field work it was observed that the former is a specialised and the latter a local market. So they have

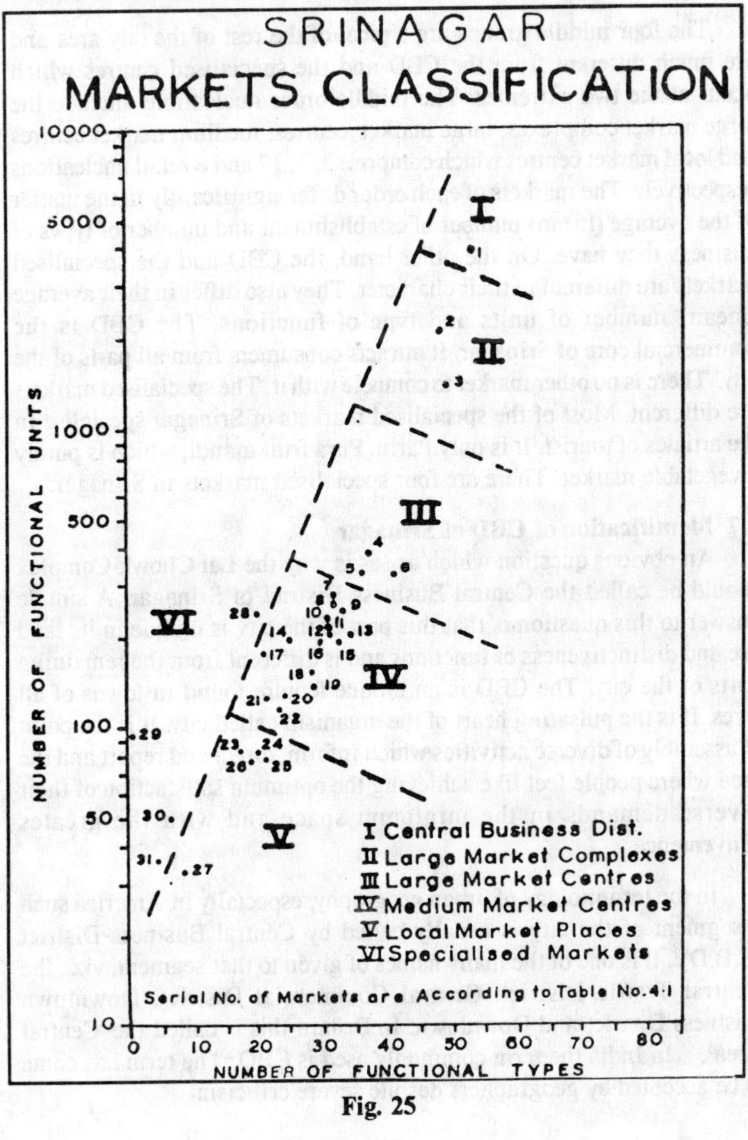

Fig. 25

been kept in the categories to which they belong. The specialised market group is clearly illustrated by the cluster of dots representing higher number of establishments, but very low values pertaining to types of business. All of these centres with the exception of the Parimpura Fruit Mandi specialise in goods of tourist interest. The Parimputa Fruit Mandi specialises in fruit vegetables.

The four middle groups are typical of the rest of the city area and are much different from the CBD and the specialised centres which occur at the two extremes. The middle order nucleations inclüde the large market complexes, large market centres, medium market centres and local market centres which comprise 3, 3, 17 and 6 retail nucleations respectively. The markets of each order differ significantly in the matter of the average (mean) number of establishment and number of types of business they have. On the other hand, the CBD and the specialised markets are different in their character. They also differ in their average (mean) number of units and type of functions. The CBD is the commercial core of Srinagar. It attracts consumers from all parts of the city. There is no other market to compete with it. The specialised markets are different. Most of the specialised markets of Srinagar specialise in the articles of tourist. It is only Parim Pura fruit mandi, which is purely a vegetable market. There are four specialised markets in Srinagar.

3.7 Identification of CBD of Srinagar

An obvious question which arises is why the Lal Chowk Complex should be called the Central Business District of Srinagar. A simple answer to this question is that this part of the city is unique in its land use and distinctiveness of functions and is different from the remaining parts of the city. The CBD is an unique feature found in towns of all sizes. It is the pulsating heart of the organism called city. It is the point of assembly of diverse activities which inform, direct and report and the area where people feel like achieving the optimum satisfaction of their diverse demands in the minimum space and with the greates convenience.

In the terminology of urban geography, especially in America such a segment of the city is usually called by Central Business District (C.B.D)[2]. It is one of the many names of given to that segment, viz., the Central Traffic District, Central Commercial District, Downtown Business District and Downtown. In Britain this is called the 'Central Area[3]. In India the term commonly used is CBD. The term has come to be accepted by geographers despite severe criticism.

The Central Business Districts of Indian cities do not conform strictly to the above mentioned features found in the cities of western countries. The social, economic and cultural conditions obtaining in Indian and western countries are quite different. The spatial pattern of shops, the lay-out of the city, the structure of buildings and the behaviour of the consumers of an Indian city present a great contrast to those of the American and European cities countries. A such the CBDs of the Indian cities are bound to be different in some matters, although they may be similar in functions.

The present study reveals that Srinagar is an example of diffused C.B.D. Here the Central Business District is generally shifting from north to south with the emergence of new areas of purchasing power resulting from the growth and expansion of the city. It may be seen that there are three commercial complexes in Srinagar. These are Nauhatta-Zaina Kadal Complex, the oldest centre; Haba Kadal-Fathe Kadal Complex, of middle age; and Lal Chowk Complex a recent development. All of these are interdependent to some extent but each has considerable intensity of central functions. In such circumstances, land use alone cannot be the sole criterion for identifying the central business district. Land use has to be complemented by some other factors such as the number and types of shops, density of shops, quality of shops, land value and rent value etc.

All of these factors have been considered, in addition to land use for identifying the Central Business District of Srinagar. To begin with land use was used as the sole criterion for delimiting the commercial belts. The road frontages and back portions of the buildings were plotted as both of these are put to commercial use. Then the buildings and their portions which are put to commercial use, including wholesale trade, which cannot be separated from retail in Srinagar, were identified, thus excluding the quarters used by administrative, educational and religious functions. These have been depicted by the choropleth technique on a large-scale map with a uniform frontage of shops. This map does not take into account the floor area as suggested by Murphy and Vance, as relevant data are not available. Three zones of intensive commercial use namely, Lal Chowk, Nauhatta-Zaina Kadal, and Haba kadal-Fathe Kadal complexes are brought out clearly on the map. Of these three, the Lal Chowk complex has been identified as the Central Business District of Srinagar on the basis of following considerations:-

The Lal Chowk Complex is located in the south-central part and is easily accessible from all parts of the city. This has resulted in the concentration of the maximum number of functional units (3745) as well as the maximum number (53) of types of functions (percentage below 0.5 in functional units has been ignored). The whole of the city serves as the tributary area of this complex. Therefore Lal Chowk has the maximum number of customers. The range of specialised functions is wide. These high order funtions include Jewellery and Watches, Radio and Televisions, Fashionable garments, Shoes, Spectacles, Motor, Cars, Cinema, Banks, Life Insurance Companies, Shawls, Carpets, Leather, Fur goods, and Books etc.

The Lal Chowk Complex has the lowest density of population (25 persons per acre), but the number of shops per thousand of total population is very high (60). This clearly shows that the commercial function is dominant in the business district. The size of the day population is the largest in the Lal Chowk Complex and that of the night population is very small. The reverse is true of the Nowhatta-Zaina Kadal and Haba Kadal-Fathe Kadal Complexes. The density of population is very high (195 person per acre) in the Nowhatta-Zaina Kadal Complex comparatively high (50 persons per acre) in the Haba Kadal-Fathe Kadal Complex. The number of shops per thousand of the total populations in these complexes is 35 and 40 respectively, which is very small as compared with the Lal Chowk Complex.

In Lal Chowk the land value per sq. feet, rent value per sq. feet and premium value per sq. feet of the frontal portions of buildings are Rs. 1229.4, 2.78 and 9706.32 respectively. This is very high as compared with Nowhatta-Zaina Kadal and Haba Kadal-Father Kadal complexes. Land value, rent value and premium in these complexes are about Rs. 104.00, 2.00 and 1100.00 and 123.00 , 0.52 and 856.00 per sq. feet respectively.

Most of Srinagar's multi-stories buildings put to commercial use (double and triple storey shops) are found in the Lal Chowk Complex. This fulfills the three dimensional requirement of the CBD. as suggested by Johnson[4].

The Central Business District also has smart shops as defined by Harries and Ullman. This area has 133 neon sign-boards, which are seen rarely in other commercial complexes of the city.

The Lal Chowk Complex has also the maximum number of pucca (3401), large size (140) and broad frontage (85) shops in the city. The

Lal Chowk Complex ranks first[5] in other qualities of shops. It has the maximum number of shops having electricity, telephone, displayed show cases and good quality signboards.

Table 3.3
The Distinctive Features of the Major Commercial Complexes in Srinagar

Distinctive Features	Lal Chowk	Nauhatta Zaina Kadal	Haba Kadal-Fateh Kadal
Accessibility	Easy	Moderate	Poor
Number of Functional Units	3745	2020	1397
Type of Functions	53	48	49
Density of pop. per acre (1981)	25	195	50
Number of shops per 1000 person	60	35	40
Land value in front (per sq. ft.)	1229.4	103.70	123.46
Rent value in rupees	2.78	1.50	0.52
Premium value per sq. ft. (in Rs.)	9706.32	1066.5	8.5556
Number of shops on First Floor	172.00	20.00	11.00
Number of shops on IInd Floor	17.00	nil	nil
Number of pucca shops	13401	1863	1360
Number of large size shops	140	8	18
Number of shops having broad frontage	85	-	6
Number of good conditions shops	3565	1766	1356
Number of shops having more than three sales men	3492	1808	1293
Number of shops having electrictiy	3745	2020	1397
Number of shops having Telephones	2424	324	104
Number of shops having seating facilities	2784	1101	1293
Number of shops having steel signboard	3163	1226	965
Number of shops having Neon signboard	133	11	7
Number of shops having show-cases	1726	850	514
Parking facilities	available	nil	nil.

Source : Field work.

It also has the highest number of salesmen in its commercial units (3492) and the highest number of good condition shops (3565).

In nutshell the Lal Chowk complex has all the requisits characteristics and qualities of a western Central Business District. Hence it can with justification be designated the Central Business District (CBD) or the commercial core of the city.

3.8 Spatial Distribution of Centres by Hierarchical Levels

A number of geographers admit that the socio-economic conditions and physical build of an urban area are not uniform every where. The city can therefore be subdivided into a number of sectors or zones which differ, besides other things, in the history of the evolution of settlement growth; density another characteristics of their populations. These differences result in an uneven distribution of shopping centres, which may be manifested in the spacing of the centres or formation of different hierarchical groups different parts of the city[6].

The spatial distribution of the market centres of different hierarchicaly order in Srinagar is shown in Fig. 26. Broadly the picture comprise three distinct clusters, one in the north-centre, the second in the centre and the third in the south-centre around the Lal Chowk Area of the city. The three are separated by residential areas.

The variation in the number of markets found in the different parts of the city is the direct outcome of the basic difference in population distribution. The central and north central parts of the city, where most of the population of Srinagar resides, have eight nucleations (Two large market complexes, one large market centre and five medium market cenres). On the other hand, the group in the south-central part consisting of Lal Chowk complex comprises 3 nucleations (one CBD, one large market centre and one medium market centre) which serve a smaller proportion of the population of the city. The remaining parts of the urban area has 20 markets which are found distributed over them and comprise 2 large market centres, 9 medium market centres, 5 local market centres and 4 specialised market centres.

In general, market of different orders are not uniformly distributed over the study area. This is an expected situation because the distribution of population and thus of purchasing power are uneven. The highest level centres viz., the large market complexes and large market centres are found concentrated in the centre.

The Central Business District has developed in the area which easily accessible from all parts of the city. The two large market complexes have developed on its north. The three large market centres are loctaed one each in the central, north-central and south-central parts of the city.

Out of the sixteen medium market centres eight are in the central part of the city, located around the CBD and the large market complexes and five of them are located in the sothern part of the city, The northernmost part of the city has only two medium market centres and there is one in the western part of the city.

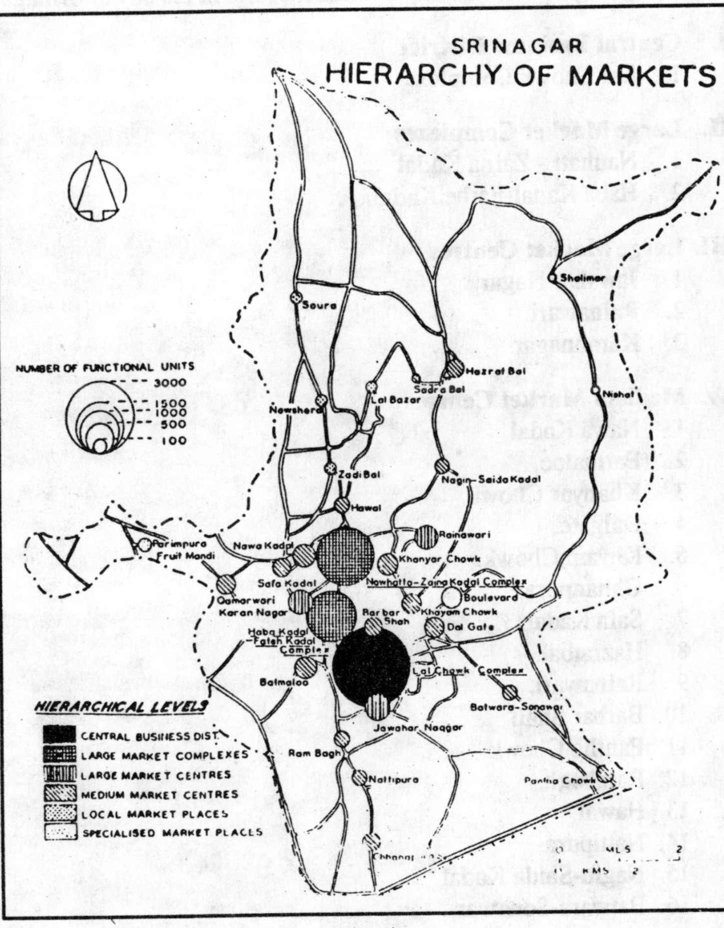

Fig. 26

It is remarkable that all of the four local market centres are located in the northern part of Srinagar. This is because of the low density of population and poor accessibility of the region.

As far as the distribution of the specialised market centres is concerned, their main concentration is found in the eastern section of Srinagar closer to the places of tourist interest, such as Nishat and Shalimar gardens and the Dal lake (Boulevard). The western most part of the city has one specialised market which is a purely vegetable market.

Following is the hierarchy of market centre in the city of Srinagar:

I. Central Business District

1. Lal Chowk Complex.

II. Large Market Complexes

1. Nauhatt - Zaina Kadal
2. Haba Kadal-Fathe Kadal.

III. Large Market Centres

1. Jawahar Nagar
2. Rainawari.
3. Karannagar.

IV. Medium Market Centres

1. Nawa Kadal.
2. Batmaloo.
3. Khanyar Chowk.
4. Dalgate.
5. Khyam Chowk.
6. Chhanpura.
7. Safa Kadal.
8. Hazratbal.
9. Rainawari.
10. Barbar Shah.
11. Pantha Chowk.
12. Rambagh.
13. Hawal.
14. Nattipura.
15. Nagin-Saida Kadal.
16. Batwara-Sonawar.

V. Local Market Places

1. Lal Bazar.
2. Zadibal.
3. Nowshera.
4. Soura.
5. Sadrabal.

VI. Specialised Market Centres

1. Boulevard.
2. Parimpura-Fruit Mandi.
3. Shalimar.
4. Nishat.

3.9 Fundamental Hierarchical Pattern

The fundamental characteristics of the market centre identified in Srinagar are shown in the following table :

Table 3.4
Summary of fundamental characteristics of market centre in Srinagar

Characteristics	CBD	Large Market complexes	Large Market centres	Medium Market centres	Local Market centres	Specialised Market centres
Average Number of Type of Functions (Mean Level).	53.0	48.5	38.0	29.0	18.0	8.0
Average number of functional units.	3745.0	1708.5	347.0	192.0	71.0	103
No. of centres.	1	2	3	16	5	4

Source : Field Work.

There is no need to compare the Central Business District with the other market centres because the former has a very high rank order. The large market complexes have on an average about 48.5 types of business and about 1708.5 commercial units. The large market centres have 38 types of function and 347 units. The medium order market centres have on the average 29 types of business and about 192 establishments. The local market places have 18 types of business and only 71 business units.

In the specialised market centres the types of functions range between 1 and 20 with an overall average of only 8. Thus they specialise in a few functions which are of tourist interest. The average number of units, however, goes up to 103 which is higher than that of the local market places. In the specialised market centres have both small and large size shops.

References :

1. Below 0.5% of total functional units of Srinagar city found in any centre has not been consider for this analysis.

2. Murphy, R. E. & Vance, J. E. jr. : "Delmiting CBD", Eco. Geog. XXX, 1954, p. 189.

3. Johnson, J. H. : Urban Geography, Report Max-Well M. C., M. P. London, 1966, p. 105.

4. Johnson, J. H. : *op. cit.*, pp. 109-113.

5. Harris and Ullman, L. : "The Nature of City,' Annals of the American Academy of Political and Social Sciences, CC X L I I, November, 1945, p. 3

6. Johnston, R. J. : *op. cit.*

4

Functional Character of the Market Centres

A variety of articles are sold in the different market of Srinagar. However, some goods are sold in some market. This leads to functional specilaisation of the different market centres. The number of establishments present and the types of goods sold, help in determining the intra-city hierarchy of markets. However the level of specialisation of individual markets is not brought out. An attempt has been made in this chapter to discuss the functional structure of the market centres of the different levels of hierarchy and to examine whether the pattern varies with levels of hierarchy.

4.1 Types of Business in Indian Cities

The types of business found in the Western cities are totally different from those of the Indian cities. This is true of the Srinagar city as well. As has been stated earlier, the social, economic and cultural conditions obtaining in India are totally different from those obtaining in the West. The commerical organization, business pattern and government regulations are also different. These differences have a direct bearing on the commercial pattern and retail establishments. For instance, in the Western countries are found three basic forms of organisation, cooperative societies, multiples and independent ownership[1]. In Britain, cooperative societies are more common in the field of retail business, each society functioning in a specified area and being controlled by the consumers[2].

There are no shops in Srinagar run by cooperative societies and multiples, i.e. groups of outlets centrally owned and to some extent centrally controlled.

There are a few retail show rooms of the important textile mills, dealing only in cloth. These are not centrally owned and controlled but function on commission basis. There is a firm of footwear (Bata Shoe Co.) run and owned by a joint stock company, but it is single outlet not groups of retail outlets such as super markets, variety stores, departmental stores, chain stores and discount stores. Such a group of retail outlets do not exist in the city of Srinagar.

In the Western countries the entry into any business is regulated by licence. In Britain from 1941 until the end of the second world war, a person was prohibited from opening a new retail shop except under licence. In Italy, licence is a normal pre-requisite, while in Netherland entry is give only to such persons who can prove that they are professionally qualified. Such regulations tend to decrease the number of shops, but, in Denmark, the number of speciality shops has increased despite regulations banning the sale of some goods together, i.e., in the same shop. In Finland the number of spatial distribution of mobile shops have been profoundly influenced by conditions, both national and provincial, under which licences are issued[3]. According to Scott. Government regulation, "National" or 'Local' influences directly or indirectly the retail structure in three ways. First, by restricting the entry of new outlets, secondly, in restricting or alternatively promoting their location and siting, and thirdly, in restricting or discriminating against particular form of organisation[4].

In Srinagar one is free to establish his own retail outlet in any part of the city without taking prior permission from any authority, Central or Local. This has lead to haphazard growth of retailing in the city.

Distributional pattern of the wholesale and retail business in the Srinagar city is totally different from that of any city of the West. Here there is generally an admixture of wholesale and retail business. A large establishment of Srinagar is engaged not only in retail but also in wholesale trade. Thus it is difficult to distinguish a wholesale from a purely retail shop. Such shops have been taken as having the same status for the purpose of the present study.

Another peculiarity of Srinagar's business is the combination of retailing and manufacturing. Making and selling of leather and fur goods, papier machie, wood and stone carvings, willow baskets, chairs wooden furniture, jewellery, bakery, steel trunk, bokhary, copper utensils, shawls, carpets etc., provide examples.

A high degree of specialisation is the common characteristics of the shops of the Western cities but this feature is rare in India. Four types of garment shops namely women's, men's, children's and families' are generally found in Western towns. This is true also of the footwear shops. In India shopkeepers generally sell all kinds of footwear in the same establishment. So far as cloth shops concerned, the only distinction may be made between those delaing in readymade garments (ladies, gents' and children's wear combined) and cloths. The cloth shops sell all kinds of textiles such as woolen, cotton, silken, tapestry and handloom products etc., used both as male and female dressing. Such shops are most common in the Srinagar city.

An appraisal of the studies made in the Western countries that there exist in the Western cities a number of types of business and commercial organisations which are not found in the Srinagar city. These include Super Markets, Discount stores. Departmental Stores, Varieties store, Weight producing shops, Pet shops, Filling stores, Candy shops and Antique stores. On the other hand there are a number of retail activities which are charactersitic of the Srinagar city and are not found in the Western cities and even in other Indian cities. Some of these which were observed during the field work include Papier Machie, Wood and stone carvings, Kangri and Bokhari, Samawar, Fur goods, Namda, Willow baskets etc.

4.2 Identification and Classification of types of functions in Srinagar

In India no official records of the retail activities of towns or cities are maintained. The Census of India has prepared a classified list of industries know as the National Industrial Classification (NIC), but the Census or, for the matter, any other agency does not collected information on the distribution, location, types and number of shops according to the list. Hence recourse was taken of detailed field work in the city of Srinagar for collecting the relevant information.

About three hundred fifty three types of business were identified during the feild investigation in the markets of Srinagar. However, many of the business establishments were merely small variations of the same type. A careful screening helped in identifying fifty three major types of business. These 53 types op functions found in the city of Srinagar have been made to match with the National Industrial Classification (N.I.C.) of India 1981[5].

It is important to mention here that National Industrial Classification consists of 10 divisions at first digit level, 66 major groups at the second digit level and 386 minor groups at the third digit level. This scheme has been adapted with minor modifications. The modified groups have been given distinctive codes by adding the suffix a, b, c, d, e, f and g, to the original code numbers. However, some functions which did not fit into the standard N.I.C. classes were classified separetely by the appropriate names, such as, second hand goods, polythene bags etc. The N.I.C. groups not found in Srinagar were dropped. Thus 53 commercial functions have been accepted for the purpose of analysis. These are given in table No 4.1.

Table 4.1

Functions Identified in Srinagar with their N.I.C. Code Numbers

SI. No.	N.I.C. Number	Types of Functions
1.	205	Bakery and Confectionery, 653: Sweet meats and Biscuits
2.	263	Shawls Carpets and Fur Goods.
3.	284	Newspaper Printing, Other Printing Press, News Agency.
4.	288	Book Binding and Envelop Making 289: Rubber Stamp and Seal Makering.
5.	322	Kangri and Earthen Pottery.
6.	340	Steel Furniture and Steel Trunk.
7.	350	Agricultural Implements and Fertilizer.
8.	355	Machine : Refrigerator and Fan.
9.	359	Metal Engineering: Welding, Battery Charging 344 : Nickel Plating, Steel Grill and Shutter.
10.	392	Auto-repairs and Spare Parts : Trunks, Cars, Motor Cycles, Bus and Tyre services.
11.	393	Watch and machine Repairs: Watch and Clock, 399 : Torch, Machine.
12.	394	Bicycle : Sale and Service.
13.	650	Grocery.
14.	651	Fruits and Vegetables, Dry fruits, Honey and Saffron.
15.	652	Meat, Fish, Chicken, Milk, and Eggs.
16.	654	Betel : Paan, Cigarette and tobacco.
17.	656	Wine shops and Bars.
18.	660	Cloth : Dupatta, Woollen Cloth, Blanket, Textile, thread and sarees.
19.	661	Readymade clothes and hosiery goods, caps.
20.	669	Bedding, Tapestry and upholstery, cotton matting, bed sheets, cotton.
21.	670	Fuel : Kerosene oil. coal, wood, gas, saw dust, wheat dust.
22.	671 (a)	Utensils : Stainless steel, stell sheets, gasware, pressure cooker, crockery.

23.	671 (b)	Utensils : Smawar, copper, brass and aluminium.
24.	672	General Merchandise : Grocery store, soap, snuff, luxury goods, super bazar, colour, provisions, cosmetic, plastic goods, sports, 679: Bangles.
25.	673	Electrical goods : Electric fittings and electrical gadgets (repairs).
26.	674	Wooden Furniture : Chair, Saw mills, 271: Wood works.
27.	675	Gold and silver smiths, Jewellers.
28.	676	Foot wear : Leather shoes, Plastic shoes, cobbler, Foam shoes.
29.	680	Medical Stores : Clinics, Chemists, Drugists, 930: Clinical Laboratories.
30.	681	Books, Stationery and Greeting Cards.
31.	682	Building Materials : Cement, Sanitary and glass ware, 320 : Bricks Ply-wood, Limestone, steel sheets, Marble Tile, Stone Crusher, Paint, HardWare and Plumbing.
32.	683	Auto-sale : Cars.
33.	684	Petrol Pumps.
34.	689	Leather goods : Attachies and Holdalls.
35.	689 (c)	Spectacles.
36.	689 (d)	Handicraft : Paper Machine, Wood and Stone Carving, Will Work, rope, basket and Naicha Maker.
37.	689	Non-Electrical Machines : Sewing machines, Stove-sale and service, Typewriter.
38.	690	Tea-stalls, cold and hot drinks, juice, cafetaria, Soda water, coffee, Limca, Fish roster.
39.	691	Hotels and Restaurants.
40.	800	Banks.
41.	811	Life-Insurance Companies.
42.	951	Cinema House.
43.	954	Radio, Television, Cassette-Sale and Service.
44.	961	Laundries.
45.	962	Barbar and Hair Cutting Saloons.
46.	963	Photographic studio and Photo-state.
47.	964 (a)	Tailoring and Embroidery, Dyers, Rafughar, Button, saree dyer.
48.	964 (b)	Marriage and party Decorator : Camping Agency and Decorators.
49.	964(c)	Artists and Painters.
50.	964 (d)	Bokhari and Black-smiths.

51.	964 (e)	Junk-yard : Kabari, Old Tin, Second Hand Cloth, Raddi Paper, Bags, Empty Tin, Second hand carpets, bottles.
52.	964 (f)	Transport Office and Travel Agencies.
53.	964 (g)	Miscellaneous : Polythene bags, Lottery, Photoframing.

Source : Field Work.

It may be pointed out that the classified list of the N.I.C. is based on dealing in a single product, but there is hardly an establishment in Srinagar which deals in only one product. The establishments sell a number of goods and rander a number of services to their customers. In order to overcome this unmanagable situation similar business activities have been put together under appropriate code numbers of the N.I.C classification.

It is important to note that the N.I.C. classification gives a consolidated list of industrial and commercial functions. The industrial establishments and activities are outside the scope of the present study. However, the conditions obtaining in Inida and particularly Srinagar may small manufacturers accept direct orders of consumers and thus become retailers. Examples are furnished by such units as shawls and carpets, willow baskets and chairs, copper utensils, leather and fur-goods, Papier machine, wood and stone carvings etc., which are manufactured and sold in the same establishments. Some other establishments which repair or manufacture such articles as jewllery, watches, typewriters and bicycles etc. also sell them or deal in their spare parts. Other establishments which in foodgrains, fruits and vegetables, meat and milk, textile, medicine, hosiery, car and scooters, dry fruits etc. combine wholeselling and retailing provided the transaction does not involve much trouble or is in volume. A few service establishments such as dry cleaning photography, tailoring, artists and painters, are also strictly speaking included among retail business as are the banks, Insurance compaines, Cinemas, Petrol pumps, Hotels and Restaurants.

Thus all of them enter the retail market and, by virtues of their size, are oftern the most important units. There is no legal restriction on the kinds of goods an establishments deals in this has to be taken into account while preparing the list of retail functions.

The list of 53 functional groups forms the basis for the analysis of the functions and hierarchy of the market centres of Srinagar. However, for the limited purpose of high-lighting the variations of the markets of various classes as far as their major functions are concerned the 53 functional groups have been regrouped into 21 broad functional groups. This generalisation is based on convernience, shopping and other goods and has made the analysis practicable.

4.3 Ranking of the types of functions

In the present study the functions of the Srinagar city have been ranked into high and low order functions on the basis of composite index values of each function. The functional units are not uniformly distributed over the city settlement area. All functions are not present in all market centres of all hierarchical order. Some functions are found only in the higher order market centres, where also the number of the establishments is small. The functions which are common, occurring almost everywhere, should be considered of low order and those which are rare shold be considered of higher order. This is a subject decision.

Kendal's method has been used for ranking of all 53 functions in this study. To start with absolute number of functions were converted into the percentages of the total number of functions occuring at different markets. This excercise was repeated for all the 53 functions. The percentage shares of all 53 funtions belonging to an individual market were summed up and divided by 53. This gave the mean percentage of function to particular market centre. This computation was repeated for all the 42 markets. The percent shares of all 53 functions occuring to any particular market were then divided by their mean. All product values of a market were awarded weightage. The weightage is given on the basis that higher is the weightage lower is the function. Higher is the function, lower is the weightage. The quatients have been, taken as the index values of market in question in each of the 53 function. The index values of various markets belonging to each 53 functions were summed up. This gave the composite index each of the 53 functions. Theses values were ranked in asceending order. Smaller the composite index value of a function higher its rank.

The composite index of any function is calculated with help of following formula.

$$Ij = \frac{n}{i = 1} Rij$$

Wherer IJ is the composite index of the function, n is the number of selected markets and Rij is the rank of ith market in the jth area.

The composite index of different hierarchical levels of functions are shown in Table No. 4.2.

Table 4.2
Functions Ranked on the basis of Kendall's Methods of ranking in Srinagar

	Ranking	N.L.C Code No.	Name of Functions	Composite Index value
Very High	1.	683	Auto Sale	5.5
	2.	251	Cinema	17.0
	3.	355	Machine: Refrigerator & Fan.	30.6
	4.	288	Book Binder.	38.0
	5.	684	Petrol Pump	40.5
	6.	811	Life Insurance Companies	58.5
	7.	689 (c)	Spectacle	74.5
	8.	964 (c)	Artist & Painter	86.0
	9.	689 (a)	Leather goods.	87.0
High	10.	350	Agricultural Implements.	103.5
	11.	689 (e)	Non-Electrical Machine.	127.0
	12.	656	Wine and Bar.	152.0
	13.	964 (f)	Transport and Travel Agencies.	155.6
	14.	284	Printing Press.	159.0
	15.	964 (d)	Bokhari	165.0
	16.	340	Steel Furniture	165.5
	17.	800	Bank	169.5
	18.	322	Kangri	169.5
	19.	964 (e)	Junkyard.	195.0
Medium	20.	964 (b)	Marriage & Party Decorator	201.0
	21.	674	Wooden Furniture	214.0
	22.	961	Laundries	243.1
	23.	670	Fuel	260.0
	24.	669	Bedding and Tapestry	265.5
	25.	681	Books & Stationery	312.0
	26.	691	Hotel and Restaurant	342.0
	27.	963	Photographic Studio	350.5

	28.	359	Metal Engineering	355.0
	29.	689 (d)	Handicraft.	377.2
	30.	671 (b)	Utensils : Copper & Brass.	410.0
	31.	394	Bicycles : Sale & Service	418.2
	32.	671 (a)	Utensils : Stainless Steel.	422.5
	33.	393	Watch and Machine Repair.	422.5
	34.	675	Jewellers.	36.1
	35.	962	Barber	481.0
	36.	690	Tea Stall	486.0
	37.	673	Electrical Goods.	492.3
	38.	654	Betel	502.3
	39.	676	Foot Wear	507.6
	40.	263	Shawl	514.0
	41.	392	Auto Repairs.	550.5
Low	42.	954	Radio & Television Sale and Service.	612.0
	43.	682	Building Materials.	652.5
	44.	650	Grocers.	689.5
	45.	680	Medical Store	733.5
	46.	205	Bakery	742.1
	47.	652	Meat-Fish-Eggs.	769.0
	48.	661	Readymade clothes.	789.5
Very	49.	660	Cloth	800.0
Low	50.	651	Fruit and Vegetable	818.5
	51.	964 (a)	Tailoring	899.5
	52.	672	General Merchandise	1001.3
	53.	964 (g)	Miscellaneous	420.5

Source : Field Work.

The composite index given in Table No. 4.2 shows the overall importance of each function in all the 42 market centres taken together.

The Table shows that the shops selling Autos and cars rank first among the functions scoring the lowest, index value of 5.5 while vegetable, tailoring and general merchandise shope rank last with the three highest index values of 818.5, 899.5 and 1001.31 respectively because these functions are present in almost all markets i.e. frequency of their occurrence is high and thus they can be classified as three of the lowest order functions.

4.4 Hierarchical grouping of Functions

For the purpose of classifying the functions into hierarchical grouping they were arranged in an asccending order on the basis of thieir composite indices. Then such class interval was selected which gave five hierarchical groups. Those groups were designated very high, high, medium, low, and very low.

4.4.1 Very High Order Function

Functions with rank orders 1 to 9 and composite indices below 100 have been kept in the very high order included in this group. The function of the highest order is auto sale and that of the lowest order is leather goods stores (attachi and holdalls) with composite indices of 5.5 and 87.0 respectively.

The other functions of this group are Cinema Houses, Machines, Book-binding and envelop making stores, Petrol-pumps and insurance companies with indices of 17.0, 30.6. 38.0, 40.5 and 58.5 respectively. Still other very high rank order functions are spectacle stores and establishments of artists and painters with indices of 74.5 and 86.0 respectively. Some of these functions are found in the high order market centres, These are machines and refrigerators stores and auto sale establishments. Cinemas, insurance companies, petrol pumps, spectacles shops etc. are also associated with the higher order market centres (CBD).

4.4.2 High Order Functions

Functions with orders from 10 to 19 and index values between 100 to 200 have been put in the high order group. This group consists of 10 fuctions. The index values of these functions vary between 103.5 and 195.0. The functions included in this group are agricultural implements and fertilizer, non-electrical machines including typewriters and sewing machines, wine shops and bars, travel agencies and newspaper printing and news agencies and other printing press, with index values of 103.5, 127.0, 152.0, 155.6 and 159.0 respectively.

Other functions of this group are bokhari and blacksmith, steel furniture and steel trunk, banks, kangari and earthen pottery and junk-yard with index values of 165.8, 165.5, 169.5, 169.5 and 195.0 respectively.

4.4.3 Medium Order Functions

Functions with rank orders from 20 to 41 and composite index values from 200 to 600 have been grouped under medium order category.

The highest order function of this group is marriage and party decorators and that of the lowest order is auto-repairs and spare parts with composite index values of 201.0 abd 550.0 respectively. This group consists of 23 functions.

Other important functions of this group are wooden furniture, laundries, fuel, tapestry and upholstery, Books and stationery and Hotels and restaurants. Their composite index values are 214.9, 243.1, 260.0, 265.5, 312.0 and 342.0 respectively.

Other functions of the medium order group are photographic studio, metel engineering handicrafts, utensils (copper and brass), bicycle (sale and service), utensils (steel), watch and machine repairs and jewellery and goldsmith. Their index values range between 342.0 and 436.1. Electrical goods, Betel, Footwear, Shawl, Carpet and fur-goods with composite index values of 492.3, 502.5 and 514.0 respectively are the other functions of the medium order group. The majority of the functions of this group are generally of higher order nature, but categorised in the medium order group. This is due to the fact that the establishments of this category such as gold smithy, carpets and shawls making, handicrafts, tapestry and upholstery, hotels, electrical goods and footwear are found presnt even in the lower order market centres. This increases the total number of shops and establishments brings them to the medium order group.

4.4.4 Lower Order Function

Functions with index values from 600 to 800 and rank orders between 42 to 48 have been grouped as low order functions. This group includes only seven functions. The highest order function of this group is radio and television with an index value of 612.0 and the lowest order function is readymade clothes with an index values of 789.5. The main functions of this group are building material, grocery and medical stores with index values of 652.5, 689.5 and 742.1 respectively.

The remaining functions of this category are bakery and meatfish and eggs with composite index values of 442.1 and 769.0 respectively.

Radio and television, which apparently appears to be a higher order function, has been categoriesed as low order function. This is only because of the fact that the establishments also include servicing which by its very nature must be available in most of the markets. This increases the total number of shops and brings them to the low order function group.

4.4.5 Very Low Order Functions

The remaining functions belong to the very low order. These functions have rank order from 49 to 53 and index values more than 800. There are four functions in this group. These functions are more common in their occurence and are of the convenience type, such as general merchandise and fruits and vegetables and clothing shops, and low order personal services such as tailoring. Their composite index values range between 800.5 for clothing to 1001.31 for general merchandise. The other two functions i.e. fruits and vegetables and tailoring shops have index values of 818.5 and 899.5 respectively.

The ranking of functions and their distribution by markets of different levels have been shown in a diagram (Fig. 27), which collaborates the preceeding discussion.

4.5 Fundamental characteristics of Ranking of Functions

The average composite index values of the functions of different hierarchical groups is shown in Table No. 4.3

Table 4.3
Fundamental Characteristics of Ranking of function

Rank order	Hierarchical Group	Classified Index value	Average No. of Index value
		<100	48.6
I	Very High	100- 200	156.2
II	High	200-200	156.2
III	Medium	200-600	390.5
IV	Low	600-800	711.3
V	Very Low	>800	879.9

Source : Field Work.

The table shows that the low average composite index values are associated with the higher order functions and the high average compostie index values are related with the lower order functions.

The average composite indices for the very high and high rank order functions are 48.6 and 156.2 respectively. On the other hand the

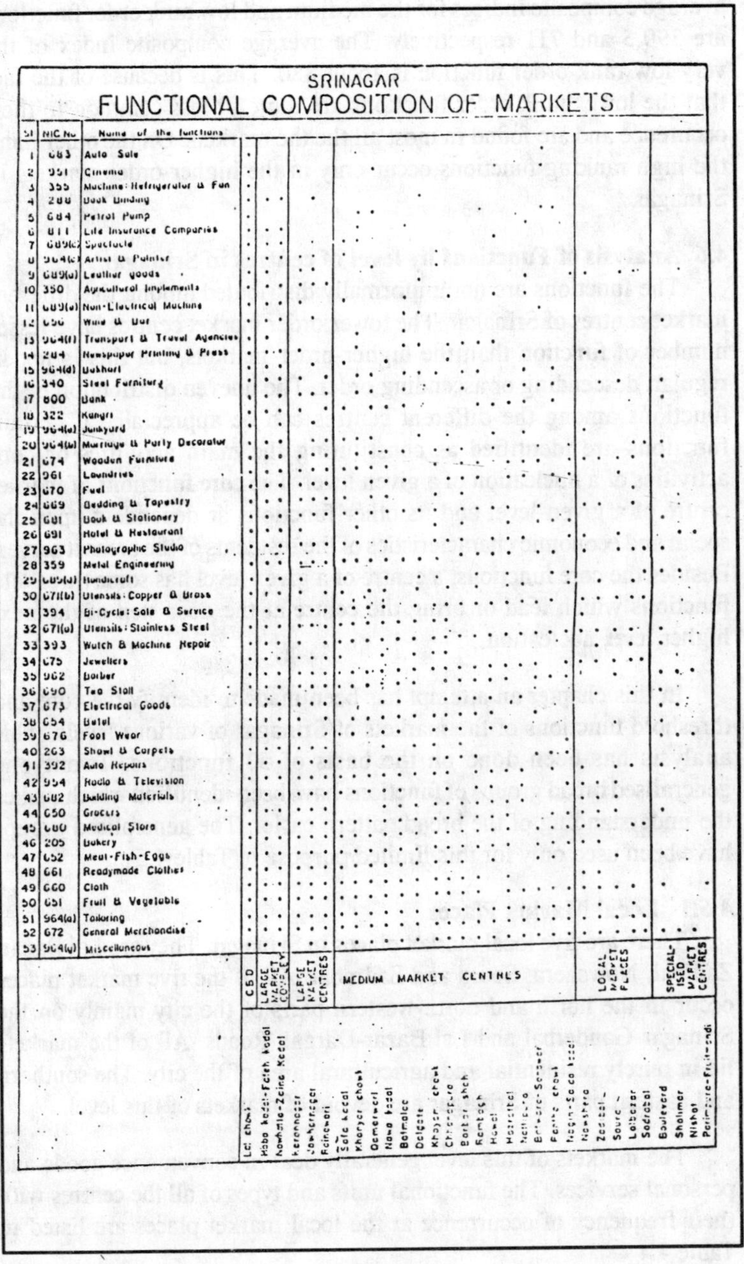
SRINAGAR
FUNCTIONAL COMPOSITION OF MARKETS
Sl
NIC No
Name of the functions
1 683 Auto Sale
2 951 Cinema
3 355 Machine: Refrigerator & Fan
4 288 Book Binding
5 684 Petrol Pump
6 811 Life Insurance Companies
7 689(c) Spectacle
8 964(c) Artist & Painter
9 689(a) Leather goods
10 350 Agricultural Implements
11 689(a) Non-Electrical Machine
12 656 Wine & Bar
13 964(f) Transport & Travel Agencies
14 284 Newspaper Printing & Press
15 964(d) Dukhari
16 340 Steel Furniture
17 800 Bank
18 322 Kangri
19 964(e) Junkyard
20 964(b) Marriage & Party Decorator
21 674 Wooden Furniture
22 961 Laundries
23 670 Fuel
24 669 Bedding & Tapestry
25 681 Book & Stationery
26 691 Hotel & Restaurant
27 963 Photographic Studio
28 359 Metal Engineering
29 685(a) Handicraft
30 671(b) Utensils: Copper & Brass
31 394 Bi-Cycle: Sale & Service
32 671(a) Utensils: Stainless Steel
33 393 Watch & Machine Repair
34 675 Jewellers
35 962 Barber
36 690 Tea Stall
37 673 Electrical Goods
38 654 Betel
39 676 Foot Wear
40 263 Shawl & Carpets
41 392 Auto Repairs
42 954 Radio & Television
43 682 Building Materials
44 650 Grocers
45 680 Medical Store
46 205 Bakery
47 652 Meat-Fish-Eggs
48 661 Readymade Clothes
49 660 Cloth
50 651 Fruit & Vegetable
51 964(a) Tailoring
52 672 General Merchandise
53 964(g) Miscellaneous
CBD
LARGE MARKET COMPLEX
LARGE MARKET CENTRES
MEDIUM MARKET CENTRES
LOCAL MARKET PLACES
SPECIALISED MARKET CENTRES
Lal chowk
Haba kadal-Fateh kadal
Nowhatta-Zaina Kadal
Karannagar
Jawaharnagar
Rainawari
Safa kadal
Kharyar chowk
Nawa kadal
Batmaloo
Dalgate
Khayam chowk
Chanapora
Barbarshah
Nowshera
Zadibal
Soura
Lalbazar
Sadrabal
Boulevard
Shalimar
Nishat

Fig. 27

average composite indices for the medium and low rank order functions are 390.5 and 711 respectively. The average composite index of the very low rank order function is about 880. This is because of the fact that the lower rank order functions are more or less common in their occurence and are found in most all the the markets. On the other hand the high ranking functions occur only in the higher order markets in Srinagar.

4.6 Analysis of Functions by level of centres in Srinagar

The functions are not uniformally distributed among the different market centres of Srinagar. The lower order market centres have lesser number of function than the higher order markets, but this is not in regular, descending or ascending order. The uneven distribution of the functions among the different centres can be appreciated if certain functions are identified as constituting the main activities or core activities of a nucleation of a given level. The core functions of market centre of a given level and its other functions ar dependent upon the social and economic characteristics of the residents of the areas it serves. Besides the core functions, a centre of a given level has some threshold functions which lead or bring the centre at the door step of the next higher level nucleation.

In this chapter an attempt has been made to identify the core and threshold functions of the markets of Srinagar of various levels. This analysis has been done on the basis of 53 functions. Twentyone generalised broad groups of functions have been identified which makes the understanding of the broad pattern easier. The generalised groups have been used only for this limited purpose in Table 4.5

4.6.1 Local Market Places

There are five local market places in Srinagar. They are Lal Bazar, Zadibal, Nowshera, Soura and Sadrabal. All of the five market places occur in the north and north-western parts of the city mainly on the Srinagar-Ganderbal and Lal Bazar-Dargah Roads. All of the markets lie in purely residential and agricultural area of the city. The southern and eastern parts of Srinagar are devoid of markets of this level.

The markets of this level generally deal in convenience goods and personal services. The functional units and types of all the centres with their frequency of occurrence at the local market places are listed in Table 4.4

Table 4.4
Functional Structure of Local Market Places

Sl. No.	N.I.C Code No.	I	II	II	IV	V	Total	Frequency
01.	205C	3	2	5	-	2	12	4
02.	350	-	-	1	1	-	2	2
03.	359	2	-	2	1	1	6	4
04.	393T	2	1	3	2	-	8	4
05.	394C	4	3	1	2	1	11	5
06.	650C	-	9	4	20	-	33	3
07.	651C	7	8	6	6	-	27	4
08.	652C	-	4	8	-	-	12	2
09.	660t	-	6	9	-	-	15	2
10.	661	-	-	-	4	-	4	1
11.	669	2	-	-	-	-	2	1
12.	670	-	-	-	1	-	1	1
13.	671(a)	-	-	3	-	-	3	1
14.	671(b)	5	2	-	-	-	7	2
15.	672C	18	12	11	7	14	62	5
16.	673T	2	3	-	-	-	5	2
17.	674	1	-	-	-	2	3	1
18.	675	3	2	-	-	-	5	2
19.	676	-	-	-	2	-	2	1
20.	680T	-	6	4	6	-	16	3
21.	681	1	2	1	-	-	4	3
22.	682T	-	4	3	3	-	10	3
23.	689	-	-	-	-	2	2	1
24.	690	-	-	-	3	-	3	1
25.	800	-	1	-	1	-	2	2
26.	954	2	-	3	3	-	8	3
27.	961T	1	2	1	1	-	5	4
28.	962C	1	1	2	1	1	6	5
29.	963	-	-	2	1	-	3	2
30.	964(a)	15	6	-	-	-	21	2
31.	964(b)	-	-	2	-	-	2	1
32.	964(d)	-	1	2	-	-	2	2
33.	964(g)	14	6	5	12	13	50	5
	Total	83	81	78	77	36	355	

Source : Field work

I.	Lal Bazar	C = Core functions
II.	Zadibal	T = Threshold functions
III.	Nowshera	
IV.	Soura	
V.	Sadarbal	

Thirty-three functions have been identified as being common to markets of this level. Seven of these are core functions, while six of them are regarded threshold functions. The core functions comprise mostly goods of daily use and very low order personal services and perishable goods. They include general merchandise, bakery, grocery, fruits and vegetables, meat-milk-chincken and such services as bi-cycle repairs, and hair cutting. Among the threshold functions are watch and clock, clothes, electrical goods, medicines and building materials.

Other functions are of mixed variety. Some such as tailoring, hosiery, ready-made garments are commonly and fully represented here. Former belongs to very low and latter with low order group. On the other hand the medium order functions such as metal engineering, tapestry and upholstery and high order functions such as agricultural implements are also found in the markets of this level, but the number of units is insignificant. They are not typical of the markets of this level.

The functional composition of the local market places according to a generalised grouping of function is shown in table 4.5. This table reveals that there is dominance of convenience functions. The largest number of units are those of food materials, general merchandise, personal services, miscellaneous shops etc. which account for 24.50, 18.88, 17.47 and 14.09 percent of the total number of functional units respectively (Table 4.5). Other major function units of the local market places are dress and dress materials, medicines, building materials, electrical appliances and earthen pottery and kangari which account for 5.36, 4.50, 3.67, 3.63 and 1.98 percent respectively. The majority of the functions of the local market places belong to the very low order functional group.

4.6.2 Medium Market Centre

There are sixteen medium market centres in the Srinagar city. Two of these markets-Hazratbal and Nagin-saida Kadal occur in the northern part of the city of the Srinagar-Daragah Road. Four of the markets namely Hawal, Nawa kadal, Safa Kadal and Khanyar Chowk occur here and three in the north-central part of the city. Barbar Shah and Kyham Chowk are in the central part of the city. Batmaloo is in the south-central part

Table 4.5
Generalised groups of functions (figures are in percentage)

S. No.	Name of functions	C.B.D.	Large market Complexes	Large market Centres	Medium market Centres	Local market Centres	Specialised market Centres
1.	Food materials	13.06	18.52	28.43	22.80	24.50	34.30
2.	General Merchandise	8.43	12.18	12.59	15.69	18.88	-
3.	Earthern Pottery & Kangari	0.50	4.41	2.01	1.80	1.98	0.49
4.	Medical Stores	3.10	3.99	5.48	3.43	4.50	0.72
5.	Building Materials	5.27	3.17	4.80	4.26	3.67	0.24
6.	Personal Services	14.84	15.49	23.15	23.29	17.47	6.08
7.	Travelling Agency & Firms	1.69	0.02	-	0.17	-	0.24
8.	Leather Goods & & Fur Materials	4.76	4.60	1.72	5.14	1.12	11.20
9.	Steel Furniture & Steel Utensils	1.87	2.01	1.92	1.87	0.84	-
10.	Jewellery & Spectacle	2.89	6.27	1.63	1.01	1.41	2.68

11.	Electrical Appliances	4.40	4.44	3.84	3.08	3.63	0.98
12.	Hotel & bar	3.98	0.97	0.39	1.73	-	13.39
13.	Non-Elec. machine	1.07	1.81	0.77	0.91	1.41	-
14.	Automobile	0.05	-	-	0.03	-	-
15.	Financial Service	1.26	0.30	0.68	0.59	0.57	0.72
16.	Shawls & Carpets	11.32	2.87	2.89	3.28	-	26.52
17.	Tapestry & Upholstry	0.82	1.25	0.97	0.51	0.57	-
18.	Electrical Machines	0.17	-	-	-	-	-
19.	Printing Press & Book Binders	1.22	0.52	0.19	0.51	-	-
20.	Dress & Dress Materials	12.20	16.13	7.20	6.32	5.36	0.98
21.	Miscellaneous	7.10	1.05	1.34	3.60	14.00	1.46
	Total	100	100	100	100	100	100

and Rambagh, Chhana-pura, Batwara–Sonawar, Nattipara and Pantha Chowk are found scattered in the southeastern parts of the city. Nattipura, Ram-bagh and Chhanapura are on the Srinagar-Chhanapura road and Batwara-Sonawar and Pantha Chowk are on the National Highway IA.

The other two medium level markets are in the eastern and western parts of Srinagar. They are Dalgate and Qamarwari on the Srinagar-Dargah and Srinagar-Baramulla roads respectively.

The functional units and the types of fuctions they discharge and occurrence are shown in Table 4.6.

Fortyone functions have been identified in the markets of this level. Of these thirteen are core functions and fourteen are threshold functions. It is impoprtant to note here that all the functions common to the local market places are found in the markets of this level also. The centres of this level, however, have a larger number of functional units and functional types. Generally, the centres of this level are more complex than the lower order local market places. The types of functions and the number of establishments with their frequency of occurrence in different centres are given in Table 4.6. Most of the threshold functions of the local market places constitute core functions in the medium market centres. The core functions of the markets of this level are generally two types. They include firstly the threshold functions of the local market places such as watch and clock repairs, cloth, electrical goods, medicines and building materials and secondly, the funtions of medium order such as shawls, fuel, foot-wear, medicines, tea-stalls, radio, T.V. shops and laundries.

The threshold functions comprise costly consumer goods such as, engineering, auto-repairs and spare parts, tapestry and upholstery, wooden furniture, jewellery, books, auto and car sale, petrol pumps, hostels and restaurants, banks, cinemas, photographic studios, and marriage and decoration belong to different functional groups.

Table 4.5 clearly indicates an increase in the personal services as against convenience goods. This is the most striking difference between the market places and the medium market centres. There is significant decrease in food material shops (22.80%), general merchandise shops (15.69%), and medicine stores (3.43%).

On the other hand there is sharp increase in the number of establishments dealing in building materials (4.20%), personal services

Table 4.6
Functional Structure of Medium Market Centres

Sl. No.	N. I. C. Code No.	I	II	III	IV	V	VI	VII	VIII	IX	X	XI	XII	XIII	XIV	XV	XVI	Total	Frequency
1.	205	13	6	5	14	6	6	8	18	7	3	10	12	9	7	3	3	130	16
2.	263C	5	-	-	21	41	-	-	-	-	13	-	-	-	-	20	-	100	5
3.	284	-	-	-	4	-	1	-	-	-	1	-	1	-	-	-	-	14	7
4.	288	-	-	-	1	-	-	-	-	-	-	-	-	-	-	-	-	1	1
5.	322C	3	1	-	-	-	-	1	3	6	-	3	1	2	1	-	-	21	9
6.	340	-	2	1	1	4	-	-	-	3	1	1	1	-	2	-	-	16	9
7.	350	-	-	-	1	-	-	-	-	-	-	-	-	-	3	1	-	5	3
8.	359T	2	4	10	1	2	2	4	6	5	1	1	1	5	-	-	1	45	14
9.	392T	-	64	5	-	4	4	5	-	4	11	30	11	-	-	4	21	163	11
10.	393C	5	3	3	6	2	5	4	2	5	2	3	3	1	2	1	2	49	16
11.	394	2	-	4	3	7	6	2	4	4	2	8	9	10	7	-	2	70	14
12.	650	23	8	-	7	8	9	-	34	-	7	-	14	7	19	-	-	136	10
13.	651	11	18	4	15	7	12	11	4	21	9	4	10	-	3	3	11	143	15
14.	652C	25	9	11	13	12	10	16	5	15	9	19	8	3	-	6	6	167	15
15.	654	4	6	4	4	7	14	-	-	5	2	-	4	3	-	-	11	64	11
16.	656	-	2	-	1	-	-	-	-	-	-	-	-	-	-	-	2	5	3
17.	660C	20	23	10	10	9	14	13	8	9	8	-	4	-	-	-	-	128	11
18.	661C	10	7	4	5	3	5	10	-	3	3	3	-	6	-	-	6	65	12

19.	669T	4	-	-	-	2	-	3	-	4	2	-	-	-	-	-	-	15	5
20.	670C	3	3	-	-	-	2	5	2	1	6	1	2	-	1	2	-	28	11
21.	671(a)	8	10	2	5	2	4	6	-	4	-	-	-	-	-	-	-	41	8
22.	671(b)	12	-	-	3	-	2	5	2	3	-	-	2	-	2	3	-	34	9
23.	672	26	22	58	27	20	41	20	28	48	43	19	14	12	16	26	9	429	16
24.	673T	5	3	-	-	-	3	9	-	-	2	-	4	4	2	-	-	32	8
25.	674T	1	1	1	-	8	3	-	-	3	8	-	-	4	-	1	1	31	10
26.	675T	12	-	-	5	2	5	4	-	-	-	-	-	-	-	-	-	28	5
27.	676C	5	14	2	-	5	5	7	6	-	2	-	-	3	-	-	-	49	9
28.	680C	11	5	19	6	5	10	11	9	4	7	3	5	6	-	4	-	105	14
29.	681T	6	2	1	2	1	-	1	3	1	1	-	2	1	-	-	1	22	12
30.	682C	7	12	26	-	-	8	9	-	4	-	-	5	13	12	3	-	99	10
31.	683T	-	-	-	-	-	-	-	-	-	-	-	-	-	-	-	1	1	1
32.	684T	-	-	3	-	-	-	-	-	1	-	2	1	-	-	-	2	9	5
33.	689(a)	-	-	-	-	4	-	-	-	1	-	-	-	-	-	-	-	5	2
34.	689(c)	-	-	1	-	-	-	1	-	-	-	-	-	1	-	-	-	3	3
35.	689(d)	4	-	-	15	16	-	3	17	-	-	36	3	-	-	9	-	103	8
36.	689(e)	-	2	-	-	-	1	1	-	-	-	-	-	1	2	-	-	7	5
37.	690C	-	9	6	2	-	3	2	5	5	2	3	3	5	-	3	8	56	13
38.	691T	-	-	3	2	13	-	-	5	-	12	5	-	-	-	4	6	48	8
39.	800T	-	2	4	-	-	-	-	2	1	1	1	-	-	1	-	2	14	8
40.	811	-	1	2	-	-	-	-	-	-	-	-	-	-	1	-	-	4	3
41.	951T	-	-	-	-	-	-	-	-	1	-	-	-	1	-	-	1	3	3
42.	954C	6	4	4	5	2	10	9	3	5	-	5	2	4	3	-	-	62	13

43.	961C	3	-	2	-	4	-	1	3	1	2	-	3	2	1	2	1	25	12
44.	962	9	3	2	8	2	4	2	3	4	6	-	5	2	2	3	4	59	15
45.	963T	2	-	4	6	3	1	2	2	2	3	-	-	3	1	2	-	31	12
46.	964(a)	24	4	29	25	14	16	14	18	8	22	17	14	13	19	14	9	260	16
47.	964(b)T	-	-	4	1	-	3	2	-	4	-	-	-	3	1	-	-	18	7
48.	964(c)	-	-	-	-	2	-	2	-	-	-	-	-	-	-	-	-	4	2
49.	964(d)	6	-	-	-	-	1	7	-	-	-	-	-	-	2	-	-	16	4
50.	964(f)	-	3	2	-	-	-	-	-	-	-	-	-	-	-	-	-	5	2
51.	964(g)	1	5	3	3	4	1	2	6	5	3	7	6	17	8	7	85	16	
	Total	278	259	244	222	221	211	202	198	197	194	179	150	132	127	122	117	3053	

Source : Field Work

C = Core function

T = Threshold function

I Nawa Kadal
II Batmallo
III Khanyar Chowk
IV Dalgate
V Khayam Chowk
VI Chhannapura
VII Safa Kadal
VIII Hazratbal
IX Qamarwari
X Barbershah
XI Pantha Chowk
XII Rambagh
XIII Hawal
XIV Nattipura
XV Nagin-Saida Kadal
XVI Batwara

(23.29%), Leather goods (5.10%), dress and dress materials (6.32%) as compared with the local market places. Another feature of the medium level market is the occurrence of new higher order functions not found in the local level markets. These are shawls and carpets, hotels and bars, printing press, travel agencies and auto sale. They account for 3.28, 1.73, 0.51, 0.17 and 0.03 percent of the units repectively.

4.6.3 Large Market Centrs

There are three large market centres in the city of Srinagar. They are Jawahar Nagar, Karan Nagar, and Rainawari.

Jawahar Nagar occurs in the south-central part of Srinagar on the Lal Chowk-Chinar Jawahar Road close to CBD. Karan Nagar on the Lal Chowk-Safa kadal Road in the central part of the city and Rainawari is in the north-central part of the city on the Lal Chok-Dargah Road.

Table 4.7
Functional structure of Large Market Centres

Sl. No.	N.I.C. Code No.	I	II	III	Total	Frequency
01.	205	19	20	27	66	3
02.	263C	4	10	16	30	3
03.	284	-	-	1	1	1
04.	288	1	-	-	1	1
05.	322C	-	7	3	10	2
06.	340	-	3	5	8	2
07.	350C	1	2	2	5	3
08.	359C	1	3	6	10	3
09.	392C	9	13	16	38	3
10.	393	-	1	3	4	2
11.	394	2	6	2	10	3
12.	650	51	12	22	85	3
13.	651	20	18	10	48	3
14.	652	12	27	20	59	3
15.	654C	-	2	8	10	2
16.	656	2	-	-	2	1
17.	660	12	17	18	47	3
18.	661	13	4	11	28	3
19.	669C	2	5	3	10	3
20.	670	6	3	4	13	3

21.	671(a)T	3	2	7	12	2
22.	671(b)	-	4	7	11	2
23.	672	43	50	15	108	3
24.	673	5	5	6	16	3
25.	674C	1	9	3	13	3
26.	675C	4	6	3	13	3
27.	676	-	5	4	9	2
28.	680	24	17	16	57	3
29.	681C	3	4	3	10	3
30.	682	20	5	12	37	3
31.	689(a)T	1	-	3	4	2
32.	689(c)	4	-	-	4	1
33.	689(d)T	-	-	5	5	1
34.	689(e)T	-	-	2	2	1
35.	690	18	4	6	28	3
36.	691T	-	-	2	2	1
37.	800C	4	1	2	7	3
38.	951	-	-	1	1	1
39.	954C	15	2	7	24	3
40.	961	5	3	3	11	3
41.	962	5	8	10	23	3
42.	963C	3	3	5	11	3
43.	964(a)	34	46	25	105	3
44.	964(b)C	32	1	-	33	2
45.	964(c)T	1	-	2	3	2
46.	964(d)T	1	-	-	2	1
47.	964(e)T	2	-	-	2	1
48.	964(g)	3	1	-	4	2
	Total	386	326	326	1041	

Source : Field Work

I Jawahara Nagar
II Rainawari
III Karan Nagar

C = core function
T = Threshold function

The functional structure of the large market centres is characterised by duplication of all the lower level functions (Table 4.7). Six new functions namely printing press, junkyard, book-binding, wine and bar, spectacles and non-electrical machine shops are added to the functions of the market centres of this level. Three Functions are not found in the markets of this level. They are auto sale, petrol pump and travel agencies. Thirteen functions are recognised as core functions of the markets of this level. Although nine functions have been identified as the threshold functions, practically there is little differnece between the large market centres and medium market centres in this regard.

The core functions of the market centres of this level are costly items like shawls and carpets, agricultural implements, metal engineering, books and stationery and radio and television sets etc.

The threshold functions deal in goods such as steel utensils, leather goods, handicrafts, non-electrical machines, artists and painters, junkyard, bokhari and black-smith and services such as banks and hotels and restaurants.

The percentages of the generalised groups of functions shown in Table No. 4.5, clearly indicate an increase in the establishments dealing in dress (7.20), electrical appliances (3.84), steel utensils (1.92), financial services (0.68), and tapestry and upholstery (0.97). On the other hand there is a sharp decrease in percentage of functions as general merchandise, hotels and restaruants, leather goods and non-electrical machines. They account for 12.59, 0.39, 1.72 and 0.72 respectively.

4.6.4 Large Market Complexes

Three large market complexes have been identified in the city of Srinagar. These are Nawhatta-Zaina Kadal and Habakadal-Fathe Kadal complexes. Both of these complexes occur north of the CBD in Nawhatta-Zaina Kadal area and Habba Kadal-Fateh Kadal area in the north-central and central parts of the city respectively.

The Nawhatta-Zaina Kadal Complex consists of five small market centres namely, Nawhatta, Bori Kadal, Zaina Kadal, Maharajganj and Rajauri Kadal occurring around Nawhatta on the main road and side lanes of the respective localities.

The Haba Kadal-Fathe Kadal complex consists of three markets. They are Haba Kadal, Azad Market and Chhotta Bazar. All of these markets occur in the central area of the city close to the CBD.

The functions of the large market complexes are to a considerable extent duplications of the functions of the lower level markets (Table 4.8). Two of the functions namely, Insurance companies and Travel Agencies are new additions to the functions of the markets of this level.

Three of the functions namely auto sale, petrol pump and machines and refrigerators are not found in the market centre of this level. Fifteen of them are recognised as core functions and eight are recognised as threshold functions. However, there is practically little difference in the functional structures of the large market complexes and central business district. Nawhatta and Zaina Kadal areas are the oldest commercial centres of Srinagar.

The core functions of the markets of this level include transactions of costly goods such as shawls and carpets, tapestry and upholstery, steel utensils, handicraft, non-electrical machines, television and radios and services such as banks, insurance companies and marriage and party decoration. These functions belong to the different hierarchical groups of functions.

Table 4.8
Functional Structure of Large Market Complexes

Sl. No.	N.I.C. Code	I	II	Total	Frequency
01.	205	70	54	124	2
02.	263C	73	25	98	2
03.	284T	6	7	13	2
04.	288	3	2	5	2
05.	322	5	2	7	2
06.	340	1	3	4	2
07.	350T	3	15	18	2
08.	359	27	6	33	2
09.	392	18	36	54	2
10.	393	24	10	34	2
11.	394	8	17	25	2
12.	650C	112	37	149	2
13.	651	77	56	133	2
14.	652	73	61	134	2
15.	654C	25	38	63	2
16.	656T	12	3	15	2
17.	660	221	144	365	2
18.	661	114	72	186	2
19.	669C	22	21	43	2
20.	670	14	10	24	2
21.	671(a)C	42	23	65	2

22.	671(b)	115	29	144	2
23.	672	200	156	356	2
24.	673	41	35	76	2
25.	674	6	14	20	2
26.	675	137	63	200	2
27.	676	58	45	103	2
28.	680	56	80	136	2
29.	681T	16	20	36	2
30.	682	72	16	88	2
31.	689(a)T	-	3	3	1
32.	689(c)C	5	9	14	2
33.	689(d)C	38	13	51	2
34.	689(e)C	10	11	21	2
35.	690	20	10	30	2
36.	691C	6	12	18	2
37.	800C	4	4	8	2
38.	811C	1	1	2	2
39.	951T	-	1	1	1
40.	954C	37	39	76	2
41.	961	9	14	23	2
42.	962	17	24	41	2
43.	963	10	18	28	2
44.	963(a)	152	114	226	2
45.	964(b)C	7	7	14	2
46.	964(c)C	6	8	14	2
47.	964(d)C	21	2	23	2
48.	964(e)T	17	-	17	1
49.	964(f)T	-	1	1	1
50.	964(g)	9	6	15	2
	Total	2020	1397	3417	

Source : Field work

I Nawahatta-Zaina Kadal Complex
II Haba Kadal-Fateh Kadal Complex

C = Core function
T = Threshhold function

The threshold functions of the large market complexes include printing press, agricultural implements, wine and bar. book-sellers and stationers, leather goods and clothes. Travel Agencies and cinemas are also identified as threshold functions of the market centres of this level.

The other important functions of the large market complexes, besides the core and threshold functions are junkyards, copper and brass utensils, gold-smithy and jewellery and embroidery etc.

The percentages of the generalised groups of functions shown in Table 4.5 clearly indicates a noteable increase in leather goods, steel furniture, jewelley, electrical appliances, non-electrical machine, tapestry and upholstery and dress materials. They account for 4.60, 2.01, 6.27, 4.44, 1.81, 1.25and 16.13 percent of the establishments repectively. Food materials, personal services, and medicine stores show a considerable decrease again and share 18.52, 15.49 and 3.17 percent respectively of the total number of establishments found in the markets of this level but the number goes on decreasing when compared to the market centres of lower level.

The new entrants, i.e. the travelling firms and agencies to the generalised group of functions account for 0.02 percent of the total shops of Srinagar.

4.6.5 Central Business District

The Central Business District occurs in the south-central part of the city. The retail activities of the central business district are distributed among the Maulana Azad and Residency Roads in the east, the Government Central Market and the Airport Road in the west, Gowkadal in the north and Hazaribagh, Lal Ded and Iqbal Park in the south. Shops on the roads, lanes and streets connecting the Shergari, Shahieed Ganj constitute parts of the Central Business District.

The Central Business District of Srinagar consists of six market centres. These are Lal Chowk, Bad Shah Chowk, Bund, Maharaj Bazar, Shergari and Government Central market. The functional types and units of the main market area are shown in Table 4.9. Only the core functions have been recognised beacuse no threshold function was identified here. The centre has varying numbers of more specialised functions. Three new function namely auto sale, machine and refrigerators and petrol pumps have been added to the traditional ones in the market centres of this level. There is less duplication of the lower order functions here. All of the fiftythree functions identified are found in the Central Business District.

Table 4.9
Functional Structure of Central Business District

Sl. No.	N.I.C Code No.	CBD	Total	Frequency
01.	205	65	65	1
02.	263C	424	424	1
03.	284C	33	33	1
04.	288	13	13	1
05.	322	4	4	1
06.	340C	30	30	1
07.	350C	11	11	1
08.	355C	6	6	1
09.	359	48	48	1
10.	392	187	187	1
11.	393C	39	39	1
12.	394	25	25	1
13.	650	105	105	1
14.	651	106	106	1
15.	652	57	57	1
16.	654C	95	95	1
17.	656C	24	24	1
18.	660C	238	238	1
19.	661C	219	219	1
20.	669C	31	31	1
21.	670	17	17	1
22.	671(a)	40	40	1
23.	671(b)	15	15	1
24.	672	256	256	1
25.	673C	68	68	1
26.	674	15	15	1
27.	675C	98	98	1
28.	676C	89	89	1
29.	680	116	116	1
30.	681C	43	43	1
31.	682	182	182	1
32.	684C	2	2	1
33.	684C	8	8	1
34.	689(a)C	17	17	1
35.	689(c)C	10	10	1
36.	689(d)	72	72	1

37.	689(e)	14	14	1
38.	690	61	61	1
39.	691C	125	125	1
40.	800C	32	32	1
41.	811C	15	15	1
42.	951C	3	3	1
43.	954	97	97	1
44.	961	20	20	1
45.	962	27	27	1
46.	963C	45	45	1
47.	964(a)C	135	135	1
48.	964(b)	42	42	1
49.	964(c)	15	15	1
50.	964(d)	15	15	1
51.	964(e)C	196	196	1
52.	964(f)C	63	63	1
53.	964(g)	32	32	1
	Total	3745	3745	

Source : Field Work

C = Core functions
T = Threshold functions

Twentyseven functions have been recognised as core functions of the Central Business District. Most of them are threshold functions of the medium market centres, large market centres and large market complexes. The functions have achieved a higher grade in the Central Business Distict because of the specialised and better quality goods available here. Cloth, readymade garments, jewellery, shawls and carpets, printing press, steel furniture, tailoring, leather goods, photographic studio are the core functions of the Central Business District. These are also found in other lower order markets, but the quality and range offered by the Central Business District are unknown in other centres. Similarly, tailoring is a low order service in other market centres, but is identified as the core function of the CBD because hihgly fashionable dresses are stitched here. Books, steel furniture, machines and refrigerators, automobiles, watches and clocks, betel, wine tapestry and upholstery, electrical goods, foot-wear, petrol pumps, spectacles, hotels, banks, insurance companies, cinemas, and travel agencies are other core functions of the Central Business District.

Table 4.5 shows the generalised groups of functions of the CBD. The table highlights the nature of the specialisation. It shows an increase in the percentage of shopping goods and a corresponding decrease in that of convenience goods shops. There is a noteable increase in the share building materials, travel agencies, leather goods, hotels and bars, financial services, shawls and carpets, and printing press, which account for 5.27, 1.69, 4.76, 3.98, 1.26, 11.32 and 1.22 percent of the total functional units respectively.

On the other hand there is sharp decrease in the share of food materials, general merchandise, earthen pottery and personal services. They account for 13.06, 8.43, 0.5 and 14.84 percent of the total shops of Srinagar respectively. The newly added functions, such as auto sale and electrical machines account for 0.05 and 0.17 percent of total shops of the city respectively.

4.6.6 Specialised Market Centres

Specialised markets are typical of India. They are often called periodic, traditional or public markets. They are not found inAmerica, but are common enough in Europe, Africa and Asia. A periodic is defined by Scott "as a public gathering of buyers and sellers at any appointed place and at regular intervals for the purpose of doing business under specific conditions"[7].

Although this kind of market has a long history in western Europe according to Berry, it is 'purely modern' in the New World and the Southern Hemisphere[8].

These markets are present also in Australian cities, especially in Melbourne, where in the early fifties there were five public and six privately owned markets. The Queen Victoria Public Market alone housed more than a half of the 2,430 stalls of the metropolitan area and is said to attract 30,000 customers on the week days[9].

In the present study the periodical markets have not been found to conform with the hierarchical pattern and have therefore been classified separetely as specialised market centres.

There are four specialised markets in the city of Srinagar, of which three occur in its eastern part along the Dal Lake and one occurs in the western part of the city at Parimpura. The names of the specialised markets occuring in the eastern part of the city are Boulevard, Nishat and Shalimar markets on the Lal Chowk-Harwan Road.

Parimpura-fruit mandi is the only specialised market found in the western part of Srinagar. All of these markets open every day, but the peak hours of the three markets namely, Boulevard, Nishat and Shalimar are from 10 a.m. to 6 p.m. The peak season is from April to October. The peak hours of Parimpura-fruit-mandi is the early morning hours only.

The markets differ from the traditional and pereodical markets found in Europe, Africa and other Asian countries in many respects.

The peculiarity of most of the specialised markets of Srinagar except Parimpura fruit-mandi which specialises in fruits and vegetables, is that they are oriented towards catering of the needs of tourists.

Twentyone functions have been identified frequenting in the specialised markets. The outstanding feature of the Parimpura-fruit-mandi is the concentration here of shops of perishable goods such as fruits and vegetables (both wholesale and retail).

The other three specialised market centres are oriented purely towards tourists industry. Generally, hotels, restaurants, tea stalls, leather and fur goods, dry fruits, handicrafts, photographic studios etc. are found in the market centres of this level (Table 4.10).

Six functions have been recognised as the core functions of the specialsied markets, while fruits and vegetables are the core function of the Parimpura-fruit-mandi because this is the only function discharged by the Parimpura-fruit-mandi. This is exclusively a vegetable market. The core functions of the remaining three specialised markets are Shawls, Handicraft goods (leather and fur goods), tea stalls, hotels and restaurants and photographic studios.

Table 4.5 shows the composition of functions by generalised groups and clearly indicates the degree of specialisation of these markets. The table shows besides food materials the dominance of shawls and carpets, hotels and restaurants and leather and fur goods in the specialised centres. They account for 26.25, 13.39 and 11.80 percent of total number of shops of Srinagar. This is due to the inclusion of the Parimpura-fruit-mandi in the specialised group of markets.

4.7 Summary of Functional Structure

The study of the functional structure of the market of different hierarcical levels reveals that an increasing functional complexity is associated with the higher order markets. On the other hand a decreasing trend in the number of functions is noticeable in the lower order centres. Moreover, the lower order centres deal in convenience goods while the higher order centres deal in both in conveniecne and shopping goods.

Table 4.10

Functional structure of Specialised Market Centres

Sl. No.	N.I.C. Code No.	I	II	III	IV	Total	Frequency
01.	263C	85	-	10	14	109	3
02.	322	2	-	-	-	2	1
03.	359	3	-	-	-	3	1
04.	393	1	-	-	-	1	1
05.	651C	4	95	-	-	99	2
06.	654	3	-	9	-	12	3
07.	661	4	-	-	-	4	1
08.	673	2	-	-	-	2	1
09.	674	1	-	-	-	1	1
10.	675	11	-	-	-	11	1
11.	676	2	-	-	-	2	1
12.	680	3	-	-	-	3	1
13.	689(d)C	40	-	4	-	44	2
14.	690C	5	-	12	13	30	3
15.	691C	55	-	-	-	55	1
16.	800	3	-	-	-	3	1
17.	954	2	-	-	-	2	1
18.	961	3	-	-	-	3	1
19.	963C	-	-	12	6	18	2
20.	964(f)	1	-	-	-	1	1
21.	964(g)	1	-	2	3	6	4
	Total	231	95	49	36	411	

Source : Field Work

I Boulevard
II Parimpura Fruit Mandi
III Shalimar
IV Nishat
C = Core functions

Table 4.11
Core and Threshold functions at different levels of Market

Local Market Places		Medium Market Centres		Large Market Centres		large Market Complexes		CBD		Specialised Markets	
205	Bakery	263	Shawls	263	Shawls	263	Shawls	263	Shawls	263	Shawls
394	Bi-cycle sale & Service	322	Kangri	322	Kangri	650	Grocer	284	Printing Press	651	Fruit & Veg.
650	Grocer	393	Watch & Machine	350	Agriculture Implement	654	Betal	340	Steel furniture	689(d)	Handicraft
651	Fruit & Veg.	652	Meat-fish-Egg.	359	Metal Engineering	669	Bedding tapestry & upholstry	350	Agr. Implement	690	Tea Stall
652	Meat-Fish-Egg	660	Cloth	392	Auto repair	671 (a)	Utensil : Stainless Steel	355	Machine & refrigerator	691	Hotel & Restaurant
672	General Merchandise	661	Readymade garment	654	Betal	689 (c)	Spectacles	393	Watch & Clock	963	Photographic Studio
962	Barber	670	Fuel	669	Bedding : Tapestry & upholstry	689 (d)	Handicrafts	654	Betal		
		676	Footwear	674	Wooden furniture	689 (e)	Non-electric machine	656	Wine		
		680	Medical store	675	Jewellery	691	Hotel & Restaurant	660	Cloth		
		682	Building material	681	Books & Stationery	800	Bank	661	Readymade garments		
		690	Tea Stall	800	Bank	811	Life Insurance	669	Bedding, Tapestry & upholstry		

	954 Radio & T.V.	954 Radio & T. V.	954 Radio & T.V.	673 Electrical goods	
	961 Laundry	963 Photographic Studio	964 (b) Marriage & Party Decorator	675 Jewellery	
		964(b)Marriage & Party Decorator	964 (c) Artist & Painter	676 Foot wear	
			964 (d) Bokhari	681 Book & Stationery	
				683 Automobile	
				684 Petrolpump	
				689(a)Leather goods	
				689(c)Spectacles	
				691 Hotel & Restaurant	
				800 Bank	
				811 Life Insurance	
				951 Cinema	
				963 Photographic Studio	
				964(a)Tailor	
				964(b)Marriage & Party Decorator	
				964(e)Junk yard	
				964(f) Travelling firms	
Local Market Places	Medium Market Centres	Large Market Centres	large Market Complexes	CBD	Specialised Markets
393 Watch & Clock	359 Metal Engg.	671 Utensil : Stainless Steel	284 Printing Press		
660 Cloth	392 Auto-repair	689(a)Leather goods	350 Agriculture Implement		
673 Electrical goods	669 Bedding, Tap-estry &	689(d)Handicraft	656 Wine & Bar		

			Upholstry						
680	Medical Store	673	Electrical goods	689(e)	Non-electrical machine	681	Books & Stationery	NONE	NONE
682	Building materials	674	Wooden furniture	691	Hotel & Restaurant	689(a)	Leather goods		
961	Laundary	675	Jewellery	964(c)	Artist and Painter	951	Cinema		
		681	Books & Stationery	964(d)	Bokhari	964(e)	Junk yard		
		683	Automobile	964(e)	Junk yard	964(f)	Travelling firms		
		684	Petrol pump						
		691	Hotel & Restaurant						
		800	Bank						
		951	Cinema					NONE	NONE
		963	Photographic studio						
		964(b)	Marriage and Party decorator						

It may be pointed out that higher order centres have the functions common in the lower order centres besides the functions typical of them. This is clear from Table 4.11 which shows the core and threshold functions of the markets of all levels. The threshold functions of the lower level centres become the core functions of the higher level centres, but the threshold functions of the higher level centres are also found frequently in the lower level centres. If a higher order function is found in a lower level centre, the physical condition of the establishment is decidedly poor. The establishment keeps cheap varieties of merchandise in stock. On the other hand, whenever a lower order function is found in a higher level centre, the physical condition of the shop is much better. The establishment keeps good variety and better quality merchandise. It may also be housed in a pucca building with all necessary infrastructures.

For example, it is observed from Table 4.11 that cloth and footwear are available in the markets of almost all levels, but ther is a great difference in the quality of goods sold. The lower order markets deal in ordinary cloth of daily use. Fancy and costly cloth such as woolen, polyster, rayon, silken, and costly brocades and embroidered silk etc. are sold in the central business district, and occassionally, in large market complexes. Similar is the case ith footwear. The medium, and large market centres and large market complexes sell ordinary variety of footwear while the CBD sells fashionable foot wear of high quality and provides wider choice.

Similarly, a few of the lower order functions such as tailoring and embroidery are recognised as the core functions of the CBD. This is because fashionable stitching and quality work is done here. The tailoring of the low order markets do cheap stitching requiring poor workmanship. But for the commoisseur and fastidious the CBD is the only choice.

These are the main reason why some of the lower order centres have higher order functions while the higher order centres have lower order functions, especially in the CBD. Hence it can be concluded that specialisation and quality are the only characteristics of the CBD.

References :

1. Scott, P. : Geography of Retailing : Hutchinson University Library, London, 1971, p. 30.

2. Ibid.

3. Hall, R. : Retailing in Northern Finland, Particularly by mobile Shops, 1964, p. : op., p. 55.

4. Scott, P. : op. cit., p. 55.

5. National Industrial Classification (Adopted by the Registrar, General of India) Census of India, 1981, Registrer General of India, New Delhi-11.

6. Scott, P. : op. Cit. p. 127.

7. Berry, B. J. L. : Geography of Market Centres and Retail Distribution, Printice Hall Inc, EngleWood Cliffs, New York, 1967, p. 13.

8. Melbourne and metropolitan Board of Workers, Melbourne Metropolitan Planning Scheme Report : Survey and Analysis, Melbourne, 1954, p. 102.

5

Quality of Buildings Housing Shops and Markets

Market centres vary widely among them selves with respect to the quality of shops. The shops in general may be housed on all floors of well built multi-storeyed pucca buildings in the market centres of higher hierarchical orders. The shops may be larger in size with well-stocked show rooms, may have wide frontage and all kinds of customer attracting devices s''ch as arrangments for seating them, rolling shatters, steel sighnboa.ds or those with neon lights, attractive show cases in front or inside with large glass panes, good sanitation, better internal lighting with generators for emergency, a number of employees (salesmen), telephone connections and other infra structural facilities. On the other hand the medium and low order market centres may have double storeyed buildings, but only their ground floors are put to commercial use; their upper floors being used as residences or the structures housing the shops may be wooden with tin roofs or the shops may be under open sky. The shops are comparatively small, may have not so wide frontage and the customer attracting in-frastructures may not be as good. These shops may have electric, but may or not have telephone connections.

These are the common features of the market centres of the Indian towns and cities. Srinagar is no exception. These are proposed to be studied thoroughly by the present work. However, the conclusions arrived at may not match with the conclusions of studies undertaken in Western countries because the conditions obtaining in those countries are totally different from those obtaining in India.

A study of the materials of which the buildings housing the shops of the market centres of various hierarahical orders in Srinagar are constructed, other characteristics of these shops and the infrastructural facilities available in them is likely to reveal several interesting facts. The characteristics of the shops and the infrastructural facilities available in them which were observed in the course of the field observation included the size of the shops (floor area), their frontage, their general look (appearance), the number of persons employed as salesmen, the kind of shutters, presence or otherwise of electricity and telephone connections, arrangement for seating the customer, types of signboards and show-cases etc.

5.1 Classification of Buildings Housing the Shops

The quality of the buildings in which the shops of Srinagar are housed was examined in course of the field work. The buildings have been grouped into five categories-pucca, semi-pucca, kutcha, stalls and open to sky-on the basis of building materials.

Pucca : The pucca buildings housing the shops are those which are built of bricks and cement concrete. They might be being used either as shops and dwellings or only for commercial purposes.

Semi-Pucca : This group consists of buildings with wooden structures tin roofs, brick or mud walls with cement or mud floors, It also includes buildings having cement floors, tin roofs, supported by wooden walls.

Kutcha : If the buildings which accomodate shops have mudwalls plasterd with mud, tin-roofs and mud floors they have been put into this category.

Stalls : There are a number of small shops in Srinagar which are housed in different kinds of buildings. Some of the latter have wooden frames tin roofs and mud floors, or the whole structure is of tin sheets with cemented floor. Both are generally small in size (4 ft. to 8 ft. wide and 6 ft. to 10 ft. deep) and located separately. These have been grouped in the category of stalls. This category also includes the pucca stalls or very small size shops which are found in the markets of Srinagar of different hierarchical order.

Open to sky : Shops of this category have no (Structure) on the ground. They are in the open fields, yet are permanent in nature The hawkers are not included in this group. They are rare in Srinagar. They have been excluded from the present study on account of their changing nature both with respect to the locality in which they operate and type of goods sold. Only such open shops have been included in this study as have been operatiiing for a long time (8-12 years) at the same place and doing their original business. These shops sell fuelwood and stone chips and are found in the medium market centres only.

Other facilities : Besides the quality of the structures housing the shops other characteristics of the commercial premises and the infrastructural facilities available in them were also noted during the field investigation. These include the size of shops, their frontage, their general look (appearance), the number of person employed as sales men by them, the kind of shutters used, presence or otherwise of electric connections, telephones and arrangement for seating the customers, type of signboards and show-cases etc.

The size of the shops : The shops have been grouped into three categories on the basis of their size. Shops with below 100 square feet of floor area have been classified into small shops, those between 100 and 300 square feet have been grouped into medium and those over 500 square feet of floor area have been called large shops.

The Frontage of shops : The shops have also been classified into four groups on the basis of their frontage. These are narrow (upto 5 feet), medium (5-10 feet), normal (10-12 feet) and wide (over 20 feet).

The General Look of shops : The genral condition or look of the building in which the shops are housed have also been kept under three heads: new, old but good and poor.

The Number of Persons Employed : The number of persons employed by the owner of the shop is an indicator of the standard of the shop. The small and low order shops are run by only one person, i.e. by the owner of the shop him self, but the larger shops are required to have more persons for serving the customers. The data relating to this have been grouped into three categories, e.g. shops of self employed persons shops employing one to three persons, and shops employing more than three persons.

Kind of shutters : The shops of the lower order market centres generally have poor quality of shutters. The quality of the shutters were observed during the feild investigation and the shops have been grouped into those with wooden, collapsible steel, and shops without closing devices.

Other Infrastructural Facilities : Other facilities such as presence or otherwise of electricity, telephone, arrangement for seating the customers and quality of show-cases were also observed during the field survey.

5.2 Buildings Housing Shops of Srinagar

The quality of the buildings housing the shops in the market centres of the various hierarchical orders in Srinagar are shown in Table No 5.1.

Building Materials : The different categories of shops as classified on the basis of the materials of which they are built are not uniformly distributed among the different market centres. Most of the shops are found in pucca buildings both in the higher and lower order market centres. The relatively higher percentage of pucca shops found in the lower order market centres is beacuse these have come up in newly settled areas, where people prefer to build pucca buildings in order to make their shops more attractive. The shops in semi-pucca, and kutcha, buildings and stalls and open to skey shops are found in larger numbers

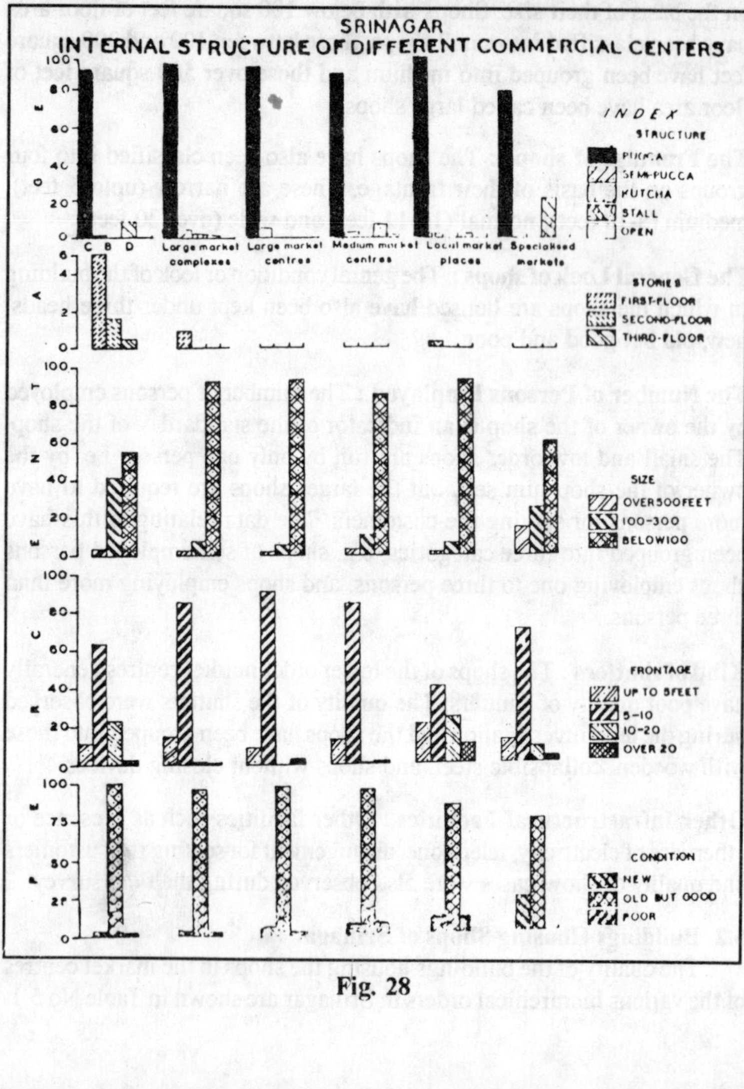

Fig. 28

in the lower order market centres. The higher order market centres also have large number of stalls which can be put up on the foot paths which exist in the higher order market centres (Fig. 28).

Table 5.1
Building materials & quality of shops of Commercial Centres of Srinagar (Figures are in Percentage)

	Quality	I	II	III	IV	V	VI	Total
Building Materials	Pucca	90.81	94.32	92.31	88.77	97.74	79.31	91.23
	Semi-pucca	0.40	4.38	5.96	2.49	1.13	-	2.56
	Kutcha	-	0.30	1.73	-	-	-	0.23
	Stall	8.79	1.00	-	7.50	1.13	20.69	5.67
	Open to Sky	-	-	-	1.24	-	-	0.31
	Total	100.00	100.00	100.00	100.00	100.00	100.00	100.00
Stories	First floor	4.60	0.90	-	-	0.29	-	1.70
	Second floor	1.60	-	-	-	-	-	0.49
	Third floor	0.45	-	-	-	-	-	0.14
Size	Large	3.74	0.76	1.82	3.34	0.29	14.36	2.89
	Medium	41.33	7.46	5.28	10.88	6.48	25.54	19.28
	Small	54.93	91.78	92.90	85.78	93.23	60.10	77.83
	Total	100	100	100	100	100	100	100
Frontage	Narrow	11.64	14.82	8.64	12.51	5.07	20.69	12.48
	Medium	63.33	80.27	90.40	85.10	92.38	40.88	77.23
	Normal	22.76	4.49	-	1.18	2.53	24.81	8.68
	Wide	2.27	0.42	0.96	1.21	-	13.62	1.61
	Total	100	100	100	100	100	100	100
Condition	New	4.08	6.00	5.48	3.77	12.11	23.11	5.56
	Old but good	95.20	91.42	93.94	90.08	85.36	76.89	91.80
	Poor	0.72	2.58	0.58	6.15	2.53	-	2.64
	Total	100	100	100	100	100	100	100

	Self	4.61	26.83	25.08	20.40	13.80	0.72	16.86
Employees	1-3	23.26	48.00	48.22	43.14	61.98	18.50	38.49
	>3	72.13	25.17	26.60	36.46	24.22	80.78	44.65
	Total	100	100	100	100	100	100	100
	Wooden	6.76	19.24	10.48	15.13	7.60	-	9.70
Shutter	Collap-sible	93.24	80.76	89.52	84.87	92.40	100	90.30
	Total	100	100	100	100	100	100	100
	Electri-city	100.00	93.39	100.00	99.80	99.71	100.00	98.0
Facilities	Telep-hone	64.72	16.95	10.57	13.47	9.30	73.00	32.09
	Seating	74.33	54.89	42.93	42.75	39.72	87.10	56.85
	Steel	84.46	63.95	66.67	65.14	57.47	85.89	71.43
Signb-oards	Neon	3.56	0.52	0.39	1.74	-	14.11	2.21
	Front	34.53	25.76	27.19	22.28	-	51.59	27.84
Show case	Inside	11.67	14.67	9.31	6.91	29.86	7.55	11.33

Source : Field work.

I = C. B. D
II = Large Market Complexes
III = Large Market Centres
IV = Medium Market Centres
V = Local Market Places
VI = Specialised Market Places

The pucca shops are thirty-five times as many as the semi–pucca shops in Srinagar. The percentages of buildings built of different materials found in the market centres of different hierarchical order in Srinagar are shown in Table No. 5.1. It will be seen in the table that out of a total of 12022 shops, 10968 (91.23%) are pucca and 307 (2.56%) are semi-pucca in the city as a whole. The kutcha and open to sky shops are almost equal in number. These are 28 (0.23%) and 38 (0.31%) in number respectively. The stalls are twice as many as the semi–pucca shops in the city as a whole. They number 681 (5.67%) and 307 (2.56%) respectively. The number of pucca shops is higher in the CBD followed by Large

Market Complexes and Medium Market Centres. The number of pucca shops is comparatively small in the large Market Centres than in the Medium Market Centres because most of the markets of the Medium order Market Centres have come up recently in the newly settled areas.

The semi-pucca shops occupy the dominating position in the Large Market Centres followed by Large Market Complexes where their percentages are 5.96 and 4.38 respectively. The kutcha shops are the largest in number in the Large Market Centres followed by Large Market Complexes.

Storeys of Buildings : Commercial activities carried on the multistoreyed buildings are associated with the C. B. D. of Srinagar. Here most of the shops are housed on the first, second and third-floors of the buildings. The C. B. D. is followed in this respect by the Large Market Complexes. The numbers of shops on the first second, and third floors are 172 (4.60%), 60 (1.60%), and 17 (0.45%) respectively in the C. B. D. In the Large Market Complexes 31 (0.90%) shops are found on the first floor while one of the Local Market Centres has one shop on the first floor. Shops are not found on the upper floors in the other market centres (Fig. 28). Here the upper floors of buildings are used for residential purposes.

Size of shops : The medium size shops are nearly seven times as many as the large shops in Srinagar. Of a total of 12022 shops of Srinagar 2318 (19.28%) are of medium size 347 (2.89%) are of large size. More than 75 per cent of the shops of Srinagar are of small size. Their number is 357 (77.83%). The small shops occupy the leading position in all the markets. The number of large shops is comparatively small except in the C. B. D. where there are 140 large shops (Fig. 28).

Frontage of Shops : The shops having medium frontage are the largest in number (77.23%) in the Srinagar city as a whole. They are followed by shops having narrow frontage (12.48%). The numbers of shops having normal and wide frontage are 1043 (8.68%) and 194 (1.61%) respectively. The narrow and medium frontage shops are most frequent in all the markets of the city. Normal and wide frontage shops are found mostly in the C. B. D. The proportions of the wide frontage shops are negligible in other markets. There are no wide front shop in Local Market Centres. Some 56 wide frontage shops are found in the specialised markets. Most of them are found in the Boulevard market.

General condition : More than 90 per cent of the shops of Srinagar are found in buidings which are old but in good condition. Their absolute number is 11036 (91. 80%) 668 (5.56%) shops are hous. l in the newly constructed buildings. Only about 2.64 per cent (318) of the shops are

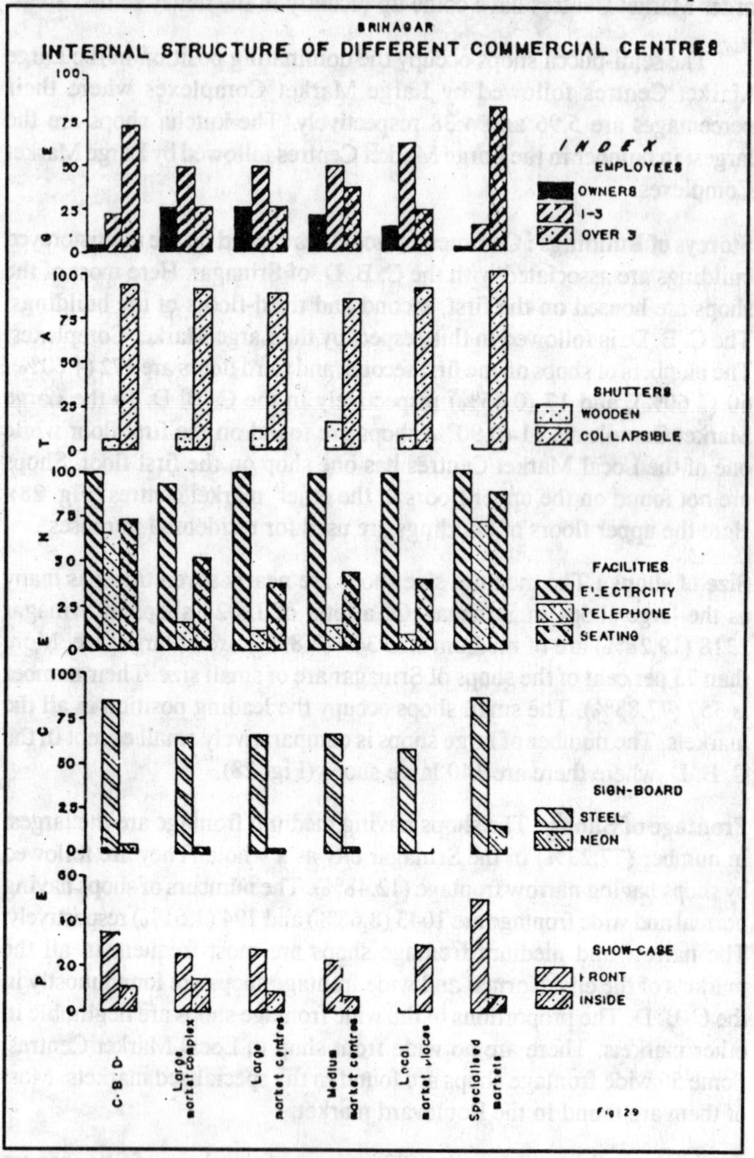

Fig. 29

found in buildings in poor conditon.

Persons employed : The shops run by more than three persons are the largest in number in Srinagar. They number (44.65%) in all. The shops having 1 to 3 employees come next. They number 4627 (38.49%). The shops run by their owners only number 2026 (16.86%). More than 70 per cent of the shops having more than three employees are found in the Central Business Districts. Of a total of 5369 shops with more than 3 employees 2701 occur in the C.B.D. This is because of the fact that the shops are of larger size in the C.B.D. and the number of the customers visiting them is also larger (Fig. 29)

Type of shutters : Of a total of 12022 shops of the city of Srinagar 1167 (9.70%) have wooden doors and 10855 (90.30) have collapsible shutters. The shops with wooden doors are most frequent in the Large Market Complemx (19.24%). Those with collapsible shutters are more frequent (93.24%) in the C. B. D.

Other facilities : As far as other facilities available in the business establishment of Srinagar are concerned, some 98.07 per cent of them have electricity but only 32.09 per cent of them have teleophone connection. Arrangements for seating the customers are also found in most of the shops (56.86%) of Srinagar. About 71.43 per cent of the shops of Srinagar have steel signboards and 2.21 per cent of them have neon signboards. These shops are found generally, in the C. B.D. In the rest of the city their proportion is negligible. As far as shops with show-cases with glass panes for displaying important items they sell are concerned 27.84 per cent of them have glass show-cases in their front and 11.33 per cent of them have show-cases inside order centres such as the C.B.D., Large Market Complexes, and Larger Market Center where their percentage is higher. The lower order centres have less of these facilities (Fig. 29).

5.3 Building materials and quality of shops by level of Hierarchy of Markets

5.3.1 The Central Business District

Lal Chowk complex is the Central Business District of Srinagar. The shops of this complex are generally, of good quality and have all the infrastructural facilities. The Central Business District consists of six markets. The building materials, the quality of the shops and the infrastructural facilities of each of them have been shown in Table No 5.2.

The pucca shops occupy the leading position in all these markets except Sherghari where the stalls are more frequent. More than 90 per cent of all the shops in each of these markets except Sherghari, are in pucca structures. In Sherghari the percentage is 40. The stalls occupy the first position in Sherghari while in Maharaj Bazar and Bud Shah Chowk they occupy the second and in Lal Chowk the third position. The

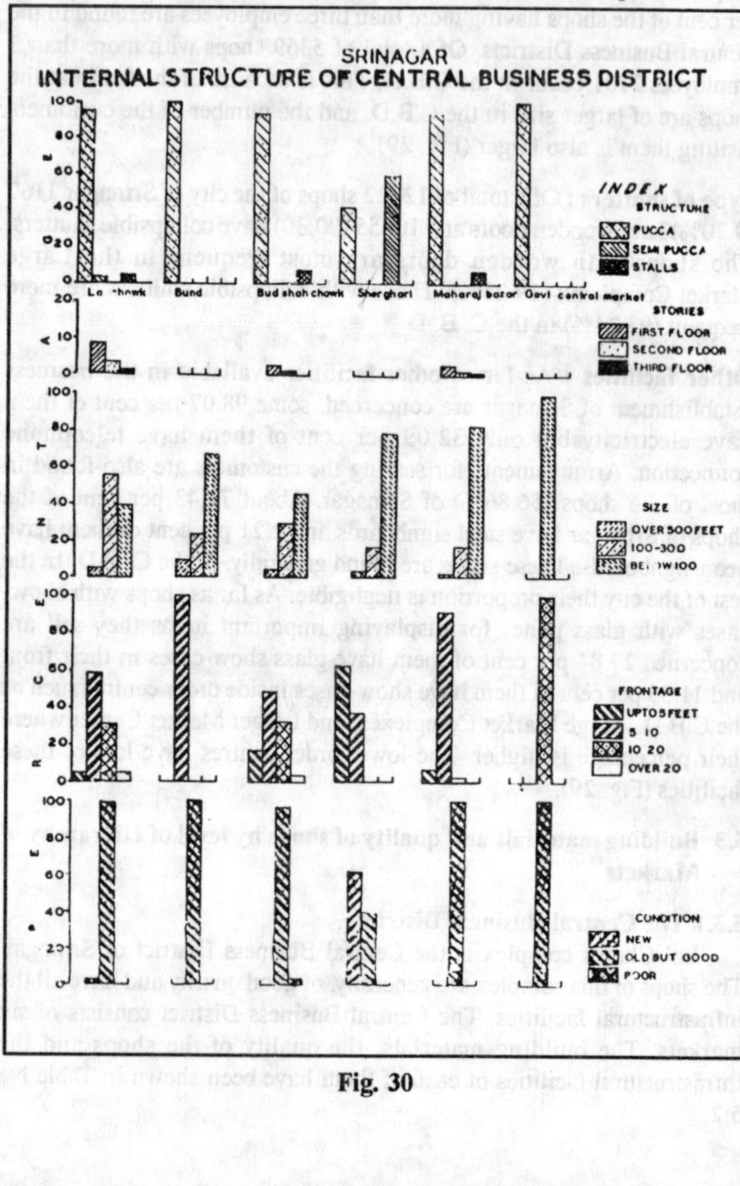

Fig. 30

Semi-Pucca shops are found only in the Lal Chowk, where their percentage is negligible. No shop in open field is found in this complex. All the shops have pucca structures in the Government Central Market and Bund Market (Fig. 30). The shops housed on the first second and third floors are predominant in Lal Chowk with 119 (8.42%) 47 (3.33%) and 16 (1.14%) in number respectively. The second Position in this respect is that of Maharaj Bazar where they are 30 (2.81%) 6 (0.56%) and 1(0.09%) in number on the first, second and third floors respectively. Bud Shah Chowk has 23 (2.86%) and 7 (0.87%) shops on the first and second floors respectively. Multi-storeyed building with commercial activities are not found in Bund, Sherghari and Govt. Central Markets of the C.B.D.

Table 5.2

Building Materials and Quality of Shops of Central Business District (Figures are in Percentage)

	Quality	I	II	III	IV	V	VI	Total
	Pucca	94.97	100.00	93.41	40.32	93.24	100.00	90.81
	Semip-pucca	1.06	-	-	-	-	-	0.40
Building Materials	Kutcha	-	-	-	-	-	-	-
	Stall	3.97	-	6.59	59.68	6.67	-	8.79
	Open to sky	-		-	-	-	-	-
	Total	100	100	100	100	100	100	100
	First floor	8.42	-	2.86	-	2.81	-	4.06
Stories	Second floor	3.33	-	0.87	-	0.56	-	1.60
	Third floor	1.14	-	-	-	0.09	-	.45
	Large	5.80	9.75	3.85	3.62	0.94	-	3.74
Size	Medium	55.87	23.18	49.07	16.94	16.14	100.00	41.34
	Small	38.33	67.07	47.08	79.44	82.92	-	54.92
	Total	100	100	100	100	100	100	100

	Narrow	5.44	-	16.65	62.10	6.67	-	11.64
Frontage	Medium	58.06	100.00	49.44	37.90	91.65	-	63.34
	Normal	31.48	-	32.18	-	1.68	100.00	27.75
	Wide	5.02	-	1.73	-	-	-	2.27
	Total	100	100	100	100	100	100	100
	New	0.08	-	-	61.30	-	-	-
Condition	Old but good	99.02	100.00	96.64	38.70	100.00	100.00	95.20
	Poor	-	-	3.36	-	-	-	0.72
	Total	100	100	100	100	100	100	100
	Self	2.40	-	2.49	3.62	10.31	-	4.61
Employees	1-3	8.42	9.76	27.32	21.78	44.10	-	23.27
	>3	89.18	90.24	70.19	74.60	45.59	100.00	72.12
	Total	100	100	100	100	100	100	100
	Wooden	0.36	-	1.37	59.68	8.34	-	6.76
Shutter	Collapsible	99.64	100.00	98.63	40.32	91.66	100.00	93.24
	Total	100	100	100	100	100	100	100
	Electricity	100.00	100.00	100.00	100.00	100.00	100.00	100.00
Facilities	Telephone	78.71	68.30	65.21	18.54	51.69	100.00	100.0
	Seating	83.80	86.58	73.54	20.16	70.19	100.00	74.34
	Steel	98.79	86.56	98.26	35.48	79.64	100.00	84.45
Signboard	Neon	7.43	1.21	1.73	-	1.21	-	3.56
	Front	46.61	43.90	9.31	14.51	33.48	100.00	34.52
Show case	Inside	15.13	3.65	23.35	-	2.62	-	11.57

Source : Field work

I = Lal Chowk
II = Bund
III = Bud Shah Chowk
VI = Sherghari
V = Maharaj Bazar
IV = Govt. Central Market

As far as the size of the shops is concerned, the medium size shops occupy the first position in three markets of the C.B.D. These are Lal Chowk, Bud Shah Chowk and Government Central Market. The small shops occupy the first position in Maharaj Bazar, Sherghari and Bund. The small shops occupy the second position in Bud Shah Chowk and Lal Chowk. No shop of this size is found in the Govt. Central Market. The very large shops rank third in all the retail nucleation of the Central Business District. Lal Chowk has the largest number of very large shops of all the markets of the Central Business District. It is followed by Budshah Chowk, Maharaj Bazar Sherghari and Bund Markets (Fig.30). The medium frontage shops have the dominant position in all the market centres of the Central Business Districts, except the Government Central Market and Sherghari. Above 50 per cent of the shops of all the other markets of the Central Business Districts have medium frontage. Normal and narrow frontage shops occupy the second and third positions respectively in all retail nucleations of the Central Business Districts. Two market centres namely Lal Chowk and Bud Shah Chowk have shops of wide frontage. The remaining markets have no shops of wide frontage. Maharaj Bazar is the only market which has the largest number of medium frontage shops and the Government Central Market has the largest number of the normal frontage shops and Sherghari has narrow frontage shops (Fig. 30).

A study of the general condition of the shops belonging to the markets of the C.B.D. of Srinagar reveals that the largest number of shops are found in the old but good condition building. Shop housed in old but good condition building occupy the dominant positions in all the six business centres of the C. B. D of Srinagar. More than 90 per cent of the shops of these centres, except Sherghari are housed in old but good condition buildings. The second position is occupied by the shops house in the newly constructed building in two market centres, namely Sherghari which, has a higher percentage. It is followed by Lal Chowk. No shop of this category are found in other centres. Poor quality shops are found only in one centre i.e., Bud Shah Chowk (Fig. 30).

The shops having more than three employees have the first position in more than 70 per cent of the markets of the Central Business District. These are Government Central Market, Bund, Lal Chowk, Sherghari and Bud Shah Chowk. The shops having 1 to 3 employees occupy the second position in all of the market centres of the Central Business Districts. The third position is occupied by the shops run by one employee or the owner of the shop in all the market centres of the C. B. D. (Fig. 31).

All the market centres of the C. B. D. of Srinagar except Sherghari occupy the first position in the number of shops having collapsible shutters. In Sherghari the newly constructed stalls with woodens door

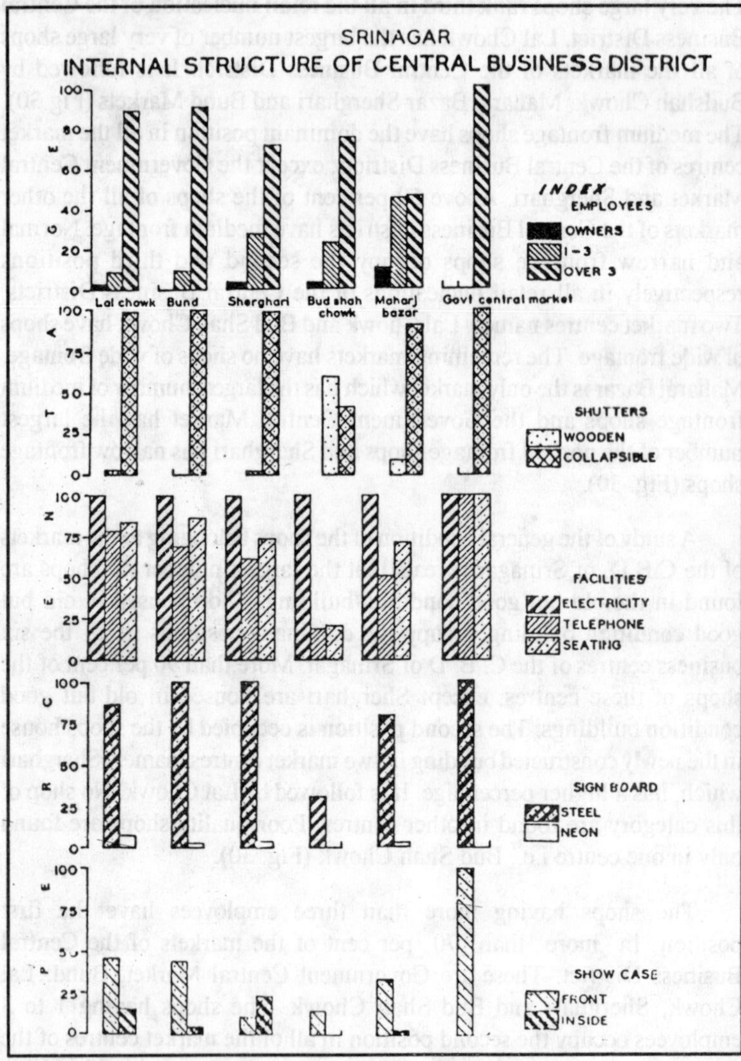

Fig. 31

predominate. These are Government Central Market, Lal Chowk, Bund, Bud Shah Chowk and Maharaj Bazar, Sherghari market occupies the first position in the number of shops with wooden doors. The remaining market centres in the number of shops with wooden doors. Bund and Government Central Markets have no shops with wooden doors. All the shops of these two markets have collapsible doors (Fig. 31).

Coming to the other facilities available in the different markets it is seen that all (100%) the shops of the C.B.D. have electricity. More than 65 percent of all the shops of the C.B.D. have telephone connections. All the (100%) shops of the Government Central Market have telephones (Fig. 31). About 75 per cent of the shops of the C.B.D. have arrangement for seating the customers. The Government Central Market with 100 per cent of its shops having arrangement for seating the customers tops the list. It is followed by Bund (86%), Lal Chowk (84%), Bud Shah Chowk (74%), Maharaj Bazar (71%) and Sherghari (20%). About 85 per cent of the shops in the C.B.D. have steel signboards. The Government Central Market ranks first with all (100%) of its shops having steel signboards. It is followed by Lal Chowk (99%) Budshah Chowk (98%), Bund (87%),Maharaj Bazar (80%) and Sherghari (35%). Only 4 per cent of the shops of the C.B.D. of Srinagar have neon signboards. Lal Chowk tops in the number of shops with neon singnboards. About 8 per cent of its shops have neon signboards. It is followed by Bud Shah Chowk (1.73%), Bund (1.21%) and Maharaj Bazar (1.21%).

The glass show-cases are there in about 35 per cent of the total number of the shops of the C.B.D. The Government Central Market tops in the number of shops with show-cases. All the 130 (100%) shops of this market have glass show-cases in their front, Lal Chowk ranks second with 47 per cent. It is followed by the Bund market with 44 per cent of its shops having glass show-cases in their front. Maharaj Bazar (34.0%), Sherghari (15.00%) and Bud Shah Chowk (10.0%) have also shops with glass show-cases in their front,. About 12 per cent of the shops of the C.B.D. have glass show-cases inside them, Bud Shah Chowk tops the list with 24 per cent of its shops. It is followed by Lal Chowk (15.13%), Bund (3.65%) and Maharaj Bazar (2.62%) (Fig. 31).

Table 5.1 highlights the dominance of pucca shops in the Central Business District. They are the largest in proposition (90.81%). Stalls and semi-pucca shops account for 8.79 and 0.40 percent of the total respectively. Kutcha and open to sky shops are not found in the C.B.D.

(Fig. 28).

Many shops of the C.B.D. are housed in multi-storeyed buldings. The percent share of the first floors is 4.60 per cent, the second floors, 1.60 per cent and the third floors, 0.45 per cent. Here the percentages of the medium and large shops are 41.33 and 3.74 per cent respectively. However, in the specialised market the percentage of large shops is 14.36 per cent. The percentage of the small shops is low (54.93%).

The majority (68.33%) of the shops of the C.B.D. have medium frontage. The normal and narrow frontage shops account for 22.76 and 11.64 per cent of the total number of the shops of the C.B.D. respectively. About 2.27 per cent of the shops of the C.B.D. have wide frontage. About 95.20 per cent of them are housed in old but good condition buildings, while only about 4.08 and 0.72 per cent of the shops are found in newly constructed and poor buildings respectively.

The largest number of shops (72.13%) of the C.B.D. are run more than by three persons. This proportion is the highest in the whole of Srinagar (except specialised market). About 23.36 per cent of the shops are run by 1 to 3 persons and 4.61 per cent of them are run by one employee or the owner himself. This proportion is the lowest after the specialised market.

The Central Business District has the largest number of shops with collapsible shutters (93.24%). Shop with wooden doors account for about 6.76 percent of the total. No shop of this complex is without doors.

All the shops of the C.B.D. are electrified. The shops with telephones account for 64.72 per cent of their total number. About 74.33 per cent of the shops of the C.B.D. have arrangement for seating the customers.

About 84.46 percent of the shops have steel signboard and 3.56 percent of them have neon signboards. About 34.54 and 11.57 percent of the shops of this centre respectively have glass show-cases in front and inside the shops. These proportions are the highest in the whole of the city (Fig. 29).

5.3.2 Large Market Complexes

There are two Large Market Complexes in Srinagar namely the Nawhatta-Zaina Kadal and Haba kadal-Father kadal complexes. The quality of the buildings in which the shops in the constituent markets of these complexes are housed is given in table No. 5.3 and 5.4.

Table 5.3
Building materials & quality of shops of Nawhatta-Zaina Kadal Complex (Figures are in Percentage)

	Quality	I	II	III	IV	V	Total
	Pucca	95.69	85.47	83.76	100.00	99.53	92.23
Building	Semi-Pucca	2.00	11.62	16.24	-	-	6.44
	Kutcha	0.15	0.59	-	-	-	0.14
	Stall	2.16	2.32	-	-	0.47	1.19
	Open to sky	-	-	-	-	-	-
	Total	100	100	100	100	100	100
	First-floor	2.61	0.88	-	-	-	.99
stories	Second floor	-	-	-	-	-	-
	Third floor	-	-	-	-	-	-
	Large	0.30	-	0.84	-	0.47	0.40
Size	Medium	7.86	2.32	9.91	5.83	12.93	8.37
	Small	91.84	97.68	89.25	94.17	86.60	91.23
	Total	100	100	100	100	100	100
	Narrow	14.02	16.87	10.55	97.5	9.93	11.99
Frontage	Medium	85.06	79.36	88.60	97.5	86.37	85.94
	Normal	0.92	3.77	0.85	2.5	3.70	2.07
	Wide	-	-	-	-	-	-
	Total	100	100	100	100	100	100
	New	17.10	17.44	5.28	-	-	9.70
Condition	Old but good	78.73	75.30	94.51	100.00	98.94	87.42
	Poor	4.17	7.26	0.21	-	1.16	2.88
	Total	100	100	100	100	100	100
	Self	21.41	54.37	24.27	14.17	27.95	28.66
Employees	1-3	49.93	27.61	66.24	58.33	38.34	47.98

		I	II	III	IV	V	Total
	>3	28.66	18.02	9.49	27.5	33.71	23.36
	Total	100	100	100	100	100	100
Shutter	Wooden	12.01	17.16	2.96	-	14.09	10.50
	Collps-ible	87.99	82.84	97.04	100.00	85.91	89.50
	Total	100	100	100	100	100	100
Facilities	Electri-city	100.00	100.00	100.00	100.00	100.00	100.00
	Telep-hone	11.71	5.81	30.38	11.67	16.17	16.03
	Seating	51.78	54.07	64.98	62.5	45.26	54.50
Signboard	Steel	64.71	36.04	61.81	72.5	69.74	60.70
	Neon	0.30	0.29	1.48	-	0.23	0.54
Show Case	Front	5.85	0.58	34.81	55.83	46.19	23.36
	Inside	30.81	35.75	8.01	-	3.92	18.71

Source : Field work

I = Nowhatta
II = Bori-Kadal
III = Maharaj Ganj
IV = Rajouri Kadal
V = Zaina-Kadal

The Nawhatta-Zaina Kadal Complexes : The majority of the shops (92.23%) of Nawhatta-Zaina Kadal complex are housed in pucca single storeyed buildings. In Rajouri Kadal and Zaina kadal all the shops are housed in pucca buildings while in the remaining three centres the pucca shops account for 95.69 (Nawhatta), 85.47 (Bori kadal) and 83.76 (Maharaj Ganj) percent respectively. The semi-pucca shops are in the largest number in Maharaj Ganj (16.24%), followed by Bohri Kadal (11.62%) and Nowhatta (2%). No shop of this category is found in Rajouri Kadal and Zaina Kadal Kutcha shops are found in Bohri Kadal (0.59%) and Nowhatta (0.15%). The remaining three centres, have no kutcha shops. The stalls occupy the first position in Bohri Kadal (3.32%), the second position in Nowhatta (2.16%) and the third position in Zaina Kadal (0.47%). No shop is found in open fields in this complex. The shops in the Double storeyed buildings are found only in Nowhatta and Bohri Kadal but the percentage shares are very small (Fig 32). The shops in multi storeyed buildings are not found in the Nowhatta-Zaina Kadal complex except in the Nowhatta and Bohri Kadal markets where 2.61 and 0.88 percent respectively of the shops are found on the first floor.

More than 91 per cent of the shops of this market complex are of

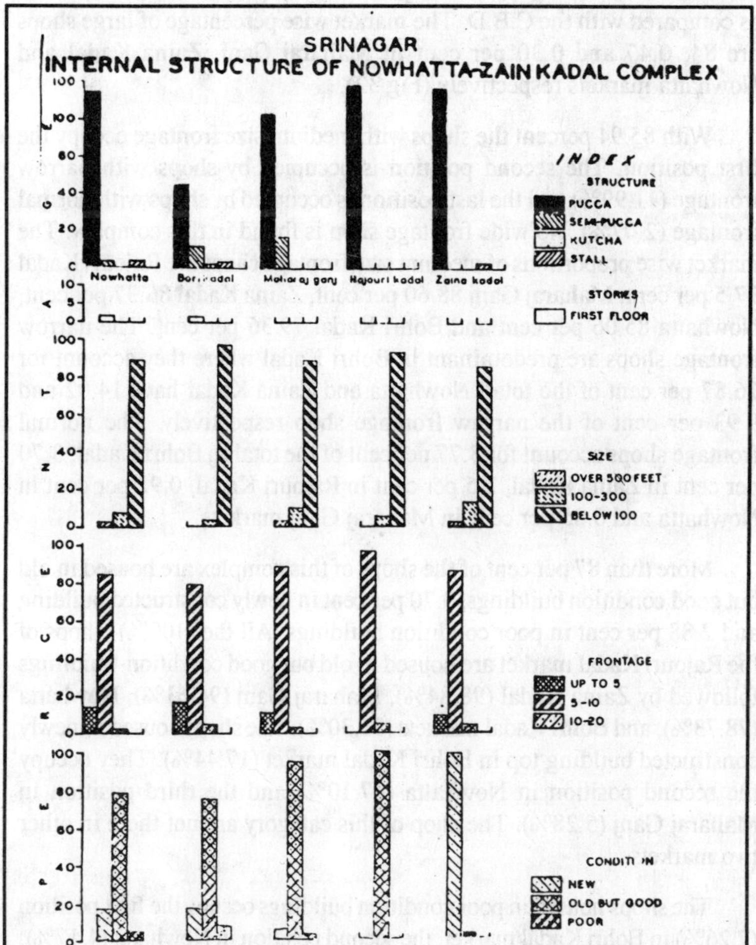

Fig. 32

small size. Almost all markets of this complex have large number of small shops. Bohri Kadal occupies the top position (97.68%). It is followed by Rajouri Kadal (94.17%), Nowhatta (91.84%), Maharaj Ganj (89.25%) and Zaina Kadal (86.60%).

The medium size shops occupy the second position (8.37%) in this complex. The percentages of medium size shops are 12.93, 9.91, 7.86, 5..83 and 2.32 per cent in Zaina Kadal, Maharaj Ganj, Nowhatta, Rajouri Kadal and Bohri Kadal respectively. The large shops constitute 0.40 percent of the total number of shops of this complex which is very small as compared with the C.B.D. The market wise percentage of large shops are 84, 0.47 and 0.30 per cent in Maharaj Ganj, Zaina Kadal and Nowhatta markets respectively (Fig.32).

With 85.94 percent the shops with medium size frontage occupy the first position. The second position is occupied by shops with narrow frontage (11.99%) and the last position is occupied by shops with normal frontage (2.07%). No wide frontage shop is found in this complex. The market wise proportions of medium size frontage shops are Rajouri Kadal 97.5 per cent, Maharaj Ganj 88.60 per cent, Zaina Kadal 86.37 per cent, Nowhatta 85.06 per cent and Bohri Kadal 79.36 per cent. The narrow frontage shops are predominant in Bohri Kadal where they account for 16.87 per cent of the total. Nowhatta and Zaina Kadal have 14.02 and 9.93 per cent of the narrow frontage shop respectively. The normal frontage shops account for 3.77 per cent of the total in Bohri Kadal, 3.70 per cent in Zaina Kadal, 2.5 per cent in Rajouri Kadal, 0.92 per cent in Nowhatta and 0.85 per cent in Maharaj Ganj markets.

More than 87 per cent of the shops of this complex are housed in old but good condition buildings, 9.70 per cent in newly constructed building and 2.88 per cent in poor condition buildings. All the (100%) shops of the Rajouri Kadal market are housed in old but good condition buidlings followed by Zaina Kadal (98.84%), Maharaj Ganj (94.51%), Nowhatta (78.73%), and Bohri Kadal markets (75.30%). The shops housed in newly constructed building top in Bohri Kadal market (17.44%). They occupy the second position in Nowhatta (17.10%) and the third position in Maharaj Ganj (5.28%). The shop of this category are not there in other two markets.

The shops housed in poor condition buildings occupy the first position (7.26%) in Bohri Kadal market, the second position in Nowhatta (4.17%). Zaina Kadal (1.16%) and Maharaj Ganj (0.21%) market follow suit. No shop of this category is found in the Rajouri Kadal market (Fig. 32).

With about 48 per cent the shops run by 1 to 3 employees top the list in this complex, shops run by one employee or by the owner himself rank second (28.66%) and those run by more than three persons rank third (23.36%). The shops run by one to three persons are predominant in Maharaj Ganj market with 66.24 per cent. It is followed by Rajouri Kadal (58.33%), Nowhatta (49.93%), Zaina Kadal (38.34%) and Bohri Kadal (27.61%) market. The shops run by the owner of the shop rank

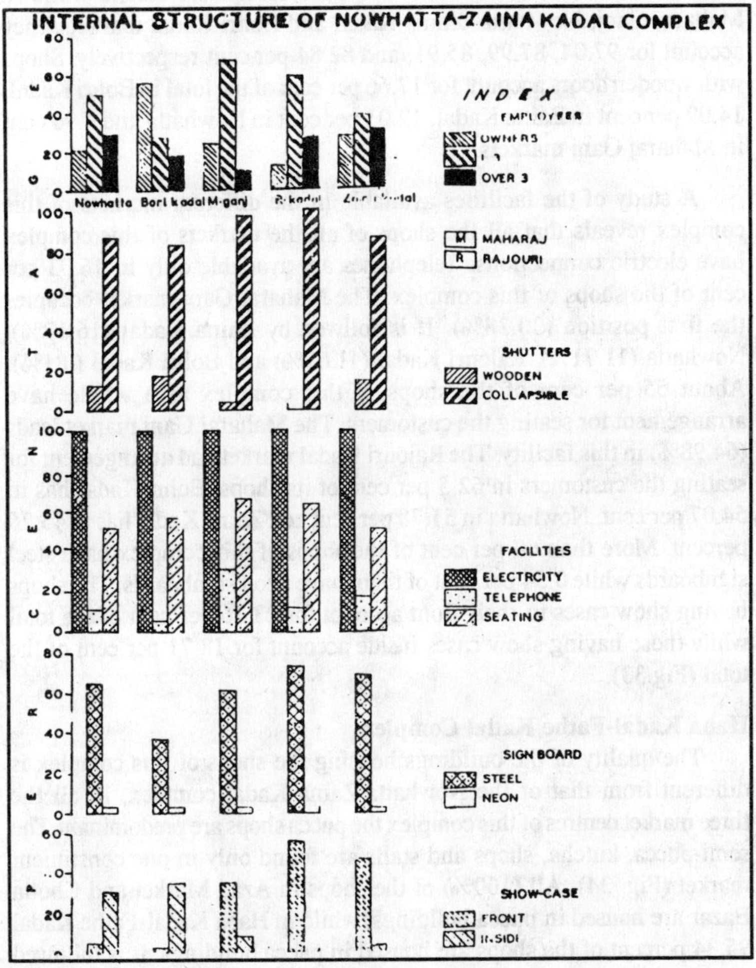

Fig. 33

first in Bohri Kadal with 54.37 per cent. It is followed by 27.95 per cent in Zaina Kadal, 24.27 per cent in Maharaj Ganj, 21.41 percent in Nowhatta and 14.17 per cent in Rajouri Kadal markets. The number of shops run by over three persons is the largest in Zaina Kadal (33.71%). It is follwed by Nowhatta (28.66%), Rajouri Kadal (27.5%), Bohri Kadal (18.02%) and Maharaj Ganj markets (9.49%) (Fig.33).

The majority of the shops of this complex (89.50%) have collapsible shutters while 10.50 per cent of them have wooden doors. In Rajouri Kadal market all the (100%) shops have collapsible sutters while in Maharaj Ganj, Nowhatta. Zaina Kadal and Bohri Kadal markets, they account for 97.04, 87.99, 85.91, and 82.84 per cent respectively. Shops with wooden doors account for 17.66 per cent of the total in Bohri Kadal, 14.09 per cent in Zaina Kadal, 12.01 per cent in Nowhatta and 2.96 cent in Maharaj Ganj markets.

A study of the facilities available in the different markets of this complex reveals that all the shops of all the markets of this complex have electric connections. Telephones are available only in 16.03 per cent of the shops of this complex. The Maharaj Ganj market occupies the first position (30.38%). It is follwed by Zaina Kadal (16.17%), Nowhatta (11.71%), Rajouri Kadal (11.67%) and Bohri Kadal (.81%). About 55 per cent of the shops of this complex as a whole have arrangement for seating the customers. The Maharaj Ganj market leads (64.98%) in this facility. The Rajouri Kadal market had arrangement for seating the customers in 62.5 per cent of its shops, Bohri Kadal has in 54.07 per cent, Nowhatta in 51.78 per cent and Zaina Kadal has in 45.26 percent. More than 60 per cent of the shops of this complex have steel signboards while 0.54 per cent of them have neon signboards. The shops having show cases in their front account for 23.36 per cent of the total while those having show cases inside account for 18.71 per cent of the total (Fig.33).

Haba Kadal-Fathe Kadal Complex

The quality of the buildings housing the shops of this complex is different from that of the Nowhatta-Zaina Kadal complex. In all the three market centres of this complex the pucca shops are predominant. The semi-pucca, kutcha, shops and stalls are found only in one constituent market (Fig. 34). All (100%) of the shops in Azad Market and Chotta Bazar are housed in pucca buildings, while in Haba Kadal-Fathe Kadal 95.34 percent of the shops are housed in pucca buildings. It is followed by semi-pucca shops (2.51%), stalls (1.26%) and Kutcha shops (0.89%).

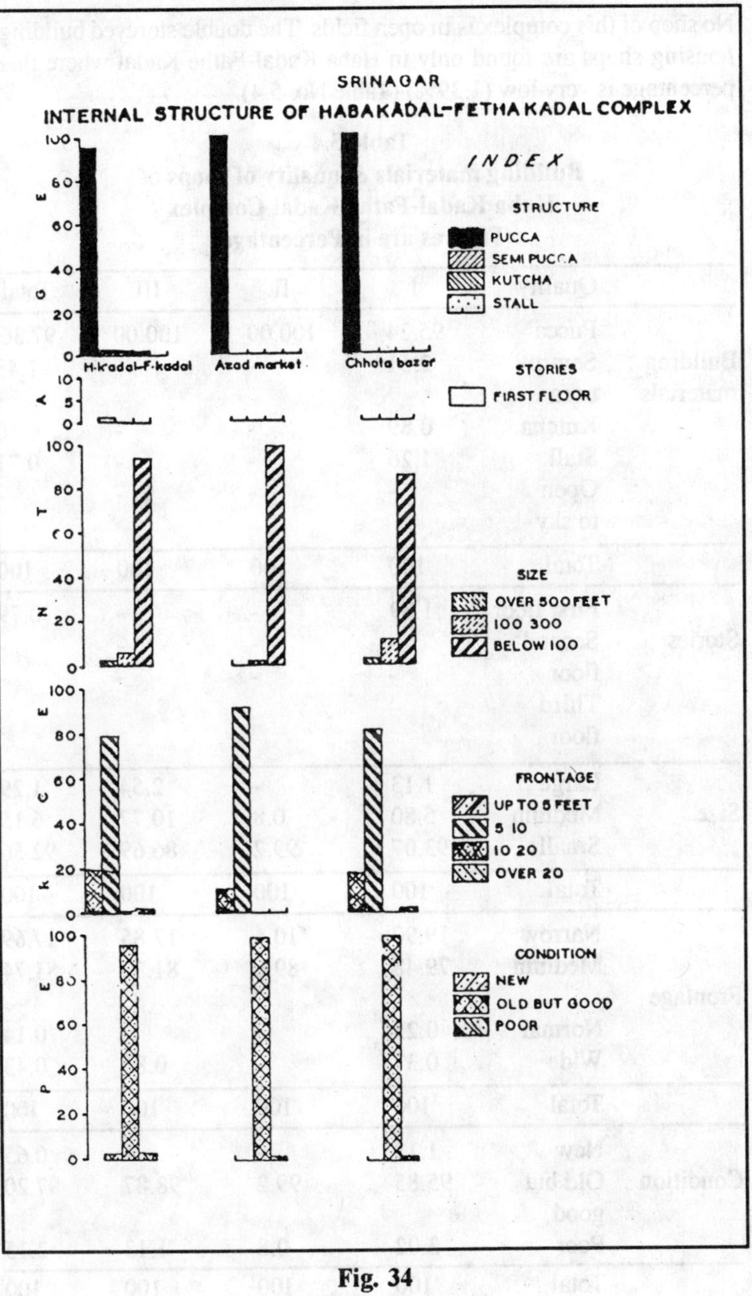
SRINAGAR
INTERNAL STRUCTURE OF HABAKADAL-FETHA KADAL COMPLEX
INDEX
STRUCTURE
PUCCA
SEMI PUCCA
KUTCHA
STALL
H-kadal-F-kadal
Azad market
Chhota bazar
STORIES
FIRST FLOOR
SIZE
OVER 500 FEET
100 300
BELOW 100
FRONTAGE
UP TO 5 FEET
5 10
10 20
OVER 20
CONDITION
NEW
OLD BUT GOOD
POOR
PERCENTAGE

Fig. 34

No shop of this complex is in open fields. The double storeyed buildings housing shops are found only in Haba Kadal-Fathe Kadal where their percentage is very low (1.39%) (Table No. 5.4).

Table 5.4
Building materials & quality of shops of Haba Kadal-Fathe Kadal Complex (Figures are in Percentage)

	Quality	I	II	III	Total
Building materials	Pucca	95.34	100.00	100.00	97.36
	Semip-ucca	2.51	-	-	1.43
	Kutcha	0.89	-	-	0.50
	Stall	1.26	-	-	0.71
	Open to sky	-	-	-	-
	Total	100	100	100	100
Stories	First floor	1.39	-	-	0.79
	Second floor	-	-	-	-
	Third floor	-	-	-	-
Size	Large	1.13	-	2.54	1.29
	Medium	5.80	0.8	10.77	6.15
	Small	93.07	99.2	86.69	92.56
	Total	100	100	100	100
Frontage	Narrow	19.90	10.4	17.85	17.69
	Medium	79.48	89.6	81.30	81.74
	Normal	0.25	-	-	0.14
	Wide	0.37	-	0.85	0.43
	Total	100	100	100	100
Condition	New	1.13	-	-	0.65
	Old but good	95.85	99.2	98.87	97.20
	Poor	3.02	0.8	1.13	2.15
	Total	100	100	100	100

Employees	Self	25.31	20.4	26.37	24.200
	1-3	47.87	54.4	43.90	48.03
	>3	26.82	25.2	31.73	27.77
	Total	100	100	100	100
Shutter	Wooden	3.02	4.00	19.83	7.44
	Collap-sible	96.98	96.00	80.17	92.56
	Total	100	100	100	100
Facilities	Electricity	100.00	100.00	100.00	100.00
	Telephone	3.02	4.00	19.83	7.44
	Seating	96.98	96.00	80.17	92.55
Signboard	Steel	65.37	82.4	66.29	68.64
	Neon	0.50	-	0.84	0.50
Show case	Front	28.84	36.4	24.92	29.20
	Inside	6.54	10.4	7.93	7.59

Source : Field work

I = Haba Kadal
II = Azad Market
II = Chhota Bazar

The majority of the shops of this complex are of small size and occupy the first position in all the constituent markets. In the Azad Market 99.2 per cent and in Haba Kadal-Fathe Kadal 93.07 per cent of the shops are of small size and occupy the first and second positions respectively. In Chhota Bazar 86.69 per cent of the shops are of small size. The medium size shops rank first in Chotta Bazar (10.77%) followed by Haba Kadal-Fathe Kadal (5.80%), and Azad Market (0.8%). Large shops are found only in two markets of these complex namely. Chotta Bazar (2.54%) and Haba Kadal-Fathe Kadal (1.13%) (Fig. 34).

With 81.74 percent of the total number the medium frontage shops have the dominating position in this complex. Narrow frontage shops account for 1 /.69 per cent of the total, while frontage shops account for 0.43 percent and the normal frontage shops for 0.14 per cent of the total.

The medium frontage shops occupy the first position in the Azad Market (89.6%) Chhotta Bazar occupies the second position (81.30%) and Haba Kadal-Fateh Kadal occupies the third position (79.48%). The narrow frontage shops pre-dominate in Haba Kadal-Fateh Kadal (19.90%). Chhotta Bazar (17.85%) and the Azad Market (10.4%) occupy the second and third positions respectively. The normal size shops are found only in Haba Kadal-Father Kadal (0.25%). While the wide frontage shops are seen also in Haba Kadal (0.37%) and Chhotta Bazar (0.85%). No wide frontage shop is found in the Azad Market (Fig. 34.).

More than 97 percent of the shops of Haba Kadal-Fathe Kadal complex are housed mostly in old but good condition buildings. Some 2.15 and 9.65 percent of the shops of this complex are housed in poor and newly constructed buildings repsectively. With 99.2 per cent of its shops housed in old but good condition buildings, the Azad Market occupies the first position, while Chhotta Bazar and Haba Kadal-Fatha Kadal occupy the second and third positions respectively with 98.87 and 95.85 per cent. The shops housed in old but good conditions buildings account for 3.02 per cent of the total in Haba Kadal-Fathe Kadal, 1.13 per cent in Chhotta Bazar and 0.8 per cent in Azad Market. The shops housed in new building are found in only Haba Kadal-Fathe kadal and account for 1.13 per cent of the total. No shops of this category is seen in the two remaining market centres of this complex. (Fig. 34).

The shops run by 1 to 3 employees occupy the first position (48.03%) in this complex. The shops run by more than three persons which account for 27.77 percent of the total occupy the second position and those run by the owner of the shop or by one employee occupy the third position. (Fig. 35.). On the whole the shope having 1 to 3 employees pre-dominate in this complex followed by shops run more than 3 employees.

It is seen that 92.56 percent of the shops have collapsible shutters while only 7.44 percent of them have wooden doors. Haba Kadal-Fathe kadal occupies the first position where shops with collapsible shutters account for 96.98 percent of the total followed by the Azad Market (96.0%) and Chotta Bazar (80.17%). Chotta Bazar (19.83%), Azad Market (4.0%) and Haba Kadal-Fathe Kadal (3.02%) have shops with wooden doors (Fig. 35).

All the market centres of the Haba Kadal-Fathe Kadal complex are electrifies. More them 7 percent of them have telephone connections. About 92.55% per cent of the shops have arrangement for seating the

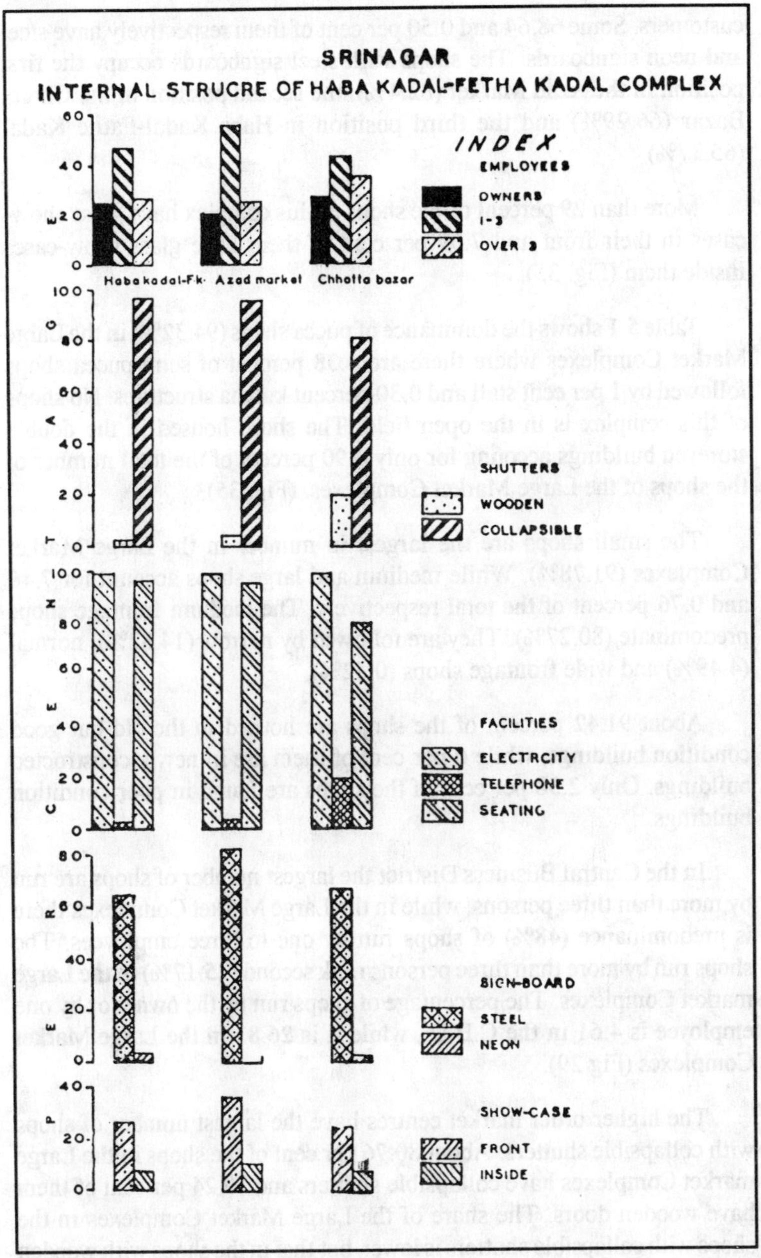
SRINAGAR
INTERNAL STRUCRE OF HABA KADAL-FETHA KADAL COMPLEX
INDEX
EMPLOYEES
OWNERS
1-3
OVER 3
Habakadal-Fk.
Azad market
Chhatta bazar
SHUTTERS
WOODEN
COLLAPSIBLE
FACILITIES
ELECTRCITY
TELEPHONE
SEATING
SIGN-BOARD
STEEL
NEON
SHOW-CASE
FRONT
INSIDE
PERCENTAGE

Fig. 35

customers. Some 68.64 and 0.50 per cent of them respectively have steel and neon signboards. The shops with steel signboards occupy the first position in the Azad Market (82.4%), the second position in the Chotta Bazar (66.29%) and the third position in Haba Kadal-Fathe Kadal (65.37%).

More than 29 percent of the shops of this complex have glass show-cases in their front and 7.59 per cent of them have glass show-cases inside them (Fig. 35).

Table 5.1 shows the dominance of pucca shops (94.32%) in the Large Market Complexes where there are 4.38 percent of semi-pucca shops followed by 1 per cent stall and 0.30 percent kutcha structures. No shops of this complex is in the open field. The shops housed in the double storeyed buildings accoung for only 0.90 percent of the total number of the shops of the Large Market Complexes. (Fig. 35).

The small shops are the largest in number in the Large Market Complexes (91.78%), While medium and large shops account for 7.46 and 0.76 percent of the total respectively. The medium frontage shops predominate (80.27%). They are followed by narrow (14.82%), normal (4.49%) and wide frontage shops (0.42%).

About 91.42 percent of the shops are housed in the old but good condition buildings, while 6 per cent of them are in newly constructed buildings. Only 2.58 per cent of the shops are found in poor condition buildings.

In the Central Business District the largest number of shops are run by more than three persons, while in the Large Market Complexes there is predominance (48%) of shops run by one to three employees. The shops run by more than three persons rank second (25.17%) in the Large market Complexes. The percentage of shops run by the owner or by one employee is 4.61 in the C.B.D., while it is 26.83 in the Large Market Complexes (Fig 29).

The higher order market centres have the largest number of shops with collapsible shutters. About 80.76 per cent of the shops in the Large market Complexes have collapsible shutters and 19.24 per cent of them have wooden doors. The share of the Large Market Complexes in the shops with collapsible shutters is lower, but that in the shops with wooden doors is comparatively higher than that of the C.B.D. (Fig. 29).

The number of shops with electricity is relatively small (93.39%) in the Large Market Complexes, while all the shops (100%) are electrified in the C.B.D. The shops having telephones are comparatively few in the Large Market Complexes (16.95%). The number of shops with arrangement for seating the customers is small in the Large Market Complexes (54.89%) as compared with the CBD. The proportion of (65.95%) and neon signboards, (0.62%), Show cases, infront (25.76%) and inside (14.67%) in the Large Market Complex are much smaller then in C.B.D.

5.3.3 Large Market Centres

There are three Large Market Centres. Data relating to them are given in table 5.5. An analysis of table 5.5 reveals that the majority of the shops (92.31%) of the Large Market Centres are housed in pucca buildings. Karan Nagar occupies the first position (98.16%). It is followed by Jawahar Nagar (95.33%) and Rainawari (82.98%). The semi-pucca shops are found in Rainawari and Karan Nagar markets which account for 17.02 and 1.84 percent respectively. No shop is in kutcha building. There are stalls in a Jawahar Nagar 4.67 percent but not in the remaining two markets (Fig. 36). Similarly no shop is found in double storeyed building.

Table 5.5
Building materials & quality of shops of Large Market Centres
(Figures are in Percentage)

	Quality	I	II	III	Total
Building materials	Pucca	95.33	82.98	98.16	92.31
	Semipucca	-	17.02	1.84	5.96
	Kutcha	-	-	-	-
	Stall	4.67	-	-	10.73
	Open to sky	-	-	-	-
	Total	100	100	100	100
Stories	First floor	-	-		-
	Second floor	-	-	-	-
	Third floor	-	-	-	-
Size	Large	1.55	2.43	1.53	1.82
	Medium	2.60	2.73	11.04	5.29
	Small	95.85	94.84	87.43	92.89

		I	II	III	Total
	Total	100	100	100	100
Frontage	Narrow	5.19	12.16	9.20	8.669
	Medium	94.81	85.71	89.88	90.39
	Normal	-	-	-	-
	Wide	-	2.13	0.92	0.97
	Total	100	100	100	100
Condition	New	4.40	-	12.27	5.48
	Old but good	95.34	100.00	86.20	93.94
	Poor	0.26	-	1.53	0.58
	Total	100	100	100	100
Employees	Self	11.66	23.70	42.33	25.08
	1-3	58.54	52.89	31.60	48.32
	>3	29.80	23.41	26.07	26.60
	Total	100	100	100	100
Shutter	Wooden	1.03	21.89	10.12	10.48
	Collapsible	98.97	78.11	89.88	89.52
	Total	100	100	100	100
Facilities	Electricity	100.00	100.00	100.00	100.00
	Telephone	8.80	6.69	16.57	10.57
	Seating	47.15	33.13	47.85	42.93
Signboard	Steel	71.77	57.44	69.93	66.67
	Neon	-	0.30	0.92	0.38
Show	Front	39.11	0.91	39.58	27.19
	Inside	-	27.97	1.53	9.31

Source : Field work

I = Jawahar Nagar

II = Rainawari

III = Karan Nagar

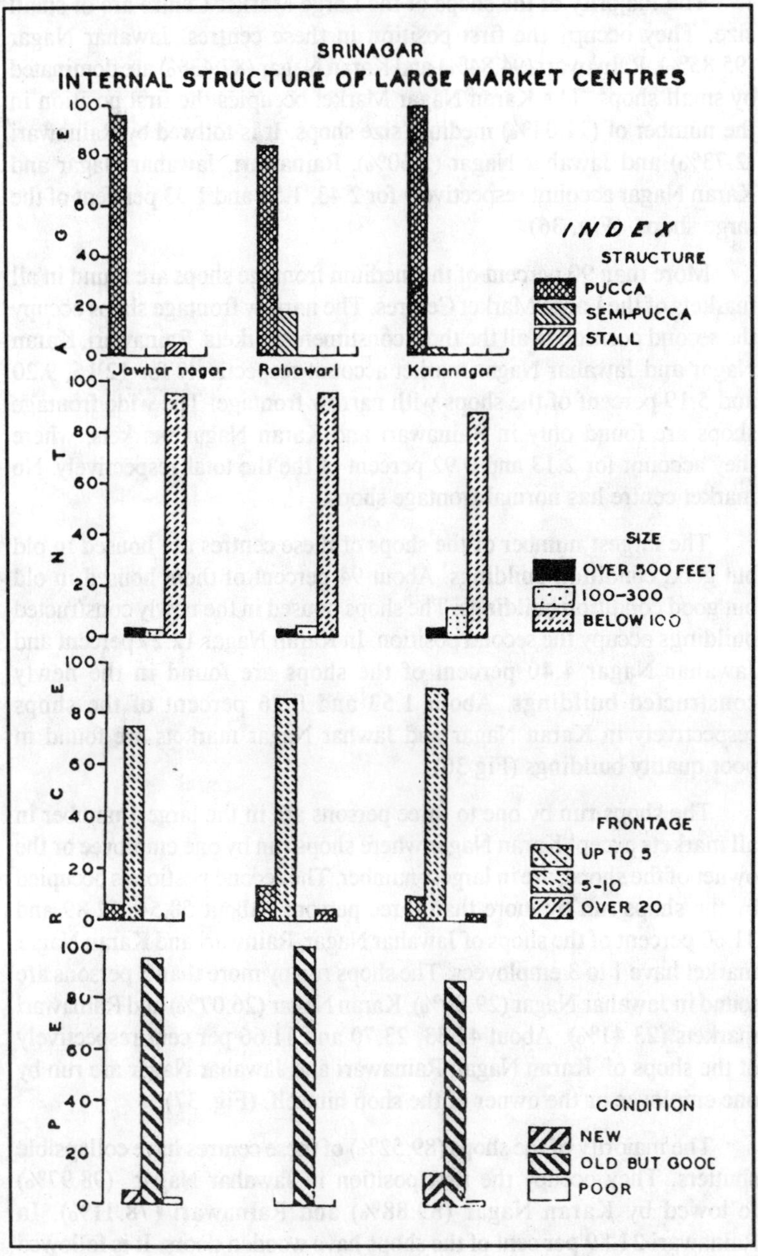
SRINAGAR
INTERNAL STRUCTURE OF LARGE MARKET CENTRES
PERCENTAGE
INDEX
STRUCTURE
PUCCA
SEMI-PUCCA
STALL
Jawhar nagar
Rainawari
Karanagar
SIZE
OVER 500 FEET
100-300
BELOW 100
FRONTAGE
UP TO 5
5-10
OVER 20
CONDITION
NEW
OLD BUT GOOD
POOR

Fig. 36

The majority of the shops of the Large Market Centre are of small size. They occupy the first position in these centres. Jawahar Nagar (95.85%), Rainawari (94.84%) and Karan Nagar (87.43%) are dominated by small shops. The Karan Nagar Market occupies the first position in the number of (11.04%) medium size shops. It is follwed by Rainawari (2.73%) and Jawahar Nagar (2.60%). Rainawari, Jawahar Nagar and Karan Nagar account respectively for 2.43, 1.55 and 1.53 per cent of the large shops. (Fig. 36).

More than 90 percent of the medium frontage shops are found in all markets of the Large Market Centres. The narrow frontage shops occupy the second position in all the three constituent markets. Rainawari, Karan Nagar and Jawahar Nagar market account respectively for 12.16, 9.20 and 5.19 percent of the shops with narrow frontage. The wide frontage shops are found only in Rainawari and Karan Nagar markets, where they account for 2.13 and 0.92 percent of the the total respectively. No market centre has normal frontage shops.

The largest number of the shops of these centres are housed in old but good condition buildings. About 94 percent of them housed in old but good condition buildings. The shops housed in the newly constructed buildings occupy the second position. In Karan Nagar 12.27 percent and Jawahar Nagar 4.40 percent of the shops are found in the newly constructed buildings. About 1.53 and 0.26 percent of the shops respectively in Karan Nagar and Jawhar Nagar markets are found in poor quality buildings (Fig 36).

The shops run by one to three persons are in the largest number in all markets except Karan Nagar where shops run by one employee or the owner of the shops, are in largest number. The second postion is occupied by the shops run by more than three persons. About 58.54, 52.89 and 31.60 percent of the shops of Jawahar Nagar, Rainwari and Karan Nagar market have 1 to 3 employees. The shops run by more than 3 persons are found in Jawahar Nagar (29.80%), Karan Nagar (26.07%) and Rainawari markets (23.41%). About 42.33, 23.70 and 11.66 per cent respectively of the shops of Karan Nagar, Rainawari and Jawahar Nagar are run by one employee or the owner of the shop himself. (Fig. 37).

The majority of the shops (89.52%) of these centres have collapsible shutters. They occupy the first position in Jawahar Nagar (98.97%) followed by Karan Nagar (89.88%) and Rainawari (78.11%). In Rainawari 21.89 per cent of the shops have wooden doors. It is followed by Karan Nagar (10.12%) and Jawahar Nagar (1.103%) (Fig. 37).

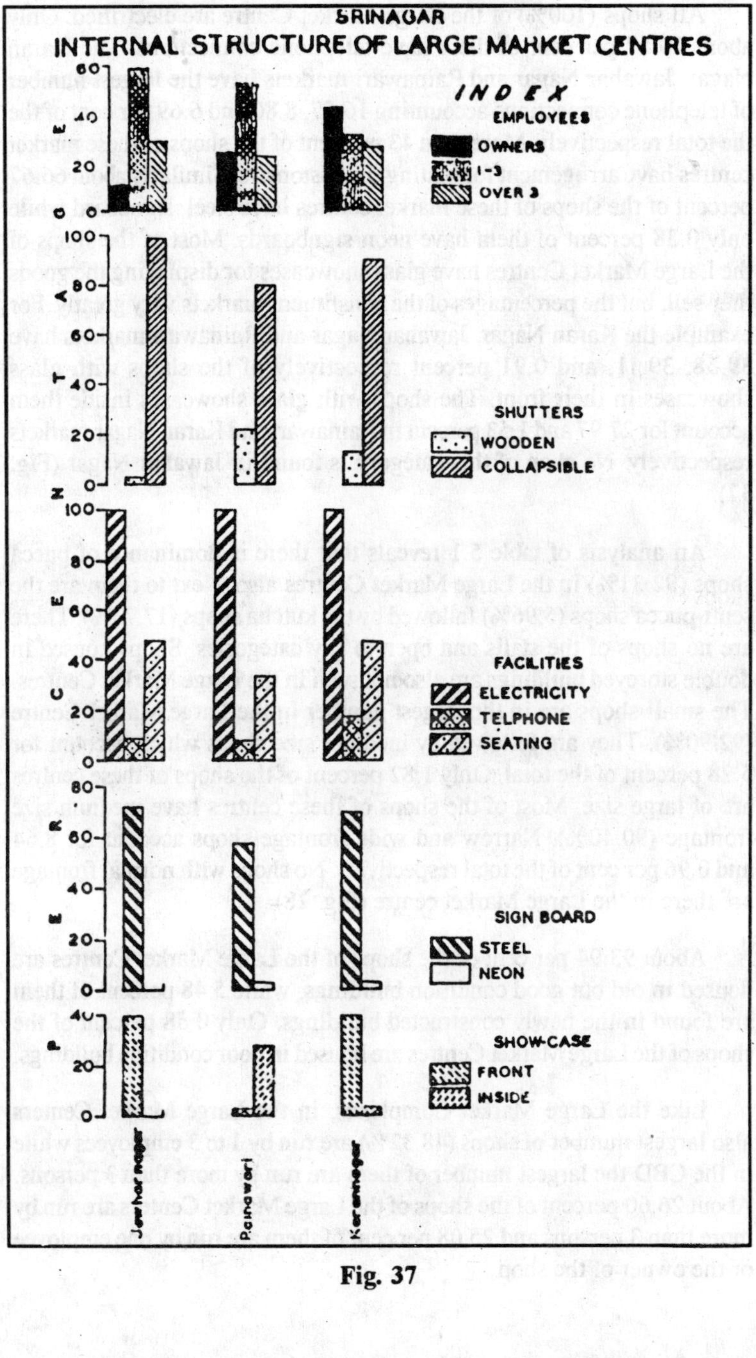
SRINAGAR
INTERNAL STRUCTURE OF LARGE MARKET CENTRES
INDEX
EMPLOYEES
OWNERS
1-3
OVER 3
SHUTTERS
WOODEN
COLLAPSIBLE
FACILITIES
ELECTRICITY
TELPHONE
SEATING
SIGN BOARD
STEEL
NEON
SHOW-CASE
FRONT
INSIDE
PERCENTAGE
Jawahar nagar
Rainawari
Karan nagar

Fig. 37

All shops (100%) of the Large Market Centre are electrified. Only about 10.57 per cent of them have telephone connections. The Karan Nagar, Jawahar Nagar and Rainawari markets have the largest number of telephone connections accounting 16.57, 8.80 and 6.69 per cent of the the total respectively. More than 43 per cent of the shops of these market centres have arrngement for seating the customers. Similarly about 66.67 percent of the shops of these market centres have steel signboard while only 0.38 percent of them have neon signboards. Most of the shops of the Large Market Centres have glass showcases for displaying the goods they sell, but the percentages of the constituent markets vary greatly. For example the Karan Nagar, Jawahar Nagar and Rainawari markets have 39.58, 39.11, and 0.91 percent respectively of the shops with glass showcases in their front. The shops with glass showcases inside them account for 27.97 and 1.53 percent in Rainawari and Karan Nagar markets respectively. No shop of this category is found in Jawahar Nagar (Fig. 37).

An analysis of table 5.1 reveals that there is dominance of pucca shops (92.31%) in the Large Market Centres also. Next to them are the semi-pucca shops (5.96%) followed by the kutcha shops (17.73%). There are no shops of the stalls and open to sky categories. Shops housed in double storeyed buildings are also not seen in the Large Market Centres. The small shops are in the largest number in the Large Market Centre (92.90%). They are followed by medium size shops which account for 5.28 percent of the total. Only 1.82 percent of the shops of these centres are of large size. Most of the shops of these centres have medium size frontage (90.40%). Narrow and wide frontage shops account for 8.64 and 0.96 per cent of the total respectively. No shops with normal frontage are there in the Large Market centre (Fig. 28).

About 93.94 per cent of the shops of the Large Market Centres are housed in old but good condition buildings, while 5.48 percent of them are found in the newly constructed buildings. Only 0.58 percent of the shops of the Large Market Centres are housed in poor condition buildings.

Like the Large Market Complexes, in the Large Market Centers also largest number of shops (48.32%) are run by 1 to 3 employees while in the CBD the largest number of them are run by more than 3 persons. About 26.60 percent of the shops of the Large Market Centers are run by more than 3 persons and 25.08 per cent of them are run by one employee or the owner of the shop.

A study of the type of doors of the shops of the market centres of the different levels brings out the difference between higher order and lower order markets. The shops with collapsible shutters occupy the first position in the C.B.D. while the Large Market Centres although the shops collapsible shutters occupy the first position, their percentage is comparatively low. The shops with collapsible shutters account for 89.52 percent of the total in the Large Market Centres. Those with wooden doors account for only 10.48 per cent of the total.

All (100%) of the shops of the Large Market Centres have electricity, but only 10.57 per cent of them have telelphone connections. This is much lower than the other higher order market centres. Similarly the proportions in these centres of shops with arrangement for seating the customers (42.93%) steel, (66.67%) and neon (0.39%) signboards, show-cases in front (27.19%) and inside (9.31%) the shops are also much lower than in the CBD and Large Market Complexes. (Fig. 29).

5.3.4 Medium Market Centres

Data relating to the Medium Market Centres are given in table 5.6.

About 89 percent of the shops of the Medium Market Centres are housed in pucca buildings. Of the sixteen in nine of these market centres all the (100%) shops are housed in pucca buildings because most of the markets of this order have come up recently in the newly settled areas. These retail nucleations are Dalgate, Chhanapura, Safa Kadal, Hazratbal, Barbar Shah, Rambagh, Hawal, Nattipura and Batwar Sonawar markets. The pucca shops are predominant in all other markets of this order except Qamarwari, where the stalls occupy the first position. The semi-pucca shops are found only in six of the sixteen markets where their percentage range between 1.43 and 15.65. No kutcha shops are found in the markets of this order. The stalls are found in four of the retail nucleations. They are Qamarwar (73.61%), Batmaloo (25.48%), Pantha Chowk (8.38%) and Khanyar Chowk (1.22%). The shops found in the open fields are found only in two market centres of this order namely Khanyar Chowk and Pantha Chowk where such shops account for 11.89 and 5.02 per cent respectively. Fuel wood and stone chips shops are found in open fields. The shops housed in double storey buildings are found only in Dalgate, where they account for 5.40 percent of the total number of shops. (Fig. 38).

Small size shops predominate in almost all the markets of this order. The largest number of medium size shops are found in Safa Kadal where

Table 5.6
Building materials & quality of shops of Medium Market Centres

	Quality	I	II	III	IV	V	VI	VII	VIII	IX	X	XI	XII	XIII	XIV	XV	XVI	Total
	Pucca	98.57	70.65	86.89	100.00	90.04	100.00	100.00	100.00	21.82	100.00	70.75	100.00	100.00	100.00	97.64	100.00	88.77
Building materials	Semipucca	1.43	3.87	-	-	9.96	-	-	-	4.57	-	15.65	-	-	-	2.46	-	2.49
	Kutcha	-	-	-	-	-	-	-	-	-	-	-	-	-	-	-	-	-
	Stall	-	25.48	1.22	-	-	-	-	-	73.61	-	8.38	-	-	-	-	-	7.50
	Open to Sly	-	-	11.89	-	-	-	-	-	-	-	5.02	-	-	-	-	-	1.20
		100	100	100	100	100	100	100	100	100	100	100	100	100	100	100	100	100
	First floor	-	-	-	5.40	-	-	-	-	-	-	-	-	-	-	-	-	0.39
Stories	Second floor	-	-	-	-	-	-	-	-	-	-	-	-	-	-	-	--	--
	Third Floor	-	-	-	-	-	-	-	-	-	-	-	-	-	-	-	-	--
	Large	-	3.09	6.56	-	5.89	-	-	1.01	1.52	6.19	12.30	2.00	3.03	3.14	3.28	9.40	3.34
Size	Medium	-	-	5.74	12.61	23.98	-	43.07	4.04	2.54	4.12	18.43	4.67	21.97	-	19.68	30.77	10.88
	Small	100.00	96.91	87.70	87.39	70.13	100.00	56.93	94.95	95.84	89.68	69.27	93.33	75.00	96.86	77.04	59.33	85.78
	Total	100	100	100	100	100	100	100	100	100	100	100	100	100	100	100	100	100
	Narrow	6.48	28.18	3.28	-	13.58	0.48	9.90	4.04	53.80	7.21	9.50	22.67	4.52	11.82	3.28	23.93	12.51
Frontage	Medium	93.52	71.04	91.80	98.20	80.54	99.52	89.60	95.96	43.14	92.79	81.00	77.33	93.89	85.03	96.72	66.67	85.10
	Normal	-	0.78	2.46	1.80	2.27	-	0.05	-	2.04	-	-	-	1.51	3.15	-	6.83	1.18

	Wide	-	-	2.46	-	3.61	-	-	-	1.02	-	9.50	-	0.76	-	-	2.57	1.21
	Total	100	100	100	100	100	100	100	100	100	100	100	100	100	100	100	100	100
	New	-	-	6.56	-	-	36.01	-	-	1.02	-	2.80	1.33	91.10	1.58	-	-	3.77
Condition	Old but good	97.49	76.44	93.44	100.00	100.00	63.99	100.00	100.00	58.33	100.00	87.00	85.34	90.90	98.42	97.54	100.00	90.08
	Poor	2.51	23.56	-	-	-	-	-	-	40.60	-	9.50	13.33	-	-	2.46	-	6.51
	Total	100	100	100	100	100	100	100	100	100	100	100	100	100	100	100	100	100
	Self	47.49	25.10	9.83	7.66	25.80	42.19	20.80	9.60	26.40	10.30	8.93	11.33	3.03	14.97	15.58	26.50	20.40
Employees	1-3	46.76	30.50	43.13	55.40	26.70	37.91	57.92	68.69	44.67	8.25	36.88	46.47	55.30	62.20	55.73	15.39	43.14
	> 3	5.74	44.40	43.03	36.94	47.50	19.90	21.28	2.71	28.93	81.25	54.19	42.00	44.67	22.83	28.69	58.11	36.46
	Total	100	100	100	100	100	100	100	100	100	100	100	100	100	100	100	100	100
	Wooden	27.33	30.11	-	-	20.37	3.80	7.42	3.03	51.78	-	50.83	15.33	0.76	10.23	3.28	-	15.13
Shutter	Collapsible	72.67	69.89	100.00	100.00	79.63	96.28	92.58	96.97	48.22	100.00	49.17	84.67	99.24	89.77	96.72	100.00	84.87
	Total	100	100	100	100	100	100	100	100	100	100	100	100	100	100	100	100	100
	Electricity	100.00	100.00	100.00	100.00	100.00	100.00	100.00	100.00	100.00	100.00	100.00	100.00	100.00	95.28	100.00	100.00	100.00
Facilities	Telephone	1.80	8.50	20.50	28.82	29.87	2.84	16.33	2.02	7.61	22.17	6.70	10.00	23.48	3.14	32.79	19.65	14.90
	Seating	43.89	27.80	53.69	52.70	54.76	46.91	53.97	23.24	30.45	47.93	24.59	32.67	53.03	27.55	56.55	50.42	42.74
	Steel	43.17	58.30	87.70	94.14	67.42	98.30	83.16	40.40	37.05	76.80	25.13	92.00	90.15	64.57	68.85	72.64	65.14
Signbord																		

	Neon	-	0.38	5.73	-	3.61	2.37	0.99	1.01	1.52	-	1.68	0.66	0.78	-	-	0.11	1.73
Show case	Front	28.41	25.86	1.22	27.02	32.12	22.74	44.55	-	15.80	38.14	10.61	24.00	-	20.48	38.96	2.79	3.38
	Inside	-	-	36.06	-	4.52	2.37	3.47	18.19	1.02	-	-	-	34.10	-	12.30	-	6.81

Source : Field work

I	=	Nawa Kadal	II	=	Bat Maloo
III	=	Khanyar Chowk	IV	=	Dal Gate
V	=	Khyam Chowk	VI	=	Chhanpura
VII	=	Safa Kadal	VIII	=	Hazarat Bal
IX	=	Qamarwari	X	=	Barbar Shah
XI	=	Pantha Chowk	XII	=	Ram Bagh
XIII	=	Hawal	XIV	=	Natti Pura
XV	=	Nagin Saida Kadal	XVI	=	Batwara Sonawar

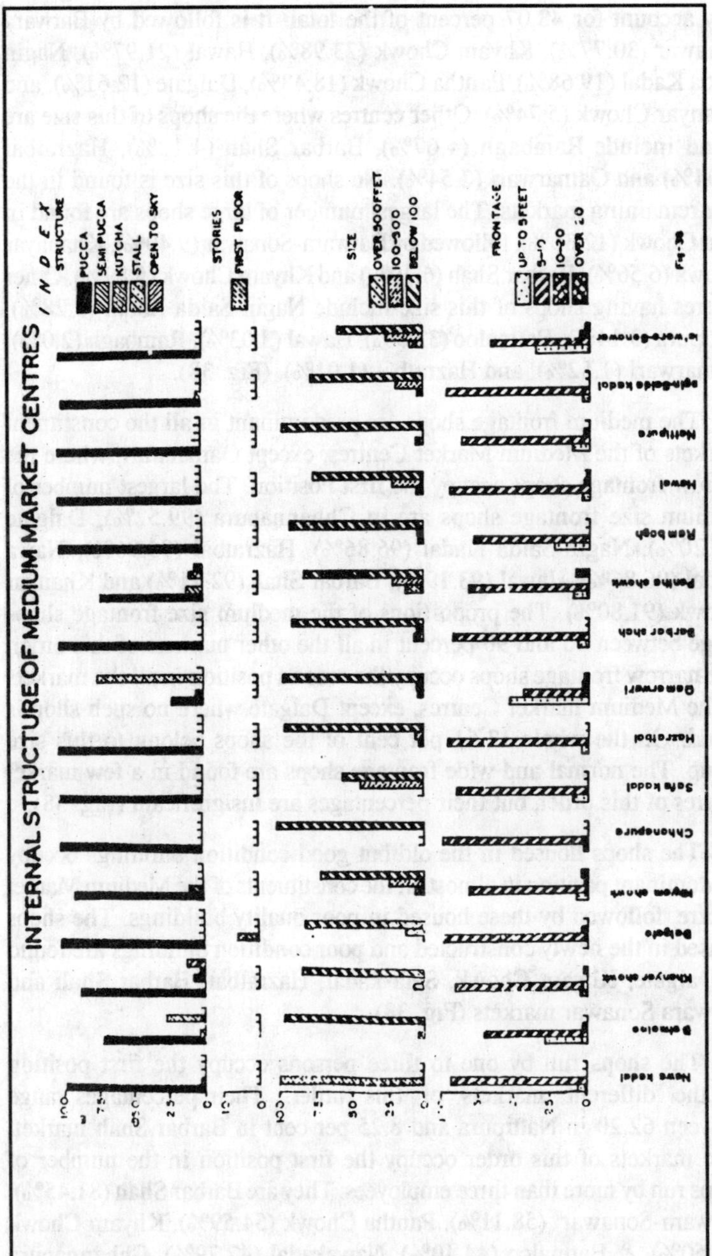
INTERNAL STRUCTURE OF MEDIUM MARKET CENTRES
INDEX
STRUCTURE
PUCCA
SEMI PUCCA
KUTCHA
STALL
OPEN TO SKY
STORIES
FIRST FLOOR
SIZE
OVER 300FFET
100-300
BELOW 100
FRONTAGE
UP TO 5FEET
5—10
10—20
OVER 20

Fig. 38

they account for 43.07 percent of the total. It is followed by Batwara Sonawar (30.77%), Khyam Chowk (23.98%), Hawal (21.97%), Nagin Saida Kadal (19.68%), Pantha Chowk (18.43%), Dalgate (12.61%), and Khanyar Chowk (5.74%). Other centres where the shops of this size are found include Rambagh (4.67%), Barbar Shah (4.12%), Hazratbal (4.04%) and Qamarwari (2.54%). No shops of this size is found in the four remaining markets. The largest number of large shops are found in Pant Chowk (12.30%), followed by Batwara-Sonawar (9.40%), Khanayar Chowk (6.56%), Barbar Shah (6.19%) and Khyam Chowk (5.89%). Other centres having shops of this size include Nagin-Saida Kadal (3.28%), Natipura (3.14%), Batmaloo (3.09%), Hawal (3.03%), Rambagh (2.0%), Qamarwari (1.52%), and Hazratbal (1.01%). (Fig. 38).

The medium frontage shops are predominant in all the constituent markets of the Medium Market Centres, except Qamarwari, where the narrow frontage shops occupy the first Position. The largest number of medium size frontage shops are in Chhannapura (99.52%), Dalgate (88.20%), Nagin-Saida Kadal (96.86%), Hazratbal (95.96%), Nawa Kadal (96.86%), Hawal (93.19%), Barbar Shah (92.71%) and Khanyar Chowk (91.80%). The proportions of the medium size frontage shops range between 66 and 90 percent in all the other markets of this order. The narrow frontage shops occupy the second position in all the markets of the Medium market Centres, except Dalgate where no such shop is found. On the whole 12.51 per cent of the shops belong to this size group. The normal and wide frontage shops are found in a few market centres of this order, but their percentages are insignificant (Fig. 38).

The shops housed in the old but good condition buildings occupy the dominant position in almost all the constituents of the Medium Market Centre, followed by these housed in poor quality buildings. The shops housed in the newly constructed and poor condition buildings are found in Dalgate, Khyam Chowk, Safa kadal, Hazratbal, Barbar Shah and Batwara Sonawar markets (Fig. 38).

The shops run by one to three persons occupy the first position in the different markets of this order. Their percentages range between 62.20 in Nattipura and 8.25 per cent in Barbar Shah market. Five markets of this order occupy the first position in the number of shops run by more than three employees. They are Barbar Shah (81.45%), Batwara-Sonawar (58.11%), Pantha Chowk (54.59%), Khyam Chowk (47.50%), & Batmaloo (44.40%). Nawakadal (47.79%), Chhannapura (42.19%), Batwars-Sonawar (26.50%), Qamarwari (44.67%), Batmaloo

(25.10%), Khyam Chowk (25.80%), Safa Kadal (20.80%) and Khanyar Chowk (9.83%) are those centres which occupy the first position in the number of shops run by one employee or the owner of the shops

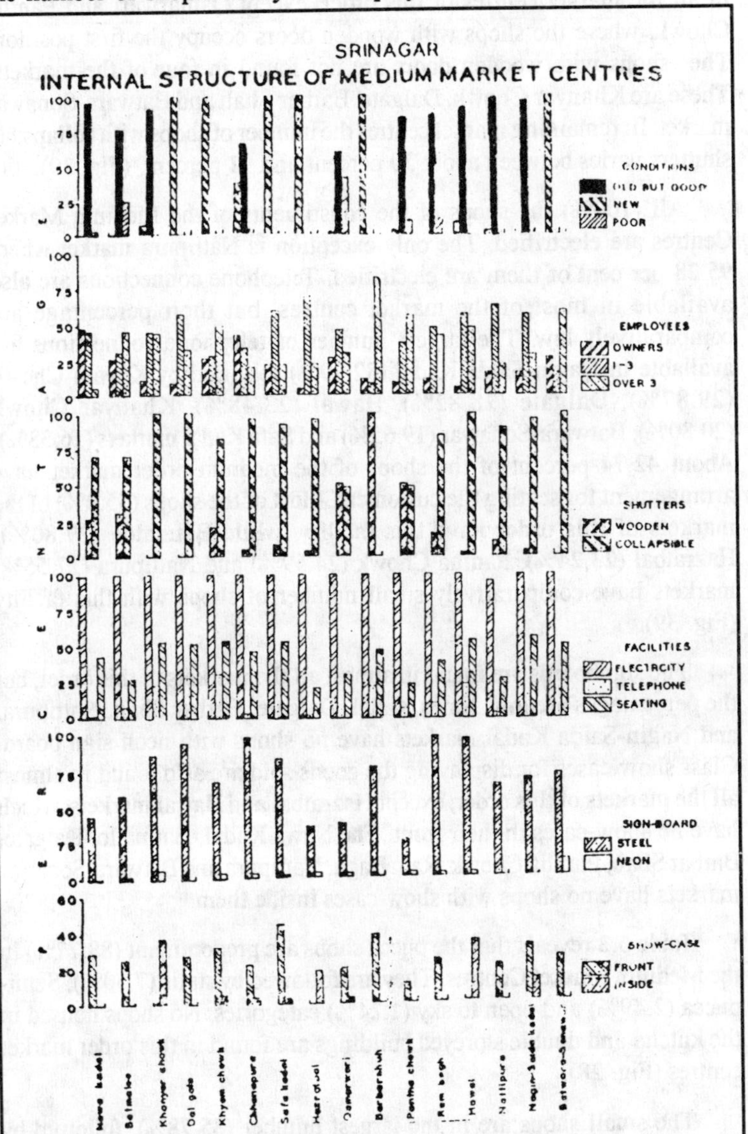

Fig. 39

himself (Fig. 39).

The shops having collpasible shutters have the dominating position in all the market centres of this order, except Qamarwari and Pantha Chowk, where the shops with wooden doors occupy the first position. The shops with wooden doors are not found in four of the markets. These are Khanyar Chowk, Dalgate, Barbar Shah and Batwara-Sonawar market. In remaining market centres the number of shops with collapsible shutters varies between about 50 percent and 91 percent. (Fig. 39).

All (100%) the shops of the constituents of the Medium Market Centres are electrified. The only exception is Nattipura market where 95.28 per cent of them are electrified. Telephone connections are also available in most of the market centres, but their percentage are comparatively low. The largest number of telephone connections are available in Nagin-Saida Kadal (32.79%) followed by Khyam Chowk (29.87%), Dalgate (28.82%), Hawal (23.48%), Khanyar Chowk (20.80%), Batwara-Sonawar (19.65%) and Safa Kadal markets (16.33%). About 42.74 percent of the shops of the medium order market have arrangement for seating the customers. Most of the shops (55.0%) of the markets of this order have this facility, while Batmaloo (27.80%), Hazratbal (23.24%), Pantha Chowk (24.59%) and Nattipura (27.55%) markets have comparatively small number of shops with this facility (Fig. 39).

The signboards are found in almost all the markets of this order, but the percentages are low. Nawa Kadal, Dalgate, Barbar Shah, Nattipura, and Nagin-Saida Kadal markets have no shops with neon sign board. Glass show-cases for displaying the goods sold are aslo found in almost all the markets of this order, except Hazratbal and Hawal markets which have no show-cases in their front. The Nawa Kadal, Batmallo, Dalgate, Barbar Shah, Pantha Chowk, Ram Bagh, Nattipura and Batwara-Sonawar markets have no shops with show-cases inside them.

Table 5.2 reveals that the pucca shops are predominant (88.77%) in the Medium Market Centres. They are followed by stalls (7.50%), Semi-pucca (2.49%) and open to sky (1.24%) categories. No shops housed in the kutcha and double storeyed buildings are found in this order market centres (Fig. 28).

The small shops are in the largest number (85.78%), followed by medium size (10.88%) and large size shops (3.34%). About 85.10 per cent of the shops of these centres have medium size frontage, followed by shops with narrow (12.51%), wide (1.21%) and normal (1.18%) frontage.

Like other commercial centres the shops housed in the old but good condition buildings are the largest here (90.08%). Only 6.15 and 3.77 percent of the shops of the Medium Market Centres are housed respectively in poor and newly constructed buildings.

The shops run by one to three persons predominate and with 43.14 percent of the total occupy the first position. The second position is claimed by the shops run by over three persons (36.46%) followed by the shops run by owner or by one employee (20.40%) (Fig. 29). About 84.87 and 15.13 percent of the shops of the markets of this order have collapsible and wooden doors respectively. These proportions are very low as compared with other higher level market centres of the city of Srinagar.

All (100%) the shops of these centres are electrified. Telephone (13.47%) and arrangement for seating the customers (42.75%) are also found here. About 65.14 percent of the shops have steel signboards and 22.28 percent shop of them have glass show-cases for displaying the goods sold by them. These propotions are also low as compared with the other higher order market centres of the city (Fig. 29).

5.3.5 Local Market Places

An analysis of the table 5.7 reveals that the quality of the shops of the Local Market Places is good. The pucca shops predominate in all the five markets of the Local Market Places. Of the five market places in three namely Zadibal, Nowshera and Soura all (100%) the shops are housed in pucca buildings while 95.19 and 88.89 per cent of the shops are housed in pucca buildings respectively in Lal Bazar and Sadarble. Pucca shops predominate here because these have come up recently mostly in the newly developed parts of the city. The semi-pucca shops and stalls are found only in Saderbal (11.11%) and Lal Bazar (4.81%). No shops is found either in kutcha building or in any open field. Only 1.30 per cent of the shops are housed in double storeyed buildings all in the Soura market. No other market has any shop housed in double storeyed building (Fig. 40).

The majority of the shops of the Local Market Places are of small size and occupy the first position in all the five market places. All the (100%) shops in Lal Bazar and Nowshera are of small size while in Sadrabal, Zadibal and Soura they constitutes 94.44, 93.82 and 77.92 per cent of the total number of shops respectively. The medium size shops are found in Soura (20.78%), Zadibal (6.18%) and Sadarbal (5.56%) while the large shops are found only in Soura market which accounts for 1.30 per cent of the total number of the shops of this market. (Fig. 40).

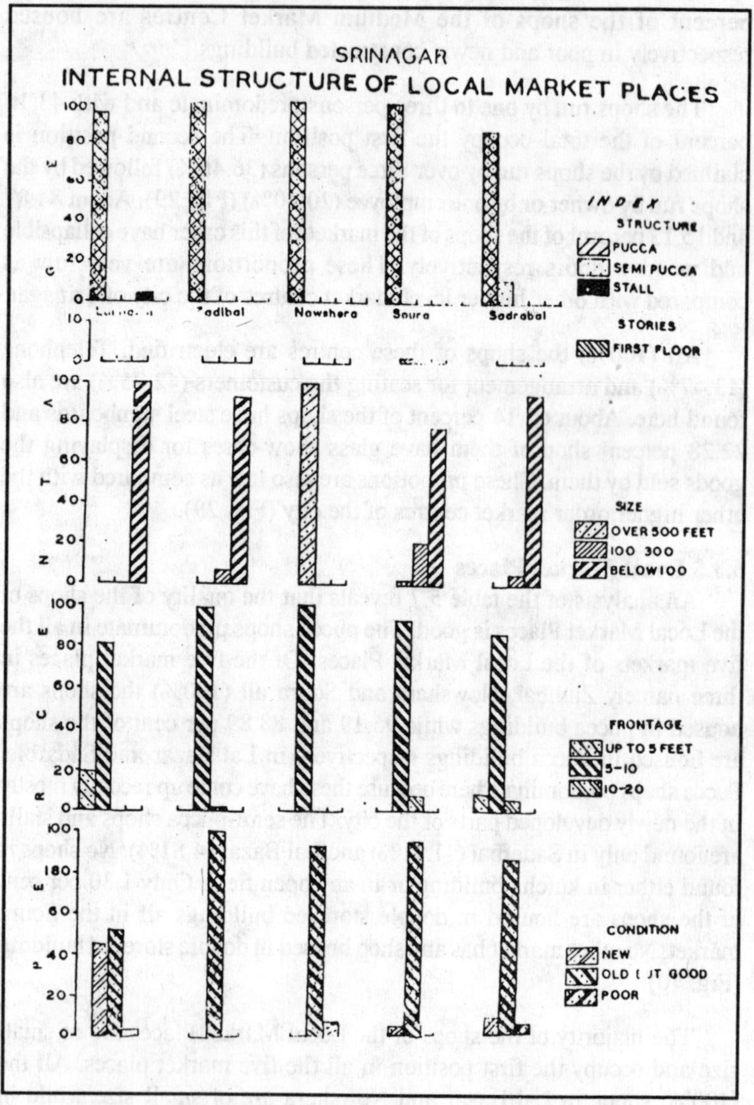

Fig. 40

Table 5.7
Building material & quality of shops of Local Market Place
(Figure are in Percentage)

	Quality	I	II	III	IV	V	Total
Building materials	Pucca	95.19	100.00	100.00	100.00	88.89	97.74
	Semi-pucca	-	-	-	-	11.11	1.3
	Kutcha	-	-	-	-	-	-
	Stall	4.81	-	-	-	-	1.13
	Open to sky	-	-	-	-	-	-
	Total	100	100	100	100	100	100
Stories	First floor	-	-	-	1.30	-	0.29
	Second floor	-	-	-	-	-	-
	Third floor	-	-	-	-	-	-
Size	Large	-	-	-	1.30	-	0.29
	Medium	-	-6.18	-	20.78	5.56	6.48
	Small	100.00	93.82	100.00	77.92	94.44	93.23
	Total	100	100	100	100	100	100
Frontage	Narrow	18.08	-	-	-	8.33	5.08
	Medium	81.92	98.77	100.00	92.20	86.11	92.39
	Normal	-	1.23	-	7.80	5.56	2.53
	Wide	-	-	-	-	-	-
	Total	100	100	100	100	100	100
Condition	New	44.50	-	-	5.200	5.56	12.11
	Old but good	51.80	100.00	92.30	94.80	94.44	85.36
	Poor	3.62	-	7.70	-	-	2.53
	Total	100	100	100	100	100	100
Emplo-	Self	24.10	8.64	19.23	7.80	2.78	13.80
	1-3	44.58	67.90	57.70	64.93	91.67	61.98

yees	>3	31.31	23.46	23.07	27.27	5.55	24.22
	Total	100	100	100	100	100	100
Shutter	Wooden	25.30	1.22	-	-	13.89	7.6
	Collapsible	74.70	98.77	100.00	100.00	86.11	92.40
	Total	100	100	100	100	100	100
Facilities	Electricity	100.00	98.77	100.00	100.00	100.00	99.71
	Telephone	-	4.93	14.10	23.38	-	9.30
	Seating	42.17	37.03	61.53	35.07	2.78	39.71
Signboard	Steel	53.01	37.03	67.94	100.00	-	57.47
	Neon	-	-	-	-	-	-
Show case	Front	-	-	-	-	-	-
	Inside	36.14	35.89	53.85	6.49	-	29.85

Source : Field work

I = Lal Bazar
II = Zadibal
III = Nowshera
IV = Soura
V = Sadarbal

The medium frontage shops have the dominating postion in all the Local Market Places. They account for 100% in Nawshera, 98.77% in Zadibal, 92.30% in Soura, 86.11% in Sadrabal, and 81.93% in Lal Bazar. The narrow frontage shops are found in Lal Bazar (18.08%) and Sadrabal (8.33%). Similarly normal frontage shops are seen only in Soura (7.80%), Sadarbal (5.56%), and Zadibal (1.23%) markets. The wide frontage shops are not found in any Local Market Place (Fig. 40).

The largest number of shops are found in the old but good condition buildings. More than 90 per cent of the shops in Soura, Sadrabal and Nowshera markets are housed in old but good condition buildings. In Zadibal 100 per cent and in Lal Bazar 51.88 per cent of the shops are housed in buildings of the same category. The shops housed in newly constructed buildings are found in Lal Bazar (44.58%). Sadrabal (5.56%) and Soura (5.20%) markets. Shops housed in poor quality building are

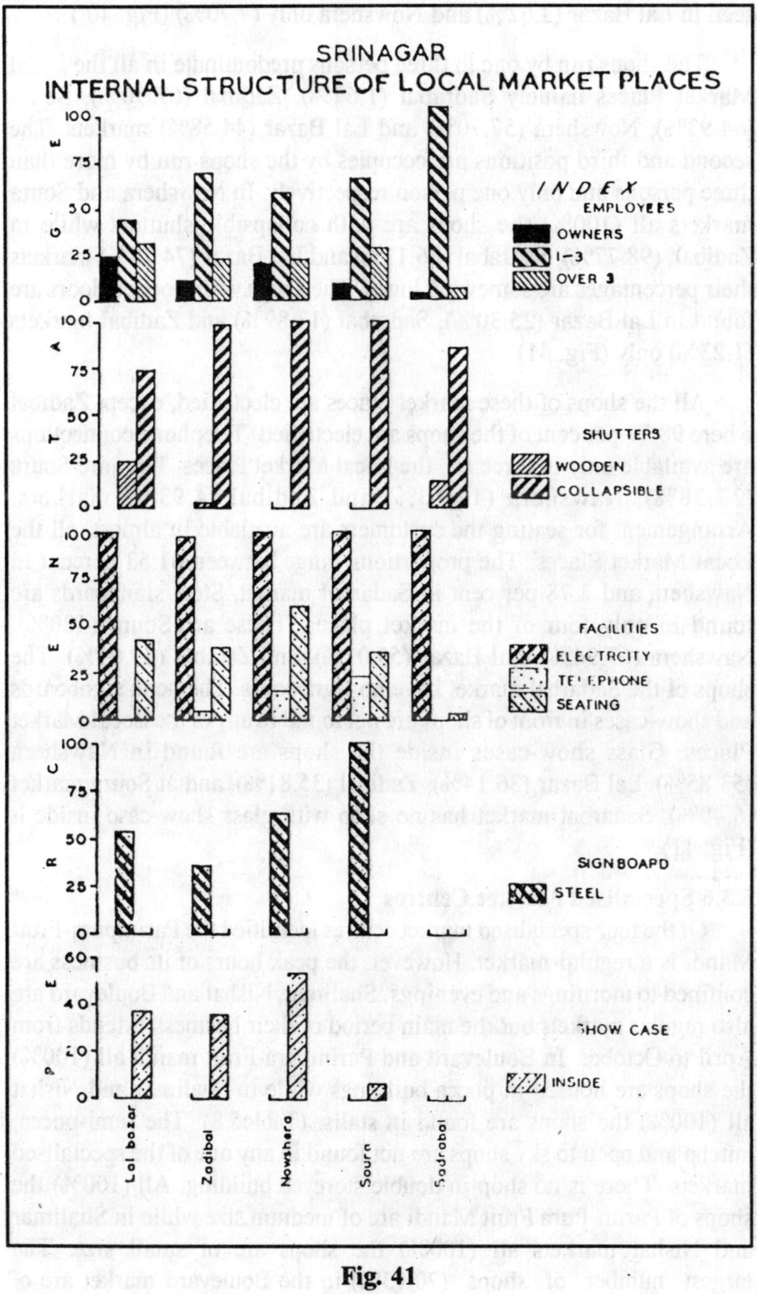

SRINAGAR
INTERNAL STRUCTURE OF LOCAL MARKET PLACES
INDEX
EMPLOYEES
OWNERS
1-3
OVER 3
SHUTTERS
WOODEN
COLLAPSIBLE
FACILITIES
ELECTRCITY
TELEPHONE
SEATING
SIGNBOAPD
STEEL
SHOW CASE
INSIDE
PERCENTAGE
Lal bazar
Zadibal
Nowshera
Soura
Sadrabal

Fig. 41

seen in Lal Bazar (3.62%) and Nowshera only (7.70%) (Fig. 40.)

The shops run by one to three persons predominate in all the Local Market Places namely Sadrabal (1.67%), Zadibal (67.90%), Soura (64.93%), Nowshera (57.70%) and Lal Bazar (44.58%) markets. The second and third positions are occupies by the shops run by more than three persons and only one person respectively. In Nowshera and Soura markets all (100%) the shops are with collapsible shutters while in Zadibal, (98.77%), Sadrabal (86.11%) and Lal Bazar (74.70%) markets their percentages are somewhat lower. The shops with wooden doors are found in Lal Bazar (25.30%), Sadrabal (13.89%) and Zadibal markets (1.23%) only (Fig. 41).

All the shops of these market places are electrified, except Zadibal where 98.77 per cent of the shops are electrified. Telephone connections are available only in three of the Local Market Places. They are Soura (23.38%), Nawshera (14.10%) and Zadibal (4.93%) markets. Arrangement for seating the customers are available in almost, all the Local Market Places. The proportions range between 61.53 percent in Nawshera and 2.78 per cent in Sadarbal market. Steel signboards are found in only four of the market places. These are Soura (100%), Nawshera (67.94%), Lal Bazar (53.01%), and Zadibal (39.03%). The shops of the Sadarbal market have no signboards. The neon signboards and show-cases in front of shops are not found in any of the Local Market Places. Glass show-cases inside the shops are found in Nawshera (53.85%), Lal Bazar (36.14%), Zadibal (35.81%), and at Soura market (6.49%), Sadarbal market has no shop with glass show-case inside it (Fig. 41).

5.3.6 Specialised Market Centres

Of the four specialised market centres identified the Parimpura-Fruit Mandi is a regular market. However, the peak hours of its business are confined to mornings and evenings. Shalimar, Nishat and Boulevard are also regular markets but the main period of their business extends from April to October. In Boulevard and Parimpura-Fruit mandi all (100%) the shops are housed in pucca buildings while in Shalimar and Nishat all (100%) the shops are found in stalls. (Table5.8). The semi-pucca, kutcha and open to sky shops are not found in any one of the specialised markets. There is no shop in double storeyed building. All (100%) the shops of Parim-Pura Fruit Mandi are of medium size while in Shalimar and Nishat markets all (100%) the shops are of small size. The largest number of shops (70.13%) in the Boulevard market are of small size. The large (25.54%) and medium size shops (4.33%) are in smaller nmbers. No large shop is found in the other specialised markets (Fig. 42).

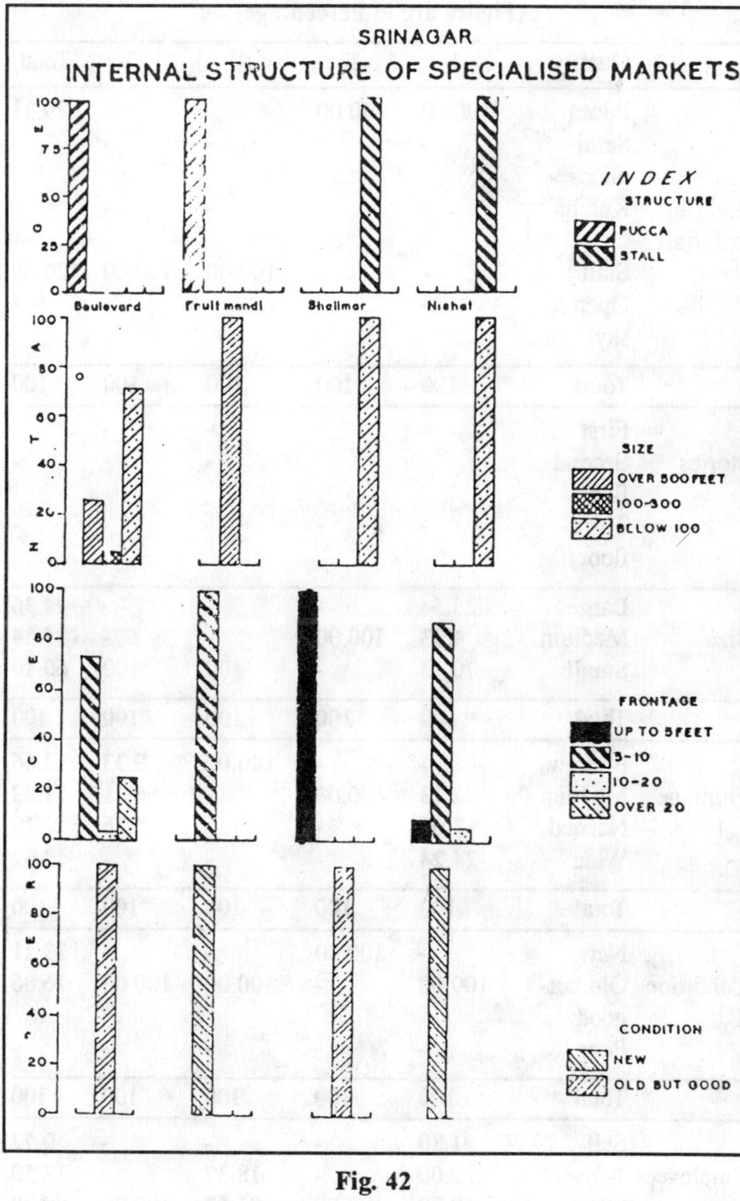

Fig. 42

Table 5.8
Building materials & quality of shops of Specialised Market Places
(Figure are in Percentage)

	Quality	I	II	III	IV	Total
Building materials	Pucca	100.00	100.00	-	-	79.31
	Semi-pucca	-	-	-	-	-
	Kutcha	-	-	-	-	-
	Stall	-	-	100.00	100.00	20.69
	Open to sky	-	-	-	-	-
	Total	100	100	100	100	100
Stories	First	-	-	-	-	-
	Second-floor	-	-	-	-	-
	Third-floor	-	-	-	-	-
Size	Large	25.54	-	-	-	14.36
	Medium	4.33	100.00	-	-	25.54
	Small	70.13	-	100	100	60.10
	Total	100	100	100	100	100
Frontage	Narrow	-	-	100.00	8.33	12.66
	Medium	72.73	100.00	-	86.11	71.53
	Normal	3.03	-	-	5.56	2.19
	Wide	24.24	-	-	-	13.62
	Total	100	100	100	100	100
Condition	New	-	100.00	-	-	23.11
	Old but-good	100.00	-	100.00	100.00	76.86
	Poor	-	-	-	-	-
	Total	100	100	100	100	100
Employees	Self	1.30	-	-	-	0.72
	1-3	29.00	-	18.37	-	18.50
	>3	69.70	100.00	81.63	100.00	80.78

	Total	100	100	100	100	100
Shutter	Wooden	-	-	-	13.89	1.21
	Collapsible	100.00	100.00	100.00	86.11	98.79
	Total	100	100	100	100	100
Facilities	Electricity	100.00	100.00	100.00	100.00	100.00
	Telephone	88.74	100.00	-	-	73.00
	Seating	95.83	100.00	69.39	100.00	93.68
Signboard	Steel	74.90	100.00	100.00	-	77.12
	Neon	25.10	-	-	-	14.11
Show case	Front	65.80	-	75.51	-	45.99
	Inside	13.41	-	-	-	7.54

Source : Field work

I = Boulevard
II = Parim-pura Fruit Mandi
III = Shalimar
IV = Nishat

The medium size frontage shops occupy the first position in three of the specialised market namely Parimpura Fruit mandi (100%), Nishat market (86.11%) and Boulevard market (72,23%). Shalimar occupies the first position in narrow frontage shops (100%). The normal frontage shops are found in two centres, Nishat (5.56%) and Boulevard (3.03%). Such shops are also found at Nishat (8.33%). The wide frontage shops are found only in the Boulevard market (24.24%).

In almost all the specialised markets all (100%) the shops are housed in old but good condition buildings except Parimpura-Fruit Mandi where all (100%) the shops are housed in newly constructed buildings. No shop is housed in poor quality building (Fig. 42.).

In Parimpura-Fruit Mandi and Nishat market all (100%) the shops are run by more than three persons while 81.63 per cent of the shops in Shalimar and 69.70 per cent of them is Boulevard are run by more than three persons. The shops run by one to three persons are found in Boulevard (29%) and Shalimar markets (18.37%). About 1.30 per cent

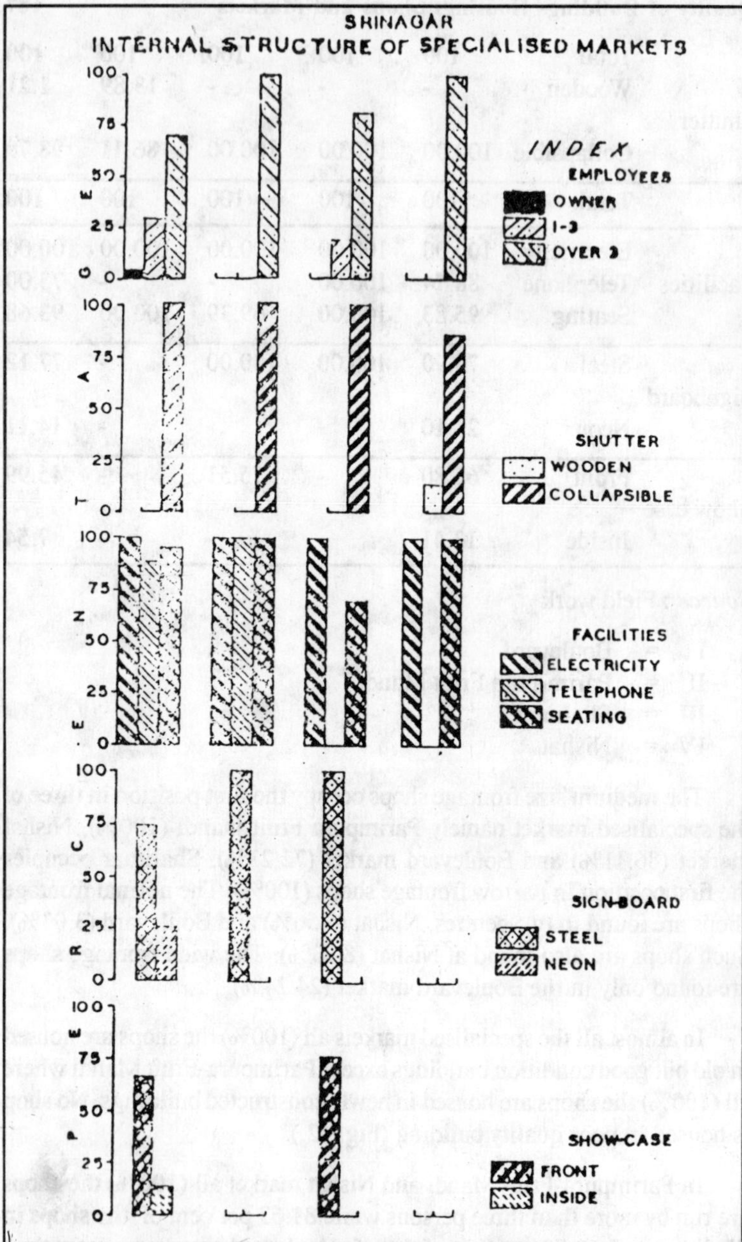
SRINAGAR
INTERNAL STRUCTURE OF SPECIALISED MARKETS
PERCENTAGE
INDEX
EMPLOYEES
OWNER
1-3
OVER 3
SHUTTER
WOODEN
COLLAPSIBLE
FACILITIES
ELECTRICITY
TELEPHONE
SEATING
SIGN-BOARD
STEEL
NEON
SHOW-CASE
FRONT
INSIDE

Fig. 43

of the shops are run by one person in Boulevard. (Fig. 43).

All (100%) the shops have collapsible sutters in all the specialised markets except the Nishat market where 86.11 per cent of the shops have collapsible shutters. The shops with wooden doors are found only in Nishat market (13.89%). (Fig. 43).

In almost all the markets all (100%) the shops are electrified. In Parimpura-Fruit Mandi (100%) the shops have telephones and seating facilities. About 88.54 per cent of the shops of Boulevard have telephone connections while there is no telephone connection in Nishat or Shalimar market. Arrangement for seating the customers are available in all (100%) the shops of the Nishat market while in Boulevard and Shalimar 95.23 and 69.39 per cent respectively of the shops have this facility (Fig. 28). Steel signboards are seen in most of the markets except Nishat where no steel signboard is there. Neon signboards are found only in the Boulevard market (25.10%).

Glass show-cases for displaying goods sold are available only in two market. The Boulevard market has glass show-cases both in front (65.80%) and inside (13.14%) the shops while the Shalimar market has glass show-cases only in front of shops (75.51%) (Fig. 29).

5.4 Summary

It is clear that the quality of shops declines with the lowering of the hierarchical order of the markets. There is predominance of inferior and poor quality shops in the lower order market centres. The pucca shops are less frequent in the lower order market centres. Their place is taken here by semi-pucca shops. The open to sky shops are not found in the CBD and the shops housed in multi-storeyed buildings are found there.

The proportion of large shops decreases with the lowering of the hierarchical order of markets. On the other hand, the number of small shops increases with the lowering of the hierarchical order of the markets. Similarly narrow frontage shops are more frequent in the lower-order markets while wide frontage shops are more frquent in the market of higher order centres. The shops are generally run by more people in the lower order market centres. Shops are run mostly by one employee or the owner himself in the latter. Similarly the shops of the higher order market centres have good quality doors. The proportion of collapsible shutter is higher in the higher order market centres. The reverse is true of the lower order market centres. The availabaility of electricity and the telephone connections decreases with the lowering of the hierarchical order of the markets. Similarly, the number of shops having glass-cases decreases with the lowering of the hierarchical order. The same is true of seating facilities. It can thus be concluded that higher. order market centres of Srinagar have good quality shops with more and more infrastructural facilities while with the lowering of the hierarchical order of market centres the quality of shops goes on declining and the infrastructural facilities go on decreasing.

6

Commercial Land Use and Land Values

6.1 Importance of Commercial Land Value in Urban Areas

In the preceeding chapters the hierarchy of the market centres has been determined on the basis of the number of establishments, types of business and quality of shops. An attempt is made here to study the rent values of shops and godowns, land values prevailing in the commercial areas in street fronts and at their backs as well as the premium paid before taking commercial space on rent. The assumption is that the rents, land values and premium increase directly with the rise in the hierarchical order of the commercial centres.

The greatest obstacle to the determination of land and rent values in the Indian cities is the use of unaccounted money in the transactions. The deeds of sales and purchases of land registered seldom show the real amount of consideration money which changes hands. The actual amount which changes hands is usually two or three times the amount recorded in the deed. Similarly in the case of rents the amount mentioned in the rent receipt is generally much less than the actual rent paid. The cash premium paid to the landlord at the time of taking the shop on rent varies between rupees 1000 to Rs. 1 lakh. The amount is not mentioned in the account books. However, if the premium paid is high the rent is generally low as the latter is partly capitalised in the form of premium. No reliance can therefore placed on officially disclosed amount which change hands in these transactions. The authors had to take recourse to field-work and personal observation invloving filling up of a large number of questionnaires and collecting primary data. It may be taken that the information given by a large number of respondents on the subject obtaining in their respective localities are nearer the truth. Unanimity has thus helped in bringing facts to the surface. Cross checking of information by means of interviews of people engaged in different economic activities and living in different localities make them still more reliable especially because the replies given by them about the state of affairs obtaining in particular localities are more or less identical. The variation of the amounts mentioned not being very great there was no difficulty in computing average land value in terms of cost, rent and permium prevailing in different parts of the city.

6.2 General pattern of Land Value

An examination of the data on land values obtaining in the city of Srinagar reveals that they differ from places to place depending upon their location, situation, approachability and future prospects. Broadly speaking the land values are the highest in south-central Srinagar (CBD). The values go on decreasing in all directions with increasing distance

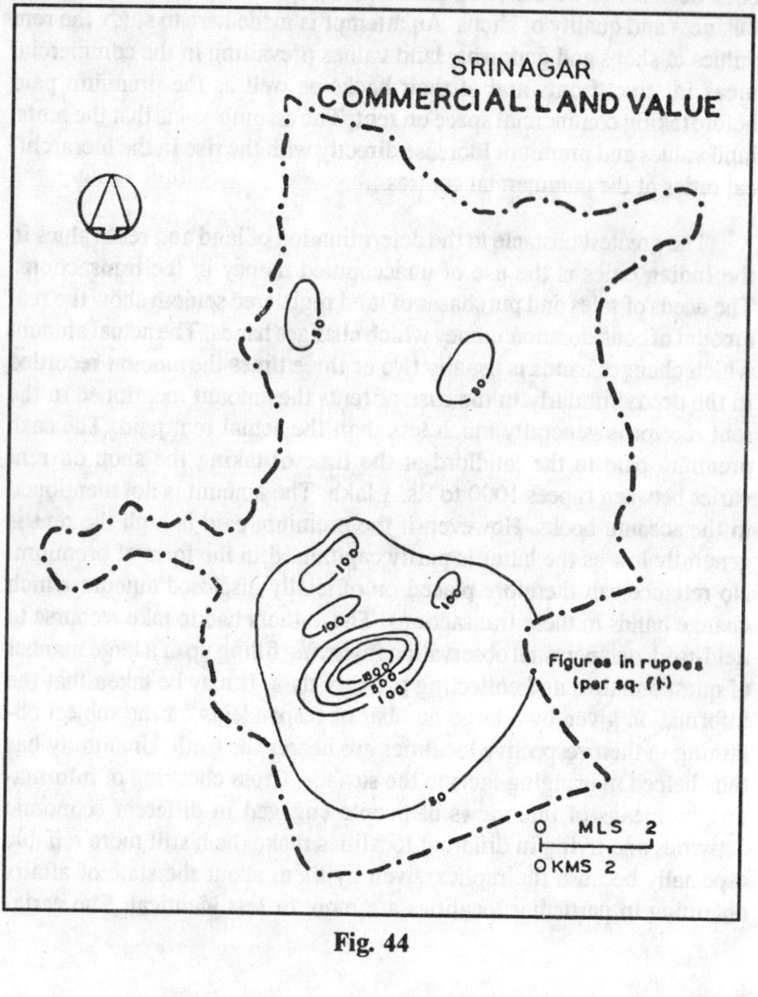

Fig. 44

from the CBD. The central part of Srinagar or the old main market centre (Nawhatta-Zaina Kadal area) has slightly lower land values than the south-central part (Fig. 44). The central and north-central parts are already overpopulated and are dominated by commercial-cum-residential uses. There is no space for any expansion. Therefore people are moving towards the southern western and northern parts of the city. Almost all the private, government and semi-government residential colonies including official quarters have been built in these parts. This has resulted in increase in price of residential plots here in recent years.

6.3. Comparision of values of lane in Commercial & Non-Commercial areas

There is great difference between the value of commercial plots having road frontage and that of the land at the back of the roads or those in the adjoining areas. Even in the same locality the property which is used for housing shops has a very high value than that which is used as a godown or residence. This is true generally of all retail nucleations of Srinagar except the Central Business District (Lal Chowk). The values of land having road frontage and the land lying at the back of the roads are almost the same in the CBD because all lands have excellent approachability. It has wide roads and is accessible from all parts of the city.

The land values are comparatively higher in the commercial areas, especially in the higher order commercial centres. This is true also of rental values of shops and godowns. The rent is higher in the higher order retail nucleations except the large market complexes, where the rent is comparatively lower because this is the old commercial area of the city. In the lower order centres the higher rent is due to the stiff competition and shortage of space. The specialised market centres also have higher rent due to their location near places of tourist interest.

The practice of charging premium before letting out commercial space is prevalent in the Srinagar city, particularly in the higher order retail nucleations. The premium is often a huge amount paid in cash to the landlords while taking the shop on rent. It is called Pagree, Mathii and Salami, etc. The amount paid is not refundable and no receipt is granted for its payment. The shopkeeper, however, manages to receive it back, sometimes with profit, when he vacates the premises in favour of any other shopkeeper. Like the land values and rents the premium also increase with the rising of the order of the commercial centres in their hierarchy.

6.4 Collection & Processing of Data

In the course of field work the authors visited all the forty-two market centres of the city of Srinagar. In each of these markets about three to five persons from different of it were interviewed in order to solicit information from them on the prevailing rates of land, rent and premium for large, medium and small shops separately. It may be mentioned here that land values were divided into two parts namely those infront and those at the back of the roads. The average of the information given by the respondents was taken as the average for the market in question. It may be recalled that the forty-two markets mentioned above constitute commercial centres of six different orders. The averages of the market centres constituting the commercial centre of each order were averaged in order to obtain the average for the markets of six different orders. The averages were then converted into rates per square feet for the sake of convenience of comparision. These rates are given in the various following tables. No agency either private or government collects or possesses data on land value. The Registrar's office where the sale deeds are registered is the only source of information. However, the price of land mentioned in the registered sale deeds were found to be much less than the values actually prevailing. It is apparent that few people state the actual price in the sale deeds in order to evade paying tax. Consequently the authors had to undertake detailed field work for gaining access to the real and currently prevailing land values, rents and premiums in the different orders of the commercial centres. The data are given in appendix.

As far as their size is concerned the shops can be grouped into three categories namely shops up to 100 sq. ft., 100 to 300 sq. ft. and 300 to 500 sq. fts. of floor area. These have been termed small, medium and large shops respectively. The lower order centres such as medium market centres and local market places have predominance of small and medium size shops, while the higher order centres, such as the CBD, Large Market Complexes, Large Market Centres have mostly large shops. Although the rents etc of the shops vary with their size in the different markets of different order. These are not related strictly with their floor area. If for example a shop has very large floor area its rent per sq. ft. would be usually proportionately less. Similarly, if the floor area of the shop is small, the rent will not decrease abruptly and the rent per sq. ft. would be proportionately more.

6.5 Land Value, Rent & Premium of Shops by Level of Centres

The values in different market centres range from Rs. 18.52 to Rs. 1851.86 per sq. ft. of land having road frontage and from Rs. 11.12 to Rs. 1851.85 in their back. Generally speaking the values of land with road frontage are almost double of those in the back. However, there are exceptions, particularly in the CBD where the two are equal. As far as the rates of rent and premium are concerned, the two have an inverse relationship. In order to integrate them the capitalised value of rent has been added to the permium. The capitalised rent is found by multiplying the rent payable per month by 120 on the assumption that the contract is for ten years. An isopleth map has been drawn on the basis of the capi-

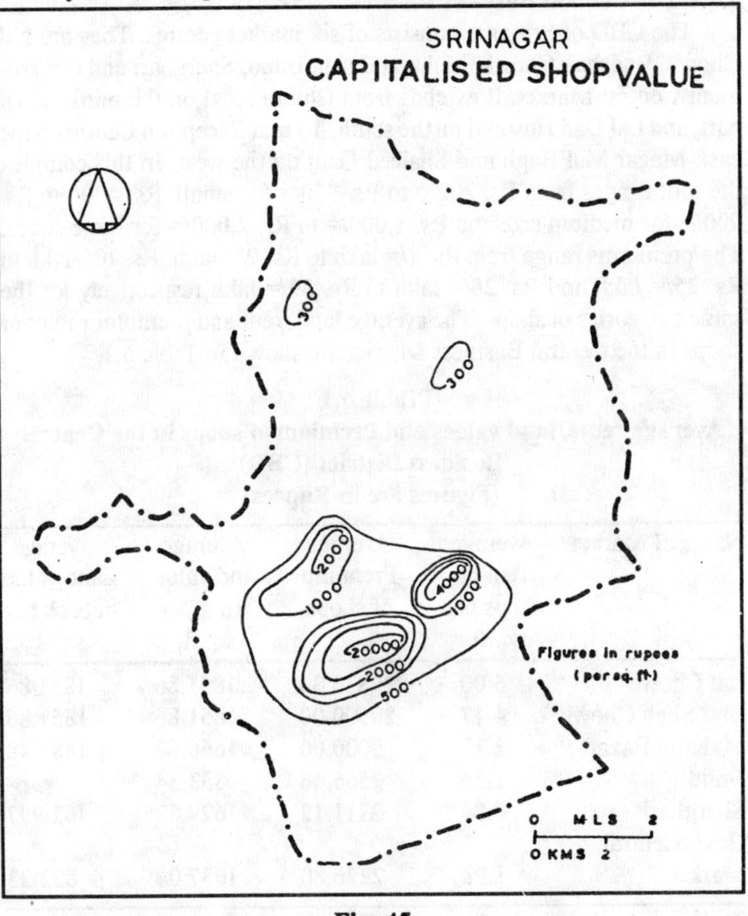

Fig. 45

talised value of rent. Five centres of increasing values emerge on the map which correspond with the five commercial zones of the Srinagar City. South-central Srinagar has the highest capitalised value of rent ranging from Rs. 1,000/= to about Rs. 20,000/=. In the west-central and east-central parts of the city the capitalised values of rent range from Rs. 1,000/= to Rs. 2,000/= and Rs. 2,000/= to Rs. 4.000/= respectively. The north-eastern and north-western parts of the city have lower capitalised values of rent. These two sections have capitalised value of rent of about Rs.300/= (Fig. 45).

6.5.1 The Central Business District

The CBD of Srinagar consists of six market centres. They are Lal Chowk, Budshah Chowk, Maharaj Bazar, Bund, Sherghari and Government Central Market. It extends from Chunti Koal on the north, Iqbal park and Lal Dad Hospital on the south, Tourist Reception Centre on the east, Magar Mal Bagh and Shaieed Ganj on the west. In this complex the rent ranges from Rs. 200/= to Rs. 350/= for small, Rs. 400/=to Rs. 900/= for medium size and Rs. 1,000/= to Rs. 2,000/= for large shops. The premiums range from Rs. 4/= lakh to Rs. 9/= lakh, Rs. 10/=lakh to Rs. 25/= lakh and Rs. 25/= lakh to Rs. 35/= lakh respectively for the same categories of shops. The average land, rent and premium values of shops in the Central Business District are shown in Table 6.1.

Table 6.1
Average rents, land values and Premium of shops in the Central Business District (CBD)
(Figures are in Rupees)

Name of Market	Average rent of shops per sq. ft.	Average Premium of shops	Average and value front per sq. ft.	Average Land value in back per sq. ft.
Lal Chowk	6.00	20833.34	1851.86	1851.86
Bud Shah Chowk	4.17	20500.00	1851.86	1851.86
Maharaj Bazar	2.17	9000.00	1666.67	1481.48
Bund	1.56	2566.66	333.34	-
Sherghari	0.84	3111.12	629.63	462.997
Govt. Central Market	1.98	2226.80	1037.04	822.23
Average	2.79	971.32	1228.40	1204.00

Source : Field Work.

The average rents range from Rs.0.84 per sq. ft. in Sherghari to Rs. 6.00 per sq. ft. in Lal Chowk. Sherghari is on the Old Secretariat Road and Lal Chowk is on the Residency Road. In Bud Shah Chowk occuring on the M.A. Road the average rent is Rs. 4.17 per sq. ft. Maharaj Bazar extending between River Jhelum on the east, Air Port Road on the west, Jahangir Chowk on the north and Iqbal Park on the south has average rent of Rs. 2.17 per sq. ft. It ranks third after Lal Chowk and Bud Shah Chowk. The Bund Market situated on the south of Lal Chowk on the right bank of River Jhelum and the Government Central Market, occuring on the right hand side of the Air Port Road near the Exhibition Ground have average rents of Rs..156 and Rs. 1.98 per sq. ft. respectively. The remaining five market centres of the Centreal Business District (CBD) have lower average rent than Lal Chowk. The Lal Chowk area of the CBD is the commercial heart of Srinagar and has the highest average rent.

All the retail nucleations of the CBD have the high rates of premium. They range from Rs. 2,226.80 per sq. ft. in the Government Central market to Rs. 20, 833.34 per sq. ft. in Lal Chowk. Bud Shah Chowk has Rs. 20,500/= per sq. ft., the second highest after Lal Chowk. The rate of premium in the Maharaj Bazar, Bund and Sherghari markets are Rs. 9,000/=, Rs. 2,566.66 and Rs. 3,111.12 per sq. ft. respectively. On the whole Lal Chowk has the highest average premium because of high competition here.

So far as land value is concerned Lal Chowk and Bud Shah Chowk top the list with average value of more than Rs. 1,85.86 per sq. ft. The average land values of Maharaj Bazar (Rs. 1,666.67), Bund (Rs. 333.34), Sheghari (Rs. 626.63) and Govt. Central Market (Rs. 1,037.04) vary greatly among themselves. The land values at the back are also the highest in Lal Chowk and Bud Shah Chowk Rs. 1,851.86 per sq. ft. each). Those in other market centres except Bund range from Rs. 462.97 to Rs. 1,48 per sq. ft. In the Bund market there is no land at the back of the buildings as the area is occupied by River Jhelum.

6.5.2 Large Market Complexes

The average land values, rents and premiums are relatively lower in the Large Market Complexes than the Central Business District of Srinagar. There are two large market complexes, namely Nawhatta-Zaina Kadal Complex, occurring in the north-central part of the city and Haba kadal-Fateh Kadal Complex which is situated in the Central part of Srinagar.

Nawhatta-Zaina Kadal occupies the first position in average rent and premium of shops while Haba Kadal-Fateh Kadal occupies the first position in average land values, both in front and at the back. Nawhatta-Zaina Kadal complex is actually the old commercial area of Srinagar. It is noted for jewellery, all kinds of utensils, cloth, tapestry and upholstry. Most of the shops here are of medium and small size. There are few large shops mainly in Maharajganj and Rajauri Kadal markets. The average rents in this complex range from Rs. 30.00 to Rs. 70.00 for small shops, from Rs. 100.00 to Rs. 250.00 for medium size shops and from Rs. 300.00 to Rs. 500.00 for the large shops. Premium is demanded in all the five market centres of this complex. The premium payable here is fairly high but it is lower than in the Central Business District (Lal Chowk). The average premiums range from Rs. 50,00/= to Rs. 70,000/= for small shops, Rs. 60,000/= to Rs. 90,000/= for medium size shops and Rs. 1 lakh to Rs. 4 lakh for large shops. The average rents, land values and premiums prevalent in Nawhatta-Zaina Kadal complex are shown in Table 6.2.

Table 6.2
Average rents, land values and Premiums of shops in Nawhatta-Zaina Kadal Complex
(Figures are in Rupees)

Name of Market	Average rent of shops per sq. ft.	Average Premium of shops	Average and value front per sq. ft.	Average Land value in back per sq. ft.
Maharaj Ganj	3.06	2277.68	148.14	111.12
Nawhatta	0.73	988.89	129.62	92.60
Bori Kadal	0.69	855.56	111.12	74.08
Zaina Kadal	0.42	511.12	92.60	37.60
Rajouri Kadal	2.61	700.00	37.04	18.52
Average	1.50	1066.5	103.70	66.78

Source : Field work.

The highest rate of rent (Rs. 3.06 per sq. ft) is prevalent in Maharaj Ganj, one of the five market centres of this complex. The same is true of the rate of Premium (Rs. 2,277.68 per sq. ft.) and land value (Rs. 148.14 per sq. ft. in the front and Rs.111.12 at the back). The Nawhatta proper and Bori Kadal markets occupy the second and third positions respectively in the matter of almost all of these rates. Rajauri Kadal which occupies the second position in the matter of rent (Rs.2.62 per sq. ft.) is the only exception.

The Haba Kadal-Fateh Kadal Complex extends from Gow Kadal on the south to Bori Kadal on the north and Karal Khud on the east to Chhota Bazar on the west. Interspersed by some medium and large ones this complex has mostly shops of small size. Most of the small shops are found from Khankhia Mulla to Basant Bagh. The roads and lanes of this area are narrow and ill-drained and have slums. The medium size and large shops are found in Chhota Bazar and Azad Markets.

The rents range from Rs. 70 to Rs. 100 for large, Rs. 50 to Rs. 65 for medium and Rs. 30 to Rs. 50 for small shops. The Premiums payable range from Rs. 90,000/= to Rs. 1 lakh for large, Rs. 60,000/= to Rs. 80,000/= for medium size and Rs. 20,000/= to Rs. 50,00/= for small shops. The rates of rent and premium are very low in Chhota Bazar than in the other market centres of this complex. Also the rates are very low in Chhota Bazar then in the other market centres of this complex. Also the rates prevalent in this commercial complex are far lower than in the Central Business District and Large Market Complex. Here the rates of rent and premium of shops are Rs. 0.40 & Rs 744.45 per sq. ft. respectively. This is because this commercial are is old. The narrow lanes and streets have compelled people to migrate to the northern, southern and western parts of the city. The average rent, land value and premium pervalent in the three market centres of Haba Kadal-Fathe Kadal Complex are given in Table 6.3.

The rates of rent, land values and permium are the highest in Haba Kadal-Fathe Kadal because this market adjoins the Central Business District of Srinagar. The average rent, premium, land value in front and land value at the back are Rs. 0.72, 1055.56, 148.15 and Rs. 111.12 per sq. ft. respectively. The other markets of this complex have lower rates. The average rent and premium of Azad Market and Chhota Bazar are almost the same. The average rent in the Azad market and Chhota Bazar are Rs. 0.42 and Rs. 0.40 per sq. ft. respectively. Similarly the average premium in the Azad Market and Chhota Bazar are Rs. 766.67 and Rs. 744.45 respectively. Chhota Bazar has the lowest land value in front (Rs. 92.60 per sq. ft.) and also at the back (Rs. 74.08 per sq. ft.). The land values in this complex are almost same as in the Nawhatta-Zaina Kadal complex but are lower than in the CBD because the two complexes except Rajouri Kadal belong to the old CBD of Srinagar.

Table 6.3
Average rents, land values and premium of shops in Habba-Kadal-Fathe Kadal Market Complex.
(Figures are in Rs.)

Name of Market	Average rent of shops per sq. ft.	Average Premium of shops per sq. ft	Average land value per sq. ft. in front	Average Land value per sq. ft. in back
Haba Kadal-Fateh Kadal	0.72	1055.56	148.15	111.12
Azad Market	0.42	766.67	129.63	92.60
Chhota Bazar	0.40	744.45	92.60	74.08
Average	0.51	855.56	123.46	92.60

Source : Field work.

6.5.3 Large Market Centres

There are three large market centres in Srinagar. They are Jawahar Nagar, Karan Nagar and Rainawari markets. Jawahar Nagar is newly developed and is situated in the southern part of Srinagar close to the Central Business District. Karan Nagar is about 5 kms. on the north-west of the CBD and Rainawari is situated in the north-western part on the Dargah road.

The average land value and premium in the Large Market Centres are relatively lower than in the large market complexes. However, the average rent is higher here than in the large market complexes. At the same time all rates here are higher than in the mdeium and local market centres. The rates of rent range from Rs. 50 to Rs. 70 for small, Rs. 100 to Rs. 250 for medium and Rs. 300 to 500 for large shops. Premium is prevalent only in two of the market centres namely Jawahar Nagar and Karan Nagar. Premium is not demanded in Rainawari. The rates of premium range from Rs. 20,000 to 30,000 for small and medium and Rs. 1 lakh to 2 lakh for large shops. The average rent, premium and land values prevalent in the Large Market Centre are given in table 6.4.

With Rs. 2.50 per sq. ft. the rate of rent is the highest in Jawahar Nagar. It is followed by Karan Nagar and Rainawari with Rs. 1.62 and

Rs. 0.85 per sq. ft. respectively. The average rent and premium are higher in the former two market centres as they are newly developed. Rainawari has lower rates of rent and premium because it is an old market. The average premium is higher in Jawahar Nagar (Rs. 933.34 per sq. ft.), but it is extremely low in Karan Nagar (Rs. 20per sq. ft.).

Table 6.4
Average rents, land values and premium of shops in Large Market Centres
(Figures are in Rupees)

Name of the Market	Average rent per sq. ft.	Average premium per sq.ft.	Average Land value per sq. ft. in front.	Average Land value per sq. ft. in Back
Jawahar Nagar	2.50	933.34	92.26	74.08
Karan Nagar	1.62	20.00	74.08	38.04
Rainawari	0.85	-	55.56	36.04
Average	1.66	476.67	74.08	49.38

Source : Field work.

The average land values in front range between Rs. 55.56 per sq. ft. at Rainawari to Rs. 92.60 per sq. ft. at Jawahar Nagar while in Karan Nagar it is Rs. 74.08 per sq. ft. The land values at the back of the roads is higher in Jawahar Nagar. It is Rs. 74.08 per sq. ft. It is Rs. 38.04 and Rs. 36.04 per sq. ft. respectively in Karan Nagar and Rainawari.

6.5.4 Medium Market Centres

There are sixteen market centre in Srinagar. Of these, four namely, Batmaloo, Barbar Shah, Rambagh and Dalgate are close to the CBD. Three of them namely, Hawal, Safa Kadal and Nawa Kadal are in the north-central part of the city. One Qamarwari is in its western part and Hazratbal and Nagin-Saida Kadal are in its northern part on the Ghulam Mohd. Ashahi Road. Two nucleations-Natiipura and Chhanapura are in the southern part of the city and another two-Pantha Chowk and Batwara-Sonawar are on the south-east of the Central Business District on the National Highway No. 1A. Khyam Chowk and Khanyar Chowk are in the central and north-central parts of Srinagar. The average rent, premium and land values of the medium market centres are given in Table 6.5.

Table 6.5
Average rents, land values and permium of shops in Medium Market Centres
(Figures are in Rupees)

Name of the Markets	Average rent of shops per sq. ft.	Average Premium of shops	Average and value front per sq. ft.	Average Land value in back per sq. ft.
Khyam Chowk	4.95	491.67	175.00	83.33
Nawa Kadai	3.06	13.15	18.52	11.12
Batmaloo	2.20	1344.45	175.08	55.56
Barbar Shah	2.09	246.67	74.08	55.56
Qamarwari	1.79	62.12	37.04	18.52
Pantha Chowk	1.62	-	18.52	15.75
Dalgate	1.14	1055.55	92.60	74.08
Rambagh	1.16	158.34	67.04	57.52
Khanyar Chowk	1.14	511.12	74.08	18.52
Hawal	1.10	66.67	37.04	37.08
Hazratbal	0.88	208.34	74.08	18.52
Sonawar-Batwara	0.85	51.12	74.08	37.04
Saidakadal-Nagin	0.79	161.12	37.03	18.52
Nattipura	0.75	-	55.56	37.04
Chhanapura	0.57	-	55.56	37.08
Safa kadal	0.52	-	55.56	37.04
Average	1.52	354.19	69.43	38.14

Source : Field Work.

The land values prevailing in these markets are mostly low ranging from Rs. 18.52 per sq. ft.in Pantha Chowk to Rs. 175.08 per sq. ft. in Batmaloo. Batmaloo and Khayan Chowk markets have high land values. The Dalgate market has Rs. 92.60 per sq. ft. in front of road. This is because these are close to the Central Business District and occur on the main roads of Srinagar.

Barbar Shah, Khanyar Chowk, Hazratbal and Sonawar-Batwara markets have comparatively higher average land values in front of the raods (Rs. 74.08 sq. ft. each). The Nattipura, Chhanapura and Safa Kadal markets having land values of Rs. 55.56 per sq. ft. each. The land values in front range from Rs. 37.03 in the Qamarwari, Hawal, Saida Kadal markets to Rs. 18.52 per sq. ft. in the Nawa Kadal and Pantha Chowk markets.

The land values at the back of the roads is comparatively low ranging from Rs. 11.12 in Nawa Kadal to Rs. 83.33 per sq. ft. in Khayam Chowk.

The system of demanding premium is prevalent in the market centres of this category except in the Pantha Chowk, Nattipura, Chhanapura and Safa kadal markets as those markets are away from the city centres. Higher premiums are demanded in the Batmaloo and Dalgate Markets. These have premiums of Rs. 1344.45 and Rs. 1055.55 per sq. ft. respectively. Khayam Chowk (Rs. 491.67 per sq. ft.) and Khanyar Chowk (Rs. 511.12 per sq. ft.) have also higher rates of premium. Nawa Kadal with Rs. 13.15 per sq. ft. has the lowest rate of premium.

The rate of rents of shops range from Rs. 4.95 to Rs.0.52 per sq. in the medium market centres. Khayam Chowk ranks first and is followed by the Nawa Kadal (Rs. 3.60), Batmaloo (Rs. 2.20) and Barbar Shah (Rs. 2.09) markets. All other markets of this group have rates below Rs. 2.00 per sq. ft. The Hazratbal, Sonawar-Batwara, Saida Kadal-Nagin, Nattipura, Chhanapura and Safa Kadal markets have the lowest rates of rent of shops (below Rs. one per sq. ft.).

The medium order markets have lower land values, rents and premiums than the large market centre, but have higher rates of all than the local markets. The average rent, premium land value in front and at the back in the medium market centres as a whole are Rs. 1.54, 364.19 69.43 and 38.14 per sq. ft. respectively.

6.5.5 Local Market Places

Five retail nucleations have been put in the category of local market places. They are the Soura, Lal bazar, Zadibal, Nowshera and Sadrabal markets. All of them are in the northern part of the City.

The average land values and premiums in the local market places are lower than in the medium market centres. The rates of rent range from Rs. 60 to Rs. 200 for small shops. Premium is not in demand except in the Soura and Nowshera markets, where the rates of premium are Rs. 8,000 and Rs.5,000 per sq. ft. respectively. The average rent. premium and land values prevalent in the local market places are shown in Table 6.6

Table 6.6
Average rents, land values and premium of shops in . Local market places
(Figures are in Rupees)

Name of the Markets	Average rent of shops per sq. it.	Average premium of shops per sq. ft.	Average Land vlaue per sq. ft. in front	Average value per sq. if. in back
Soura	2.94	61.11	74.08	18.52
Lal Bazar	1.89	-	55.56	18.52
Zaidibal	1.45	-	37.04	18.52
Nowshera	1.06	5.56	37.04	18.52
Sadrabal	0.82	-	18.51	12.35
Average	1.63	33.38	44.45	17.28

Source: Field work.

The Soura market situated near the All India Institute of Medical Sciences ranks first in all categories of land values. The average rent and premium of shops and land values in front and at the back of the roads in Soura market are Rs. 2.94, Rs. 61.11, Rs. 74.08 and Rs. 18.58 respectively. These are the highest of all the local market places.

The rates of rent in Zadibal, Nowshera and Sadrabal are Rs. 1.45, Rs. 1.06 and Rs. 0.82 respectively. Premium is demanded only in the Soura and Nawshera markets. Nowshera has the lowest rate of premium (Rs. 5.56 per sq. ft.). The next higher land value in front, after Soura market is prevalent in Lal bazar (Rs. 79.08). It is followed by Zaidibal and Nawshera markets with Rs. 37.04 per sq. ft. each. The Sadarbal market has the lowest land value of Rs. 18.51 per sq. ft. Land values of the back of the roads are almost equal in all the markets of this group. It is (Rs. 18.52 per sq. ft.) except in the Sadarbal market which has a slightly lower land value (in back) of Rs. 12.35 per sq. ft.

6.5.6 Specialised Market Centres

Four markets have been put in the category of specialised markets. These are the Boulevard, Nishat, Shalimar and Parimpura-Fruit Mandi. These markets are entirely different. They are noted for their specialised functions mostly serving the tourists. The Parimpura-Fruit Mandi is an exception and is important for fruits and vegetables. The land values range from Rs. 200 to Rs. 300 for small shops, Rs. 350 to Rs. 450 for medium size shops and Rs. 400 to Rs. 600 for large shops. The premium is in demand only in the Boulevard market where the rates are Rs. 4 lakh for small shops, Rs. 5 lakh for medium size shops and Rs. 5.5 lakh for large shops. The land values vary between Rs. 50,000 to Rs. 5.5 lakh per kanal. This high value is due to its advantageous location. The average rent, premium and land values of the specialised markets are shown in Table 6.7.

Table 6.7
Average rents, land values and premium of shops in Specialised Market Centres
(Figures are in Rupees)

Name of Market	Average rent of shops per sq. ft.	Average Premium shops sq.ft.	Average land value per sq. ft. in front.	Average Land value per sq. ft. in back.
Boulevard	5.89	4055.56	111.12	74.08
Nishat	2.00	-	37.04	16.67
Shalimar	2.28	-	20.07	3.09
Parimpura-Fruit Mandi	3.78	-	18.52	14.82
Average	3.49	4033.56	46.69	27.16

Source : Field work.

The rates of rent and premium are very high in the specialised market centres. There is predominance of small and large shops in these markets, but medium size shops are also found here. Large shops are found in the Boulevard and medium size shops are found in the Parimpura Fruit Mandi. The average rent and premium are the highest here. They are Rs. 5.89 and Rs. 4,055.56 per sq. ft. respectively in the Boulevard. The rates of rent in Nishat, Shalimar and Parimpura are Rs. 2.00, Rs. 2.28 and Rs. 3.78 respectively. The land values are the highest in the Boulevard. They are Rs. 111.12 per sq/ ft. in front and Rs. 74.08 per sq. ft. at the back of the roads. The land valueds in Nishat and Shalimar are Rs. 37.04 and Rs. 20.07 per sq. ft. respectively in front and Rs. 16.67 and Rs. 3.09 per sq. ft. at back of the roads. The Parimpura Fruit Mandi has a land value of Rs. 18.52 in front and Rs. 14.82 per sq. ft. at back. It is situated away from the Central Business District because of which the land values are very low.

6.6 Summary

The preceeding discussion reveals that the rents, land values and premiums tend to increase with the rising hierarchical position of the markets. The average rents, premiums and land values of the markets of differeent hierarchical orders are shown in Table 6.8.

Table 6.8
Average rent, Land values and premium of shops in Market Centres of Srinagar
(Figures are in Rupees)

Name of Markets Centres.	Average rent of shops per sq. ft.	Average premium of shop per sq. ft.	Average land value in front per sq.ft.	Average Land value in back per sq. ft.
CBD	2.79	971.32	1228.40	1294.00
L.M. Complexes	1.05	961.10	113.58	79.69
Large Market Centre	1.66	476.67	74.08	49.38
Medium Market Centres	1.54	364.19	69.43	38.14
Local Market Centres	1.63	33.38	44.45	17.28
Specialised Market	3.49	4033.56	46.69	27.16

Source : Field work

Barring the specialised markets the highest average rent (Rs. 2.79 per sq. ft.), Premium (Rs. 971.32 per sq. ft.) and land value (Rs. 1,228.40 per sq. ft.) are found in the Central Business District. It is followed by large market complexes in the matter of premium and land values, but by large market centre in the matter of rents (Rs. 1.66 per sq. ft.). The local market centres have average rent of Rs. 1.63 per sq. ft. and the medium market centres have Rs. 1.54 per sq. ft. because these markets are of developing nature.

The average rent and premium in the specialised markets are higher than in the CBD, because most of the specialised markets are at places of tourist interest where the rents and premiums are bound to be very high.

So far as land values in front and at the back of the roads are concerned the specialised markets have rates slightly higher than the local market centres which have the lowest (Fig. 46).

It is clear from table 6.8 that all categories of land value generally increase with the rising of the level of the market centre in the hierarchy. Kendall's method was used for ranking the land values, rents and premiums prevailing in the six different of markets orders separately (Table 6.9). Thus each category of markets has four ranks one each in respect of rent, premium, land value in front and that at the back of the roads. The

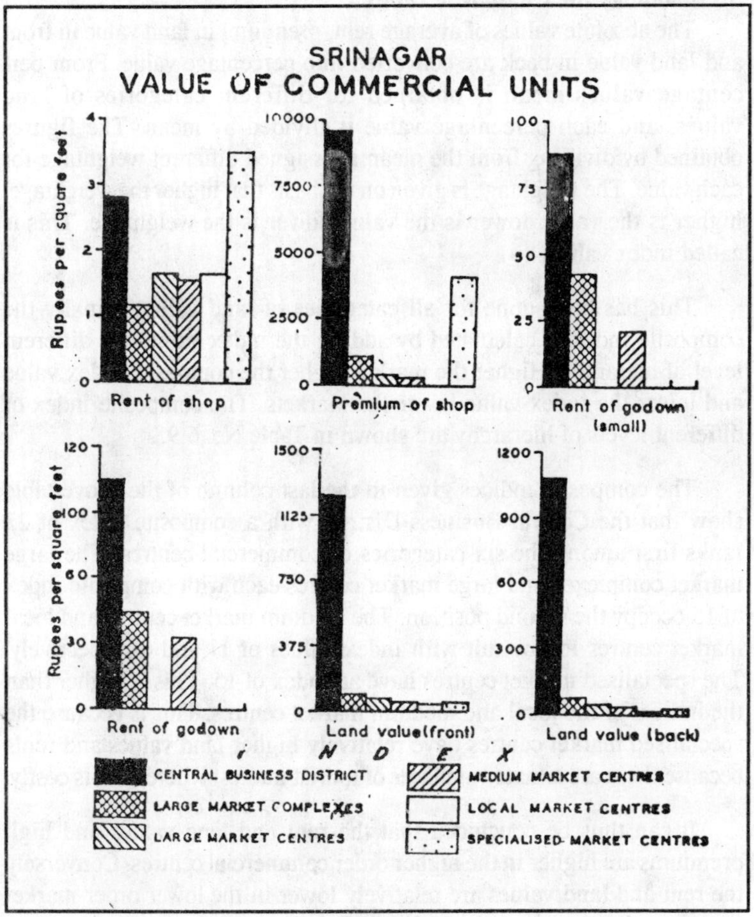

Fig. 46

sum of the four ranks of a category gives its composite score. The composite index is given by the formula :

$$I_j = \sum_{i=1}^{n} R_{ij}$$

Where Ij is the composite index of different values. n the number of selected values and Rij is the rank of ith value in the jth area.

Methodology for Composite Index

The absolute values of average rent, premium, in land value in front and land value in back are converted into percentage value. From percentage values mean is obtained for different categories of land values, and each percentage value is divided by mean. The figures obtained by dividing from the mean is assigned different weightage for each value. The weightage is given on the basis that higher the weightage, higher is the value, lower is the value, lower is the weightage. This is called index values.

This has been done for all categories of land values. Finally the composite index is calculated by adding the index values of different level of hierarchy. Higher the market higher the composite index value and lower the index value lower the markets. The composite index of different levels of hierarchy are shown in Table No. 6.9.

The composite indices given in the last column of the above table show that the Central Business District with a composite index of 23 ranks first among the six categories of commercial centres. The large market complexes and large market centres each with composite index of 15 occupy the second position. The medium market centres and local market centres follow suit with index values of 11 and 6 respectively. The specialised market centres have an index of 15. This is higher than the indices of the local and medium market centres. This is because the specialised market centres have relatively higher land values and rents because these are situated at places of tourist interest where land is costly.

It can thus be concluded that the rent and land values and high premiums are higher in the higher order commercial centres. Conversely the rent and land values are relatively lower in the lower order market centres and premiums are not demanded (Fig. 46).

Table 6.9
Composite Index of Different Values of Commercial Centres of Srinagar
(Figures are in Rupees)

Level of Commer-cial centres	Average rent of shop per sq. ft.	Average Premium of shop per sq. ft.	Average land value per sq. ft. in front	Average land value per sq. ft. in back.	Composite Index.
C.B.D.	5	6	6	6	23
Large Market Complexes	1	4	5	5	15
Large Market Centres	4	3	4	4	15
Medium Market Centres	2	2	3	3	11
Local Market Centres	3	1	1	1	6
Specialised Market centres	6	5	2	2	15

Source : Field work.

Secondly, there is a marked decrease in the rates of rent and land values with the increase in the distance of commercial centres from the Central Business District.

So far as the land values at the back of the roads (commercial premises) are concerned they also increase with the rising of the order of the markets. The maximum average land values are observed in the Central Business District and the minimum in the local market places.

Conclusion

7.1 General Summary

The study of the commercial activities of the intra-urban tracts constitutes a new speciality within the broad field of Geography. It is seen that the hierarchy of the market centres which emerge within the urban places are similar to the central places. The market centres can be calssified in basically the same way as the central places. The smaller, lower order markets, deal mianly in convenience goods, while the higher order markets, sell a wide range of goods and have larger stock.

Most works in this Specilaity have been done by western geographers including Applebaum, Proudfoot, Ratcliff, Berry, Garrison, Garner, Simons etc. Most Indian geographers have undertaken regional studies and dealt mainly with the market towns rather than the intra-city market places. However, the pioneering work done by Datta, Alam and Sami deserve mention.

The present study is based on intensive field work because relevant data relating to the city of Srinagar were not available either in published or unpublished form. Srinagar is one of the topmost tourist centres of the world and is the chief town and administrative headquarter of the Jammu and Kashmir State of India. It is also a religious and commercial centre. It extends between 34°0', and 34°14' north latitudes and 74°43' and 74°52' east longitudes. It is situated at the foot of Zabarman and Takh-te-Sulaiman mountain on both banks of river Jhelum and around the Dal lake. It has thus a picturesque and attractive location. The outer boundary of Srinagar is 109.43 Kilometers long. The city has an area of about 157 square kilometers. This includes areas under the cantonment, hill forest and water bodies. The location of Srinagar has favoured its economic and commercial development. It is situated at the most appropriate distances from almost all the commercial and marketing centres of the valley. The two other large towns and commercial centres of the valley-Anantnag and Baramulla-are only thirty Kilometers away from it towards the south-east and north-west repectively. River Jhelum has acted and continues to act as an important route of trade and passenger movement. Sringar was and still is the point of convergence of many transport routes.

The emergence of Srinagar as an important commercial and trading centre is not a recent phenomenon. The origin and evolution of the commercial centres within the city are related to its gradual growth. Ancient Srinagar had political and cultural contacts with most parts of Asia including Tibet and China. It grew as a commercial centre within the last 16th centuries. The commercial activities expanded with the growth of the population and the gradual expansion of the city settlement area. At the beginning of the present century, Zaina Kadal, Maharajganj, Haba-kadal, Fathe-Kadal, and Rainawari were the main commercial areas of old Srinagar where confectioners; cloth, shawl, and carpet dealers, coppersmiths, silversmiths, goldsmiths and general merchandise storekeepers had their business establishments along the roads and streets. The city expanded towards the south of city-settlement area during first quarter of the present century. The newly developed Lal Chowk area is purely commercial in character. It also has some offices, educational institutions, parks, clubs etc. The city then expanded rapidly towards the south, north and west. Some expansions have commercial establishments while others are purely residential.

The first census count of the population of Srinagar was taken in 1891. The total population of the city then was 1,18.960. It rose to 6,21, 621 by the year 1981. The population of the city grew steadily up to 1951. It started to grow rapidly since 1961 when the city had a population of + 16.40% which rose by +45.03% and +46.08% by 1971 and settlement area according to the Census of 1981 is 16 persons per acre. The highest density (194.86 persons per acre) is found in the old commercial area (ward No. 8). The density decreases sharply away from it. The Central Business District has a population density of 24.69 persons per acre.

Of the total land area of the city of Srinagar 43.86% is under residential use, 37.43% is under agriculture, forest, hills and open land, 16.84 is under water bodies and 1.87% is under commercial use.

The commercial establishments are found along all the important roads and streets. The important commercial belts lie along the Residency, Maulana Azad, Airport and old Hospital Roads and the Harisingh High Street in the south-central part of the city.

Field investigation reveals that a number of new functions have come up during the immediate past decades. They include automobile, radio, television and other electronic goods, machine shops and dry cleaning establishments. There are in all 12022 commercial units, which during the field work were put into 350 functional groups. The number of groups had to be reduced to 53 for the sake of convenience of analysis and given National Industrial Classification code numbers. These occur in 42 nucleations. The outer boundaries of these nucleations have been determined on the basis of the compactness of the shops, break in their continuity, their functional specialisation and intensity of commercial land use.

The 42 markets in which the commercial establishment occur, have been ranked on the basis of the number and types of establishments and their functional specialisation. Kendal's method of ranking has been used for determining the composite indices. Higher the composite index the higher the rank of the market. Lal Chowk emerges as the market with the highest rank. It is followed by Budshah Chowk and Maharaj Bazar. These markets occur in the south-central part of Srinagar. A number of markets occur in contiguous belts or nucleations and form commerical complexes. Others are separate from each other and form independent market centres of different hierarchical orders. Lal Chowk includes six retail nucleations, while the Nowhatta-Zaina Kadal and Haba Kadal-Fateh Kadal complexes include five and three retail nucleations respectively.

If the independ market centres which forms part of larger market are left out the number of market centres is reduced to thirtyone. They have been grouped into six hierarchical orders with the help of a scatter diagram. These are the Central Business District, Large Market Complexes, Large Market Centres, Medium Market Centres, Local Market Places and Specialised Market Centres. The Lal Chowk complex emerges as the Central Business District of Srinagar. Nowhatta-Zaina Kadal and Haba Kadal-Fateh Kadal complexes emerge as Large Market complexes. Three market centres come in the category of Large Market Places and four as specialised Market Centres. The 53 functions identified in Srinagar have been ranked with the help of Kendal's method of ranking into five hierarchical orders. The functional character of each market unit was examined and the core and threshold functions at each level of hierarchy identified. It is found that there are thirty three functions in the local market places. Seven of them are core function dealing in lower order goods and services and 6 are threshold function. There are 51 functions in the Medium Market Centres. Thirteen of them are core functions dealing in convenience goods and fourteen are threshold functions. Of a total of 48 the large market centres have 14 core functions dealing in shopping goods and 9 threshold function. There are fifty functions in the large market complexes. Fifteen of them are core and 8 are threshold functions. It is difficult to distinguish between the core and threshold functions in the large market centres. The Central Business District has 53 functions, Twenty seven of them are core function. All of them are higher order functions which constitute threshold functions at the lower level of hierarchy.

The study of the materials of which the buildings housing the shops of the market centres of the different hierarchical orders, the other charactersitics of the shops and the infrastructural facilities available in them reveal interesting facts. The majority of the shops of the C.B.D. and Large Market Complexes are housed in pucca and multistoreyed buildings. Most of them area of large size and have wide frontages. They have electric and telephone connections, and also seating arrangement for the customers. The shops are run generally by more hands. They have attractive show cases and highest signboards. The higher order market centres have more shops with collapsible shutters and attractive show cases.

The land value differs from one part of Srinagar to another depending upon the location, and approachability of the places. The land values are mostly higher in the commercial areas, especially in the higher order commercial centres. The rents are also high in the higher order of retail nucleations.

There is market differene between the value of commercial land in road front than that at their back. Even in the same locality the value of the land which is used for constructing buildings for housing the shops has higher value than that which is used for constructing godowns or residences. This is true of all parts of Srinagar except in the Central Business District (Lal Chowk) where the land value in front and at the back of roads are more or less equal.

The practice of charging premium for commercial space is prevalent all over the city especially in the higher order markets. The amount of premium increases with the rising of the market centres in the hierarchy.

7.2 Conclusion

Having a picturesque and tantalising situation, a pleasant climate except occasionally and serviceable people the city of Srinagar is more a tourist than a religious and commercial centre. All the same its location the heart of the Kashmir Valley, the presence of river Jhelum and the Dal lake, the convergence of many a transport arteries, its cultural and commercial relation with near and far Asian countries, its being one of the topmost tourist centres of the world and above all its rapidly increasing population and demand for goods and services have given boost to its commercial activities. Commercial activities started in the old quarters of Zaina Kadal, Maharajganj, Haba Kadal etc. The expansion of the city settlement area and the coming up of the new residential colonies with the growth of population brought about expansion of the commercial areas. Commercial establishments sprang up along all major roads, streets, lanes and bylanes. With changing times modern establishment dealing in automobiles, radio sets, televisions, other electronic goods, electrical appliances, machine tools etc. were added to the traditional ones.

Shops discharging 350 types of functions identified during field work were reduced to 53 for the sake of convenience of analysis. These shops occur in 42 market centres. As some of the markets form parts of larger market complexes the number of market centres also decreased to 31. The market centres were ranked with the help of scatter diagram. It is seen that five distinct hierarchical orders emerged which conforms the assertation that the intra city market centres are akin to the central places, which also are capable of being marked into different orders. The functions were also ranked with the help of Kendle's method of ranking. The functions were further divided into core and threshold categories. However, it is not easy to say which where are core or threshold functions. Some functions which are in the core category in the higher order market centres are in the threshold category in the lower order market centres and vice versa.

The quality of the market centres, their functional specialisation and distribution within the intra-urban tract were then studied in detail. It is seen that the higher order market centres confine themselves in the heart of the city in its south; central and north-central parts especially in the Central Business District. The concentration is on account of the locational advantage and approachability.

The number of commercial establishments, the quality of shops and the intensity of commercial land use go on decreasing from the city centre towards the peripheral zone; the medium order market centres occur around the higher order market centres, but the lower order market centres are either in the peripheral zone or in the newly settled residential colonies.

The higher order functions are more frequent in the higher order market centres. Their number goes on decreasing with the going down of the market centres in the order of hierachy.

The buildings housing the shops discharging higher order functions are of good qualtiy, the look of the shops is good, and the infrastructural facilities available in them are mostly of higher order. The reverse is true to some extent of the market centres of the lower order.

Functional complexity increases with ascent of the market centres in the ladder of hierarchy. The higher order market centres sell a wide range of goods and have adequate stock. In contrast the lower order market centres deal mainly in convenience goods, the quality of goods sold is relatively poor and their stock is limited.

The land values rents and premiums are markedly higher in the higher order market centres especially in front of the roads than at their backs. These are not true of the market centres of the lower order. The lands which have godowns and residential houses have still lower land values, rents and premiums.

7.3 Suggested Plan for Future Development

The authors are conscious of the fact that market geography is a vast subject. A modest attempt has been made in this work to answer some of the question posed by the complex relationship which exist between the nature and functions of the market centres and the urban landscape of Srinagar. Many questions pertaining to the relationship still remain unanswered which will be taken care of by the future research worker.

There is limited scope for the expansion of the city settlement area of the city of Srinagar. River Jhelum and the Dal lake occupy considerable intra-urban space. Mountains restrict the expansion of the city settlement area on the northeast, east and southeast while upper Sindh and Anchar lake do so on the north-west where the land is lowlying and marshy.

The market centres of the city of Srinagar are confined to its few parts creating thereby the problems of space, congestion and crowding of shops, compulsory flocking of the customers and traffic jams and disorders.

As Lal Chowk is hit hardest by these disabilities it is suggested that the Kashmir Drivers' and State Transport bus stands and some educational institutions such as the Biscoe Tyndale and Mallinson Girl's School should be relocated in suitable places and the land vacated by them should be used for constructing modern shopping centres and super market. These step will enhance rather than solving the problem of flocking of the customers and traffic jams and disorders.

At least no new shops should be allowed to be put up in the already congested market centres. At best the existing commercial establishment should be allowed to undergo renewal without contravening the urban regulations. Setting apart of commercial space should be made obligatory in the newly coming up residential colonies in the northern, southwestern and southern parts of the city and neighbourhood market centres should be allowed to emerge.

A number of satellite townships should be allowed to grow in the area included in Greater Srinagar. For example the land up to Pandach on the north, Zaina Kot on the west and Pampore and Khannabal on the south may be utilised for the purpose.

Geographical inertia has played its part for more than half a century and no half hearted step can solved the problems created by it. No government and no municiapl or town planning authority can take drastic step. The present unsatisfactory condition will, very likely, continue for all times to come.

Bibliography

Books

1. Alam, S.M. : Hyderabad and Secunderabad: A study in urban Geography; Allied Publishers Private Ltd. Osmania University Press, Hyderabad, 1985.

2. Alam, S.M. & Khan, W : Metropolitan Hyderabad and Secunderabad: A strategy for development; Asia Publishing House, Osmania University Press, Hyderabad, 1972.

3. Adlerson, Ulroe & Halbert, M.H. : Men, Motives and markets; Prentice Hall of India Pvt. Ltd. New Delhi - 110001, 1968.

4. Allami, Abul Fazal, : The Ain-i-Akbari; Munshilal Manchourlal Publishers Pvt. Ltd. New-Delhi.

5. Annual Administrative report of Municipal Committee, town area and vistors Bureau Deptt., J & K, 1940.

6. Applebaum, W & Schapken : Attas of Business Centres; Chincinnati, Hamilton & County. 1955.

7. Balkrishna, k. : Commercial Relations between India and England (1601-1757) London, 1924.

8. Bamzai, P. N. K. : A History of Kashmir; Metropolitan Publishers Pvt. Ltd. New-Delhi 1962.

9. Belshaw, C.S. : Traditional Exchange and Modern Markets; Englewood cliff, Prentice Hall, 1965.

10. Berry, B.J.L. : Geography of Market Centres and Retail Distribution; Prentice Hall, INC Englewood cliff N.J. 1967.

11. Berry, B.J.L. : The Commercial Structure of American Cities; A Revies, Chicago, 1962.

12. Berry, B.J.L. : Commercial Structure and Commercial Blight; Re-

tail pattern and process in the city of chicago, University of chicago, Deptt. of Geography, Research paper, 85. 1963.

13. Berry, B.J.L. & Garrison, W.L. : studies of Highway Development and Geographical Change; University of Washington Press, Washington, 1956.

14. Berry, B.J.L. & Harton, F.E. : Geographic Perspectives on Urban Systems, Prentice Hall, INC, Englewood cliff, New Jersey, 1970.

15. Berry, B.J.L. & pred, A : Central Place Studies, A Bibliography of theory and application, Regional Science Research Institute, series No. I, 1961, Spplimented through 1964, by H.G. Barnum, R. Kasperson, and S. Kuichi, 1965.

16. Bhardwaj, R.K. : Urban Development in India, National Publishing House, Delhi, 1974.

17. Borchert, J.R & Adams, R.B. : The Trade Centres and Trade Areas of the Upper Midwest, Upper Midwest Economic Study Urban Report 3, Minneapolis: University of Minnesota Press, 1963.

18. Burn, W : British Shopping Centres, Leonard Hill (book) Ltd. London, IL959.

19. Canoyer, H.G. : Selecting a Store Location (U.S. Deptt. of Commerce, Economic series No. 56), Govt. Printing office, Washington, 1946.

20. Carter, Harold, : The Study of Urban Geography, IIIrd section Edward Arnold Publiser Pvt. Ltd. London London 1982;

21. Census of India, : Series Jammu and Kashmir 1881 and 1981.

22. Chatterjee, S.P. : Fifty Years of Science in India (Geography) Indian Science Congress Association, Calcutta, 1964.

23. Chatterjee, S.P. : Progress of Geography in India, (1964-1968), Indian science Congress Association, Calcutta, 1968.

24. Christaller, W : Central Place in Southern Germany (Translated by Baskin, C.W.), Englewood cliffs, New Jersey, 1966.

25. Cox, J.L. and Son : Appendix to the Report from the Selection Committee of House of Common on the Affairs of East India Company 16th August 1832, London, 1834.

26. Daulson, John A : Retail Geography; John Willey and Sons INC. New-York 1980.

27. Dickinson, R.E. : The City Region in Western Europe, Rautladge and Kegan Paul Ltd., London 1967.

28. Dickinson, R.E. : The City Region in Western Europe, Rautladge and Kegan Paul Ltd., London 1967.

29. Elias, N. : Tarikhi Rishidi; Ed. Ross, London, (1923).

30. Foster, W. : The English Factory in India. 1622-69, Oxford, 1908.

31. Gallison, A.B. & Fisner, S : The Urban Pattern, Indian Edition, Affiliated East-West Press Pvt. Ltd., New Delhi 1956.

32. Galpin, C.J. : The Social Anatomy of on Agricultural Community. University of Wisconsin, Agricultural Experiment Station Research, Bulletin No. 34. XXX 1915.

33. Garnier, B.J. : Urban Geography; Longmanz, Green and Co. Ltd, London, 1967.

34. Garnier, B.J. : Internal Structure of Retail Nucleations, North western University studies in Geography, Evanston, 1966.

35. Garnier, J.B. : Geography of Marketing; Longman INC. group New-York 1979.

36. Gazetter of Kashmir and Ladakh, Vivek Publishing House, Delhi-7, 1974.

37. Gibbs, J.P. : Urban Research Methods, Indian edition, Affiliated East-West Press Pvt. Ltd.; New Delhi, 1966.

38. Goldberg, M. & Chinloy, Peter : Urban Land Economics; John Willey and Sons, New York 1984.

39. Goodaman, R. : Teach Yourself Statistics, English Language Book Society, London, 1965.

40. Haggett, P. : Locational Analysis in Human Geography, Edward Arnold Publishers Ltd. London, 1965.

41. Haig, R.M. : Major Economic Factors in Metropolitan Growth and Arrangement, Regional Survey of New-York and its Environs (New-York Regional Plan of New-York and its Environs, 1927).

42. Hall, M & Knapp, J and Winsten, C. : Distribution in Great Britain and North America, London, 1961.

43. Hamilton, C.J. : The Trade Relation Between England and India, (1600-1896) Calcutta, 1919.

44. Hayes, C.R. and Schull, N.W. : Greensbore Retail Core Analysis, Greenbore, N.C., 1965.

45. Herbert, D.T. and Johnston, R.J. : Geography and Urban Environment; Johan Wiley and sons, New-York, 1980.

46. Hussnain F.M. : Heritage of Kashmir; Gulshan Publishers, Srinagar (J & K), 1980.

47. James, H. R.Johnes : Urban Geography, pergamom, London, 1966.

48. Janki V.A. : Functional Classification of Towns in Gujarat, Geography Research Paper Series, No.2 University Publication Sale Unit, Baroda, 1966.

49. Johnson, J.H. : Urban Geography, second edition; Robet Maxwell, M.C. New York, 1977.

50. Jones, E. : Towns and Cities; Oxford University Press, London, 1966.

51. Jones, R. : Retail facilities in the city of Edinburgh, Edinburgh, 1963.

52. Kenney, J.F. and Keeping, E.S. : Mathematics of Statistics, Indian Edition, New Delhi, 1954.

53. Khan, Mohd Ishaqe : A History of Srinagar (1846-1947), A study in socio-cultural change; Amir Publishers Srinagar, (J & K), 1978.

54. Khan, W : Markets Settlements in the Hyderabad Metropolitan Research Project, Technical Bulletion, No. 5, 1967.

55. King, L.J. : Statistical Analysis in Geography, prentice Hall Inc. Englwood cliffs New Jersey, 1969.

56. Konard, E. & Erickson R. (Ed.) : Marketing Research; D.B. Taraporovalas Sons and Co., Pvt. Ltd., Bombay, 1971.

57. Koul, G.L. : Kashmir now and than;

58. Koul, P.A. : Report on Srinagar Municipal Administration J & K,

1920-1921.

59. Kornhauser, David : Japan : Geograhical background to urban Industrial Development; Longman group Ltd., Longman House, U.K. 1982.

60. Lawrence, W.R. : Provincial Gazetter of Kashmir; Rima Publishing House, E.R. 10, Inderpuri, New Delhi, 1985.

61. Lemis, Peter; : Maps and Statistics, Library Congress Cataloging London, 1977.

62. Lovy, H. : The Shops of Britain, London, 1948.

63. Losch, A : The Economics of Location, (Translated by Woglom, W.H. and Stopler, W.F) New Haven, 1954.

64. Mahmood Aslam : Statistical Methods in Geographical Studies; Rajesh Publications, New Delhi (India) 1977.

65. Mandal, R.B. : Statistics for Geographers and Social scientists, Concept Publishing Company New-Delhi-19.80.

66. Master Plan of Srinagar City; Town and Country Planning Deptt., Govt. of J & K, Srinagar, 1970.

67. Mayer, H.M. & Kon, C.F. : (ed) Readings in Urban Geography. Indian edition; Central Book Depot, Allahabad, 1967.

68. Matoo, A.N. : Kashmir Geographia Oour Logg; (Urdu ed.) Kapoor Brothers J & K Srinagar, 1954.

69. Misra, R. P. : Contribution to Indian Geography, Concepts and Approaches; Concept Publishing Company, New Delhi (India).

70. Moorcroft, William; : Travels Part II; Published by Director, Language Deptt. Punjab, Patiala 1970.

71. Murphy, R.E. : The American City, An Urban Geography, Mc Graw Hill book Company, New-York, 1966.

72. Pant. D. : The commercial Policy of Moguls, Bombay, 1930.

73. Parkinson, C.N. : Trade in Eastern Seas, 1793-1813, Cambridgem 1937.

74. Potter, D. : The Bazar Merchant, in Social Forces in the Middle

East, edicted by S.N. Fisher, Ithaca, N.Y. 1955.

75. Prabha, K. : Towns a Structural Analysis, Inter India Publications, Delhi-35, 1979.

76. Rao, G.R.S. : Regionalism in India; S Chand & Co. Pvt. Ltd. New Delhi,1975.

77. Ratcliff, R.U. : Urban Land Economics; Mc Graw Hill book Company; New-Delhi, 1949.

78. Ray, S.C. : Early History and culture of Kashmir; Munshilal Manoharlal Publishers New Delhi.

79. Robbani, G.M. : Kashmir Social and Cultural History, Anmol Publishers, New Delhi, 1986.

80. Rolph, I.K. : The Locational Structure of Retail Trade, Vol. 80, Domestic Commerce Series, U.S. Bureau of Foreign and Domestic Commerce, Govt. Printing Office Washington, 1929.

81. Saxena, H.M. : Geography of Transport and Market Centres; S. Chand and Co; Pvt. Ltd., New Delhi, 1975.

82. Saxena, H.M. : Geography of Marketing Concept Publishing Company, New Delhi, 19.

83. Schell, E. : Aspects of Central Place Theory Unsubstantiated by Store Facilities in Baston's Retall Land scape; Abstract of papers. 20th International Geographical Congress, London, 1964 (Edicted by F.E. Ian Hamilton)

84. Scott P. : Geography of Retailing; Hutchinson University Library, London, 1971.

85. Sharma, D.C. : Kashmir under Sikhs; Seema Publications, New Delhi-7, 1983.

86. Simmons, J.W. : The Changing Pattern of Retail Location, Research Paper No.92, Dept. of Geography, University of Chicago, 1964.

87. Simmons, J.W. : Toranto's Changing Retail Complex; Department of Geography, Research Paper No. 104 University of Chicago Chicago, Illinois, U.S.A. 1966.

88. Singh, H.H. : Kanpur; A Study in Urban Geography; B.H.U. Varansi,

1972.

89. Singh, R.L. : Banaras; A Study in Urban Geography, Nand Kishore and Brothers, 1955.

90. Singh, R.L. : Allahabad; A Study in Urban Geography; Banaras Hindu University, Vanarasi, 1955.

91. Smails, E : The Geography of Towns; Hutchinson University Library London, 1953.

92. Smith, H : Retail Distribution; A Critical Analysis, London, 1937.

93. Snedecor, G.W. and Cochran, W.G. : Statistical Methods, Indian edition, Calcutta, 1966.

94. Sofi, G.M.D : Kashmir Volume I; Light and Life Publishers, New Delhi 1974.

95. Sofi, G.M.D. : Kashmir Volume II; Light & Life Publishers, New-Delhi 1974.

96. Stamp, L.D. : Applied Geography; Harmondsworth, London, 1960.

97. Stein, Sir, M. Aurel : Rajatarangini of Kalhana volume-I; Motial Banarsidas, Publishers, New Delhi,1900.

98. Stein, Sir, M.A. : Rajatarangini of Kalhana Volume IIrd; Motilal Banarsidas Publishers, New-Delhi, 1900

99. Stein, Sir. M Aruel : Rajatarangini of Kalhana Volume IIIrd; Motilal Banarsidas Publishers, New-Delhi, 1900.

100. Stein, Sir. M. A. : Rajatarangini of Kalhana Volume IVth; Motilal Banarsidas Publishers, New-Delhi, 1900.

101. Stein, Sir. M.A. : Rajatarangini of Kalhana Volume VIIth; Motilal Banarsidas Publishers, New-Delhi, 1900.

102. Stein, Sir. M.A. : Rajatarangini of Kalhana Volume VIIIth; Motilal Banarsidas Publishers, New-Delhi, 1900.

103. Tyalor, G. : Urban Geography; Mehtuen & Co. Ltd., London; 1949.

Journals

1. Alam, S.M. : "Commercial Structure of the Cities of Hyderabad and Secunderabad". Journal of the Osmania University Arts, Com-

merce, Law and Education, Vol.-I, 1963, pp. 1-10.

2. Alexandar, J.W. : "The Basic Non-basic Concept of Urban Economic Functions", Economic Geography, Vol-30, 1954, pp.246-61.

3. Applebaum, W. : "Marketing Geography" In American Geography Inventory and Prospects, Edicted by James, P.E. and Jones, F.F. Syracuse, 1954.

4. Aurousseau, M. : "The Distribution of Population: a Constructive Problem" Geographical Review, Vol-II, 1921. pp.363-92.

5. Backmann, M.J. : "City Hierarchies and the Distribution of City Size," Economic Development and Cultural Change, Vol-VI, 1958, pp. 243-48.

6. Bengtsson, R. : "The Structure of Retail Trade in a Small Swedish Town," Lund Studies in Geography, Proceedings of the I.G.U. Symposium in Urban Geography, Lunds, 1960, K. Norborg (Ed) Gleerups Land, pp. 297-312.

7. Berry, B.J.L. : "Ribbon Development in the urban Business Pattern", Annals of the Association of American Geographers, Vol.-49, 1959, pp. 145-55.

8. Berry, B.J.L, Simmons, J.W. and Tannaut, R.J. : "Urban Population Densities; Structure and Change." Gegoraphical Review, Vol.53, 1963, pp. 389-405.

9. Berry, B.J.L. : "The Retailing Component of the Urban Model", Journal of American Institute of Planners, Vol.-31, 1965, pp. 150-55.

10. Berry, B.J. & Garriosn, W.L : "A Note of Central Place theory and the Range of a Good", Economic Geography, Vol.-34, 1958, pp. 304-11.

11. Berry, B.J.L. & Garrison, W.L. : "The Functional Basis of the Central Place Hierarchy", Economic Geography, Vol.-34, 1958, pp.145-45.

12. Berry, B.J.L. & Garrison, W.L. : "Recent Development of Central Place Theory", Paper and Proceedings of the Regional Science Association, Vol.-4, 1958, pp.107-20.

13. Boal, F.W. & Johnson, D.B. : "The Functions of Retailing and Service Establishments of Commercial Ribbions", Cannadian Geographers, Vol.-9, 1965. pp.154-69.

14. Bohnert, J.E. & Mathingly, P.F : "Delimitation of CBD Through Times", Economic Geography, Vol.-140, 1964, pp. 337-47.

15. Brush, J.E. : "The Hierarchy of Central Places in South-Western", Geographical Review, Vol.-43, 1953, pp. 380-402.

16. Bucklin, L.P. : "Retail Strategy and the Classification of Consumer Goods," Journal of Marketing, Vol.-27, 1963, pp. 50-55.

17. Carol, H. : "The Hierarchy of Central Functions Within the City," Annals of the Association of American Geographers, Vol.-50, 1960, pp. 419-38.

18. Carruthers, J : "Major Shopping Centres in England and Wales," Geographical Journal, Vol.-123, 1967, pp.371-85.

19. Canter, H. & Rowley, G. : "The Morphology of Central Business District of Cardiff," Transactions of the Institute of British Geographers, No 38, 1966, pp. 119-34.

20. Chari, C.S.S. : "Stages in the Growth of the City of Madras," Journal of Madras Geographical Association, Vol.-2, 1927, pp. 79-104.

21. Chark, W.A.V. : "Consumer Travel Patterns and the Concept of Range", Annals of the Association of American Geographers, Vol.-58, 1968,pp.386-96.

22. Clark, W.A.V. : "The Spatial Structure of Retail Functions in A New Zealand City", New-Zealand Geographers, Vol.-23, 1967,pp. 23-33.

23. Clark, W.A.V. & Rushton, G. : "Models of Intra-Urban Consumer Behaviour and their Implications for Central Place Theory", Economic Geography, Vol.-46, 1970, pp. 486-97.

24. Cohen, S.B. & Lewis, G.K. : "Form and Function in the Geography of Retailing", Economic Geography, Vol.-43, 1967, pp. 1-42.

25. Davar, S.K. : "Shopping Facilities and Trend in Delhi", Journal of the Institute of Town Planners, 1962.

26. Davies, D. : Boundary Study as a tool in CBD Analysis", Economic Geography, Vol.035, 1959, pp.322-45.

27. Davies, W.R.D. : "Centrality and Central Place Hierarchy", Urban Studies, Vol.-4, 1967, pp. 61-79.

28. Davies, W.K.D. : "The Ranking of Serice Centres; A Critical Review", Institute of British Geographers, Transactions No. 40, 1966, pp.51-56-77.

29. De Blij, H.J. : "The Functional Structure and Central Business District of Lourence Margues", Mogambique, Economic Geography, Vol-38, 1962, pp. 56-77.

30. Deshpande, C.D. : "Market villages and Periodic Fairs of Bombay", Karnatak, Indian Geographical Journal, Vol.-16, 1941, pp. 327-39.

31. Diamand, D.R. : "The Central Business District of Glasgowl", Lund Studies in Geography, Sries, B, No.24, in K. Norborg (Ed.) Proceeding of the Symposium in Urban Geography, Lund, 1960, Lund, Sweden, Gleerup, pp. 525-34.

32. Dickinson, R.E. : "Market and Market areas on East Anglia", Economic Geography, Vol.-10, 1934, pp. 172-82.

33. Dutta, A.K. : "Intra-City Hierarchy of Central Places; Calcutta, As a case Study", the Professional Geographers, Vol,-21, 1969, pp. 18-22.

34. Dutta, A.K. : Daily shipping in Howrah City; A Study in Social Geography and Planning", National Geographical Journal of India, Vol. 12, 1966, pp. 163-77.

35. Dutta, A.K. : "Daily Shopping in Calcutta", Town Planning Review, Vol.37, 1967, pp. 307-16.

36. Eldridg, M. : "The Plate Class Shop Front", Architectural Review, 1958.

37. Forrest. J. : "Retail Activity in New Zealand Town", New Zealand, Geographer Vol. 24, 1968, pp. 61-75.

38. Getis, A. & Getis, J.M. : "Retail Store Spatial Affinities", Urban Studies, Vol. 5, 1968, pp. 327-32.

39. Golledge, R.G. : Rushton, G. & Clark, W.A.V.; "Some Spatial Char-

acteristics of Iowa's Dispersed Farm Population and their Implications for the Grouping of Central Place Functions", Economic Geography, Vol. 42, 1966, pp. 261-72.

40. Harris, C.D. & Ullman, E.L. : "The Nature of City", Annals of the American Academy of Political and Social Science, Vol. 242, 1945, pp. 7-17.

41. Hayes, C.R. and Schul, N.W. : "Some Characteristics of Shopping Centres", Professional Geographer, Vol.17, 1965, pp. 11-14.

42. Hodge, G. : "The Predication of Trade Centres Viability in Great Predication of Trade Centres Viability in Great Plains", Papers of the Regional Science Association, Vol. 15, 1965, pp. 87-115.

43. Hoffer, C.R. : "Service of Rural Trade Centres". Social Forces, Vol. 10, 1931, pp. 66-71.

44. Hoyt, H. : "The Residential and Retail Pattern of Leading Latin American Cities", Land Economics, Vol. 39, 1963, pp. 449-54.

45. Hoyt, H. : "Classification and Significant Characteristics of Shopping Centers", in H.M. Mayer and C.F. Kohn (Eds.), Readings in Urban Geography, Chicago, University of Chicago Press, 1967, pp. 454-61.

46. Hurst, E.M. and Sellers, J. : "An Analysis of the Spatial Distribution of Gustomers Around Grocery Retail Operations', Professional Geographer Vol. 12, 1969.

47. Jefferson, M. : "The Distribution of World's City Folks", Geographical Review, Vol.-XXI, 1931.

48. Johnston, R.J. and Rimmer, P.J. : "A Note on Consumer Behaviour in an Urban Hierarchy", Journal of Regional Science, Vol.7, 1967, pp.191-66.

49. Kar, N.R. : "Urban Characteristics of Calcutta", Indian Population Bulletin, Vol. I, 1960, pp. 35-67.

50. Kelley, E.J. : "Retail Structure of Urban Economy", Traffic Quarterly, Vol. 9, 1955, pp. 411-30.

51. Kenyon, J.B. : "On the Relationship Between Central Functional and Size of Place", Annals of the Association of American Geogra-

pher, Vol. 57, 1967, pp. 736-50.

52. Khan, F.H. & Salahuddin, A : "The City Centre of Chittagone", The Oriental Geographer, Vol, 11, 1967, pp. 1-37.

53. Krishnan, K : "Fairs and Trade Centres of Madural and Ramnad", Journal of Madras Georaphical Association, Vol. 7, 1932, pp.237-49.

54. Krishnan, V. : "Trade Centres of Tinnevelly District", Journal of Madras Geographical Association, Vol. 15, 1940, pp. 272-46.

55. Lakshmanan, T.R. & Hansen, W.G. : "A Retail Market Potential Model" Journal of American Institute of Planners, Vol. 31, 1965, pp. 134-43.

56. Leeming, F.A. : "An Experimental Survey of Retail Shopping and Service Facilities in Part of North Leods", Transactions and papers of the Institute of British Geographers No. 26, 1956, pp. 133-52.

57. Lively, C.E. : "The Appearance and Disappearance of Minor Trade Centres in Minnesotas", 1905-1930, Social Forces, Vol. 10. pp. 71-75.

58. Lomas, G.M. : "Retail Trading Centres in the Middlands", Journal of the Town Planning Institute, Vol. 50, 1964, pp. 104-19.

59. Mabogunje, A.L. : "T Evolution and Analysis of Retail Structure of Lagos", Nigeria, Econmic Geography, Vol. 40, 1964, pp.304-23.

60. Mathur, V.S. : "Agricultural Marketing in Western United Province", Indian Geographical Journal, Vol. 16. 1941, pp. 28-41.

61. Mattingly, P.F. : "Delimitaition and Movement of CBD Boundries Through Time; The Harrisburg Example", Professional Geog., Vol. 16, pp. 9-13.

62. Mayer, H.M. : "Patterns and Recent Trends of Chicago Outlaying Business Centres", Journal of Land and Public Utility Economics, Vol. 18, 1942, pp. 4-16.

63. Hayfield, R.C. : "The Range of a Central Good in the Indian Punjab", Annals of the Association of American Geographers, Vol. 53, 1963, pp. 38-49.

64. Mcintyze, W.E. : "The Bi-weekly Markets at Modinagar", Geographi-

cal Review, Vol. 45, 1955, pp. 66-80.

65. Mukherjee, A.B. : "The Bi-weekly Markets at Modinagar", Indian Geographer, Vol. 2, 1957.

66. Murphy, R.E. : "Marketing Geography Comes of age; Introductions to Store Location and Development Studies", Economic Geography, Vol. 37, 1961, Editorial.

67. Murphy, R.E. & Vance, J.E. : Jr. "Delimiting CBD", Economic Geography, Vol. 301, 1954, pp. 189-222.

68. Nelson, L. and Jacobson, E.J. : "Recent Changes in Farm Trade Centres of Minnesota", Rural Sociology, Vol.6, 1941, pp. 99-106.

69. Nelson, R.L. : "Selection of Retail Location", Journal of American Institute of Planners Vol.25, 1954.

70. Pattaniak, N. : "Weekly Market Barpali", Geographical Review of India, Vol. 15, 1953.

71. Parr., J.B. : "City Hierarchies and the Distribution of City Size", A Reassessment of Beckman's Contribution, Journal of Regional Science, Vol. 9, 1969, pp. 39-54.

72. Percival, R.N. : "Shoppping Centres in Britain", Journal of the Town Planning Institute, Vol.51, 1965.

73. Philips, F. : " A Note on Retail Trade", Journal of Regional Science, Vol. 6, 1965.

74. Pred, A. : "Business Thoroughfares as Experessions of Urban Negro Culture", Economic Geography, Vol. 39, 1963, pp. 217-33.

75. Proudfoot, M.J. : "The Outlaying Busienss Centress of Chicago", Journal of land and Public utility Economics Vol. 13, 1937, pp. 57-70.

76. Proudfoot, M.J. : "The Outlaying Busienss Centres of Chicago", Journal of Land and Public Utility Economics Vol. 13, 1937, pp. 57-70.

77. Proudfoot, M.J. : "City Retail Structure", Economic Geography, Vol.13, 1937, pp. 425-28.

78. Ratcliff, R.U. : "The Problem of Retail Site Selection", Michigam

Business Studies, Vol. 9, Part-I, 1939.

79. Reddy, S.N. : "Vegetable Market and Regional Relationship of Hyderabad City", Geograpphical Review of India. Vol. 23, 1961.

80. Renolds, R.B. : "Retail Specialization of Central Business Districts", Journal of American Institute of Planners, Vol. 26, 1960, pp. 313-16.

81. Sami, A. & Ahmad, A. : "Hierarchy of Market Centres in the City of Gaya", Journal of Institute of Town Planners, Vol.8, Nos. 1 (139) Sept. 1989.

82. Singh, A. : "Local Business Activity Indese", Journal of Regional Science, Vol. 7, 1967.

83. Singh, K. N. : "Barhaj; A Market Town", National Geographical Journal of India, Vol. 7, 1961, pp. 21-36.

84. Singh, R.L. : "Geographical Concepts and methods of Research Work", National Geographical Journal of India, Vol. 6, 1960, pp. 127-36.

85. Singh, S.M. : "The Stability Theory of Rural Central Place Development", National Geographical Journal of India, Vol. 11, 1965, pp. 13-21.

86. Singh, U. : "Industrial and Commercial Landscape of Allahabad City", National Geographical Journal of India, Vol. 7, 1960, pp. 227-41.

87. Singh, S.: "Weekly Market at Bannia in Manbhum", Geographical Review of India, Vol. 13, 1951.

88. Skinnter, G.M. : "Marketing and Social Structure in Rural China", Journal of Asian Studies, Vol. 24, 1964, pp. 3-43, 195-228, 363-99.

89. Smailes, A.E. & Hartley, G. : "Shopping Centres in Greater London Areas", Transections of the Institute of British Geographers, No. 29, 1961, pp. 201-13.

90. Stone, G.P. : "City Shoppers and Urban Ilentification", American Journal of Sociology, Vol, 60, 1954, pp. 36-45.

91. Suresh, R. : "Parade-A Periodical Market of Kanpur", The Geographical Knowledge, Vol. 4, 1971, pp. 56-65.

92. Tamaskar, B.G. : "The Weekly Market of Sagar Damoh Plateau", National Geographical Journal of India, Vol. 12, 1966, pp. 38-50.

93. Trrant, J.R. : "A Classification of Shops Types", Professional Geographers, Vol. 19, 1967, pp. 179-83.

94. Thakur, B. : "The Central Business District of Patna", Proceedings of Symposium on Urban Land use (21st International Geographical Congress 1968), Hyderabad, National Committee for Geography, Calcutta, 1972, pp. 77-84.

95. Thorpe, D. : "The Main Shopping Centres of Great Britain in 1961", Their Location and Structural Characteristics, Urban Studies, Vol.5, 1968, pp. 165-206.

96. Thorpe, D. & Nader, G.A. : "Customer Movement and Shopping Center; A Study of Central Place System in Northern Durhum", Regional Studies, Vol.-I, 1967, pp. 173-91.

97. Ullaman, E.L. : "A Theory of Location for Cities", American Journal of Sociology, Vol, 46, 1941, pp. 853-64.

98. Vauce, J.E. Jr. : "Emerging Pattern of Commercial Structure in American Cities", Lund Studies in Geography, Series, B No. 24, in K. Norborg (Ed.) Proceedings of the I.G.U. Symposium in Urban Geography, Lund, 1960, pp.485-518, Lund, Sweden; Gleerup.

99. Veeranna, S. : "Planning of Shopping Facilities in Towns and Cities", Journal of the Institute of Town Planning, 1963.

100. Venugopal, V. : "Commercial Structure of Warangal City in Andhra Pradesh", India, Proceedings of Symposium on Urban Land use (21st. International Geographical Congress, India, 1968), Hyderabad, National Committee for Geographers, Calcutta, 1978, pp. 13-17.

101. Vining, R. : "A Description of Certain Spatial Aspects of an Economic System", Economic Development and Cultural Changes, Vol.3, 1955, pp.147-95.

Government Publications, Published & Unpublished Reports

1. Ananta Padmanabham, N. : "Some Aspects of Urban Land use in the CBD of Coimbatore City", Paper Presented at the 21st International Congress Symposium on Urban Land use, Hyderabad, 1968.

2. Anwar Ahmad : "Hierarchy of Markets in Gaya", Unpublished Ph. D, Thesis, Dept. of Geography, Patna University, 1988.

3. Jamil, A. : "Markets Heirarchy & Consumer Behavior in Patna Urban Agglomaration", Unpublished Ph. D. Thesis, Dept. of Geography, Patna University 1990.

4. Das, M. : "Dilimitation of the Central Business District of Calcutta", Paper Presented at 21st. International Congress on Urban Land use, Hyderabad, 1968.

5. United Nation Population Studies No. 8, 1950, New-York, 1950.

6. "Melbourne and Metropolitan Board of Worker, Melbourn, Metropolitan Planning Scheme Report"; Survey of Analysis, Melbourne, 1954.

7. "Shopping Centres in Greater Phonix", First National Bank Phonix 1957.

8. "The Science of Geography", National Academy of Science, National Research Council Publication, 1277, 1965.

9. Report on "Land Use Pattern of India's Cities and Towns", Town and Country Planning Organisation (Ministry of Works, Housing and Urban Development), New Delhi, 1966.

10. "Traffic and Transportation Problems in Metropolitan Cities", Metropolitan Transoport Team Committe on Plan Projets, Planning Commission, New-Delhi, 1967,

11. "A Survey of Research in Geography", Indian Council of Social Science & Redearch, New-Delhi, 1972.